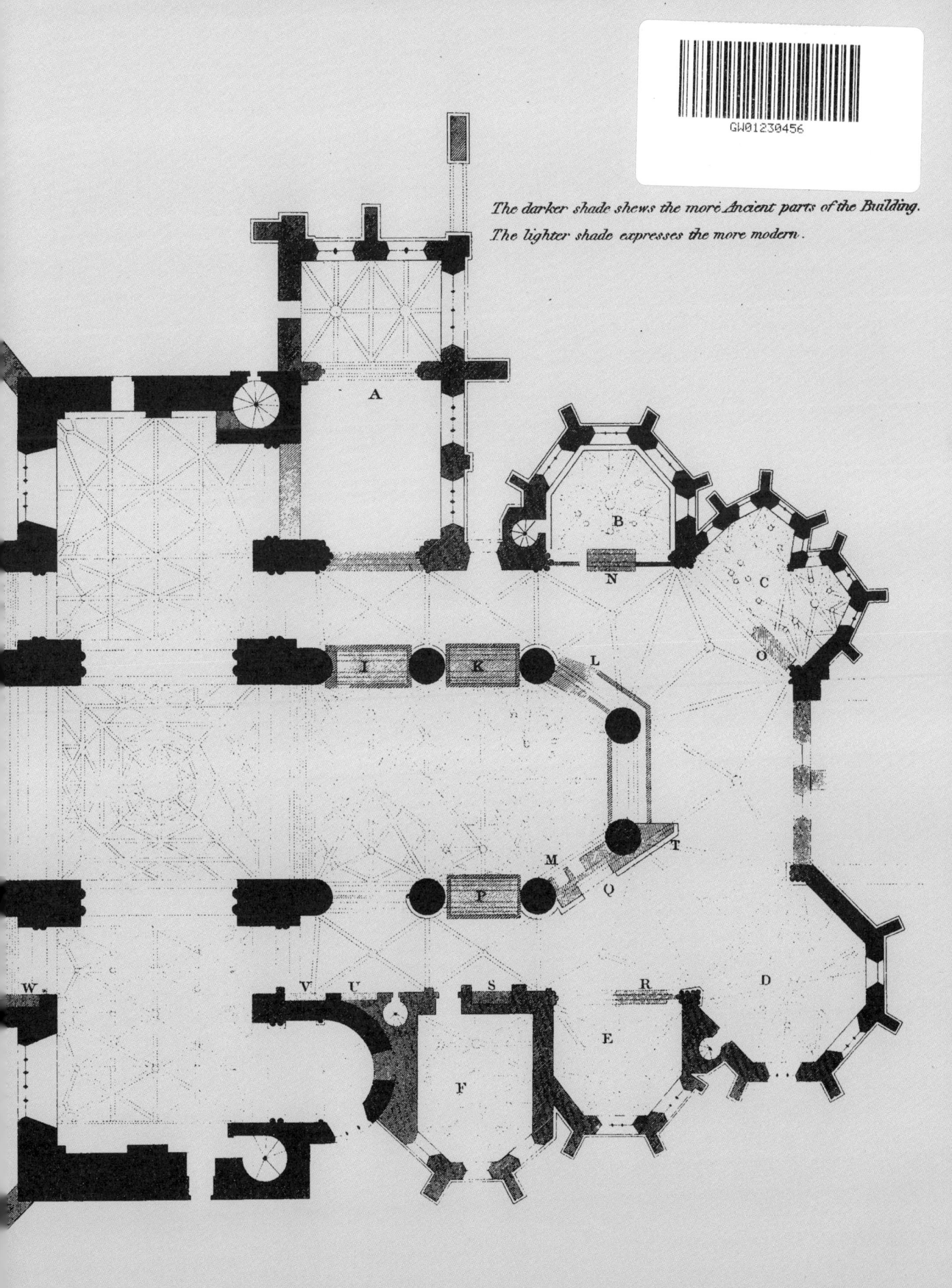

The darker shade shews the more Ancient parts of the Building.
The lighter shade expresses the more modern.

A HISTORY OF TEWKESBURY ABBEY

Celebrating 900 years

A HISTORY OF TEWKESBURY ABBEY

Celebrating 900 years

C.E. WHITNEY

Photography
JACK BOSKETT

Reconstructions
DAVID BALL

LOGASTON PRESS

First published in 2022 by Logaston Press
The Holme, Church Road, Eardisley HR3 6NJ
www.logastonpress.co.uk
An imprint of Fircone Books Ltd.

ISBN 978-1-910839-53-9

Text copyright © C.E. Whitney, 2022.
All photographs copyright © Jack Boskett
unless otherwise stated beneath each photograph.
All reconstruction illustrations copyright © David Ball
unless otherwise stated beneath each illustration.

All rights reserved.
The moral rights of the author have been asserted.

Without limiting the rights under copyright reserved above, no part of this publication may be reproduced, stored in or introduced into a retrieval system, or transmitted, in any form or by any means (electronic, mechanical, photocopying, recording or otherwise), without prior written permission of the copyright owner and the above publisher of this book.

Designed and typeset by Richard Wheeler in 10.5 on 14.5 Caslon.
Cover design by Richard Wheeler.

Printed and bound in Poland.

Logaston Press is committed to a sustainable future for our business, our readers and our planet.
The book in your hands is made from paper from sustainable sources.

British Library Catalogue in Publishing Data.
A CIP catalogue record for this book is available from the British Library.

CONTENTS

	FOREWORD	*vii*
	ACKNOWLEDGEMENTS	*ix*
ONE	Prologue: Before the Abbey	1
TWO	1090–1121: The Building, Consecration and Dedication of the Abbey	9
THREE	1122–1215: From Dedication to the signing of Magna Carta	23
FOUR	1216–1314: The Age of the de Clare family, the building of a Lady Chapel	31
FIVE	1315–1470: The Despensers, Lady Eleanor and major changes	41
SIX	1471–1540: The Battle of Tewkesbury, Henry VIII and the Abbey's Dissolution	53
SEVEN	1541–1660: The Abbey's Dissolution to the Restoration	65
EIGHT	1660–1836: The Restoration to the end of the Regency	79
NINE	1837–1920: Victorian Reordering and Restoration to the end of the First World War	97
TEN	1920–2020: From between the Wars to a twenty-first century pandemic	117
ELEVEN	2021: Celebrating the past, living the present, embracing the future	141
	ENDNOTES	149
	BIBLIOGRAPHY	163
	INDEX	167

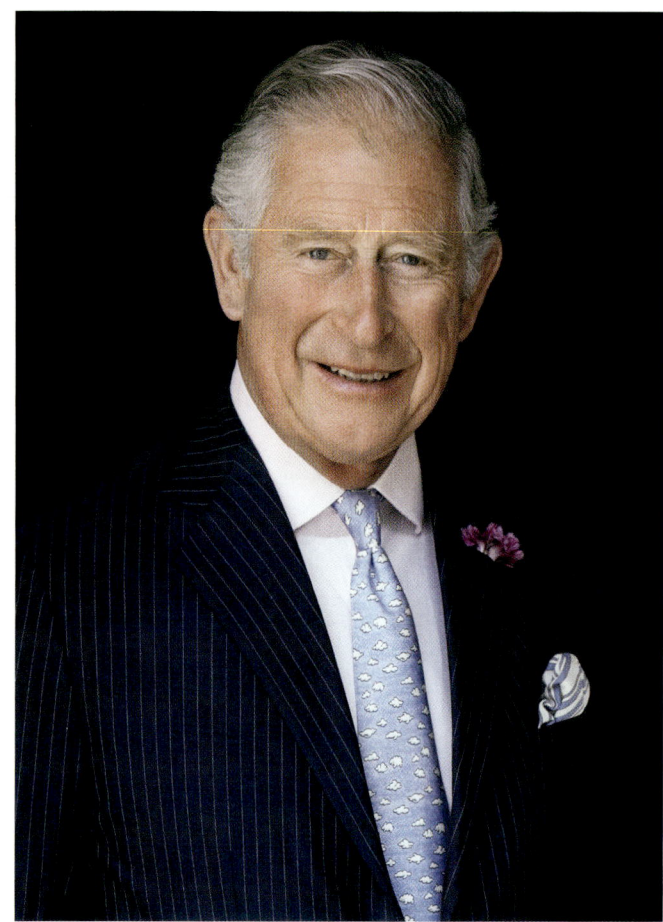

HRH The Prince of Wales

CLARENCE HOUSE

Among all the marvellous architectural riches with which this country is blessed, our incomparable abbeys and cathedrals must surely be counted with our greatest treasures.

Tewkesbury Abbey is one of England's most beautiful and majestic churches, and has been recognised as such by its many distinguished patrons since medieval times.

This fascinating book, written to mark the 900th anniversary of the Abbey's consecration and the 550th anniversary of the Battle of Tewkesbury, traces the history of the building and its community from the earliest times to the present day. Among the recent events which it records are Her Majesty The Queen's visit in 1971, the great flood of 2007 and the impact on the Abbey of the COVID-19 pandemic.

Today, Tewkesbury Abbey offers a welcome to many pilgrims, visitors and parishioners alike. It is an invaluable oasis of quiet, prayerful calm to people of all faiths and of none in the midst of a busy and fractious world. That it remains so, as well as being one of our most extraordinary architectural jewels, after 900 years is a real cause for celebration.

I warmly commend this book to you as a celebration of this special and holy place.

For the Vicar, Churchwardens and Community of Tewkesbury Abbey

And in memory of
Anne Whitney
who loved this place

ACKNOWLEDGEMENTS

I should like to thank the Revd Canon Dr Paul Williams, DL, Vicar of Tewkesbury Abbey, and the PCC for their enthusiastic support for this project. Thanks to Tewkesbury Abbey Publications, the group that oversees all Abbey publishing, for the care they took over the project. The Abbey community support has been wonderful, from the Revd Wendy Ruffle of 'Celebrate' to Philippa Shaw, Claire Redstone and Margaret Wilson in the office, together with Rebecca Duncombe, the Abbey Fabric Officer, the Abbey shop staff, particularly Maggie O'Leary, Amanda Thomas and Penelope Tubbs. Through Amanda and Penelope, I must thank members of the Tewkesbury Medieval Festival and Tewkesbury Battlefield Society for their input, especially for bringing the Tewkesbury Indenture to my attention. Thanks to all the vergers for their consistently helpful support, especially Mark Taylor, Head Verger and Operations Manager, not least for his photographic assistance, and Julia Hall, former Head Verger and Sacristan, for her considerable knowledge of matters liturgical and her editorial skills. My thanks, too, to Carleton Etherington, the Abbey's organist and Minister of Music, for checking my comments on the Abbey organs, and also to David Bagley and Malcolm Taylor for their profound knowledge of the bells, Abbey clocks and, in David's case, Peregrine falcons.

Thanks to the Tewkesbury Town Library staff for their assistance. Thanks, too, to Louise Hughes of the University of Gloucestershire Archives, including the Bristol and Gloucestershire Archaeological Society Special Collection, for her help in finding various texts. Sarah Radcliffe, archivist, St Paul's Cathedral, London, was also most helpful. The Director of the Archbishop Parker Library at Corpus Christi College, Cambridge, Dr Philippa Hoskins, and her colleagues, Anne McLaughlin and Alex Devine, helped a great deal, notably concerning the text of the *Samson Pontifical*. Louise Soothill-Ward, clerk to Slapton Parish Council, South Devon, kindly provided useful information concerning Sir Guy de Brien, KG.

I am hugely grateful to the classicist David Evans, formerly senior master at Dean Close School, for translating medieval liturgical Latin from the *Samson Pontifical* into comprehensible English with great care and elegance. Grace Pritchard-Woods,

Archivist, Dean Close Foundation, found Tewkesbury Abbey-related texts in various unlikely places, including India, and generously often acquired them for me.

I am grateful to Malcolm Thurlby, Professor Emeritus of Visual Art and Art History at York University, Toronto, Canada and to archaeologist and architectural historian Dr Stuart Harrison, York Minster Fellow of the University of York, for their expert opinions on all matters Romanesque, not least the oculus. I must thank Professor Julian Luxford, Head of Art History, St Andrew's University, for his Fitzhamon lecture on *The Founders' Book* to the Friends of Tewkesbury Abbey in 2018, and for his help on this project. Thank you to Dr Helen Gittos, Associate Professor, Balliol College, University of Oxford, for her expertise and help on liturgical matters concerning Anglo-Saxon and Norman church consecrations and dedications, and her knowledge concerning the pre-Conquest English Church. I am also hugely grateful to Professor John Harper, late Director of the Royal School of Music and an Emeritus Professor of Bangor University not just for a wonderful 2021 Fitzhamon lecture on the Abbey's consecration and dedication but for useful conversations subsequently. The list would certainly not be complete without warmly thanking Professor Joyce Hill, formerly Pro-Vice-Chancellor, Director of Medieval Studies and Head of English at Leeds University and now Emeritus Professor there, not only for her excellent Fitzhamon lecture in 2019 but also for her generous help and time in answering questions on the late Anglo-Saxon Church with deep understanding and good humour.

Sue Rundall, a seasoned genealogist, spent a huge amount of time trying to solve the problem of the identity of the recumbent knight in the recess at the east end of the north nave aisle, and for her efforts I am also very grateful.

I would like to thank John Jeffreys and Don Freeman, highly experienced Abbey guides both, for their preparedness to answer all manner of questions and for allowing me to go round the Abbey with them when they were taking tours. I am grateful to Patricia Shakesby for her boundless interest in all matters Romanesque, and for her research into, and subsequent informative paper on, Robert Fitzhamon. Thanks also to Dr Andrew Crowther, formerly Vice-Chairman of the Friends of Tewkesbury Abbey and Chairman of the Friends of St Mary's Priory Church, Deerhurst, for his support that included lending me useful texts. I would like to thank Val Proctor, the Abbey's 2021 Officer, Tracey Jaggers and, later, Rachel Trott, who followed Tracey as Tewkesbury Abbey Commercial Manager, for their commitment to this project, that went far beyond professional interest. Arthur Lawrence, of the Abbey's community, very kindly kept me 'on track' concerning my temperamental computer. He was excellent at coaxing it back to functioning properly.

Pat Webley, the Honorary Archivist at Tewkesbury Abbey, put his encyclopaedic knowledge of all things to do with the Abbey at my disposal. I am most grateful for his deep interest, many suggestions, careful advice and corrections, meticulous research and many extremely useful discussions.

I was most fortunate to benefit hugely from the thoughts and observations of Neil Birdsall, FSA, for over 30 years the Abbey's architect and surveyor. His constant, good-humoured, wise and deeply knowledgeable support throughout this project was invaluable.

Graham Finch, chairman of the Friends, formerly an English teacher of many years' experience, read my typescript and not only corrected my more glaring errors but tactfully suggested a number of improvements. I am so grateful for his editorial input, wise advice and above all his unfailing encouragement.

David Ball, both a qualified architect and an artist with considerable experience of medieval church buildings, not least as Chairman of the Gloucester Diocesan Advisory Committee, generously undertook the challenging task of attempting to reproduce various vanished views of the Abbey. He went to great trouble, assisted by his wife Anna, to ensure that the illustrations were as accurate as they could be and to him must go heartfelt thanks.

I must also gratefully thank the photographer Jack Boskett, who took immense care and artistry over the photography. Nothing was too much trouble and he was always positive, cheerful and highly professional. It was a joy to work with him, as it was with the illustrations working party that included Rachel Trott and Karen Vincent as well as Jack. Thanks, too, to Nick Jones of the Photo Studio for his technical assistance and to Ian White for a photograph in Chapter 11.

Thank you to Richard and Su Wheeler of Logaston Press for their customary warm welcome, efficient, understanding care and attention to detail.

This project would not have come to fruition without the generous financial help of our sponsors. I am more grateful than I can say to Dean Close Foundation, Cheltenham; Tewkesbury's Civic Society; the Friends of Tewkesbury Abbey and to Tewkesbury Abbey Parochial Church Council.

Finally, my very grateful thanks to His Royal Highness the Prince of Wales for graciously consenting to write his thoughtful Foreword to the book.

Although great care has been taken to maintain accuracy, inevitably there will be found sins of both omission and commission, for which I apologise.

Charles Whitney
Bushley Green, Tewkesbury

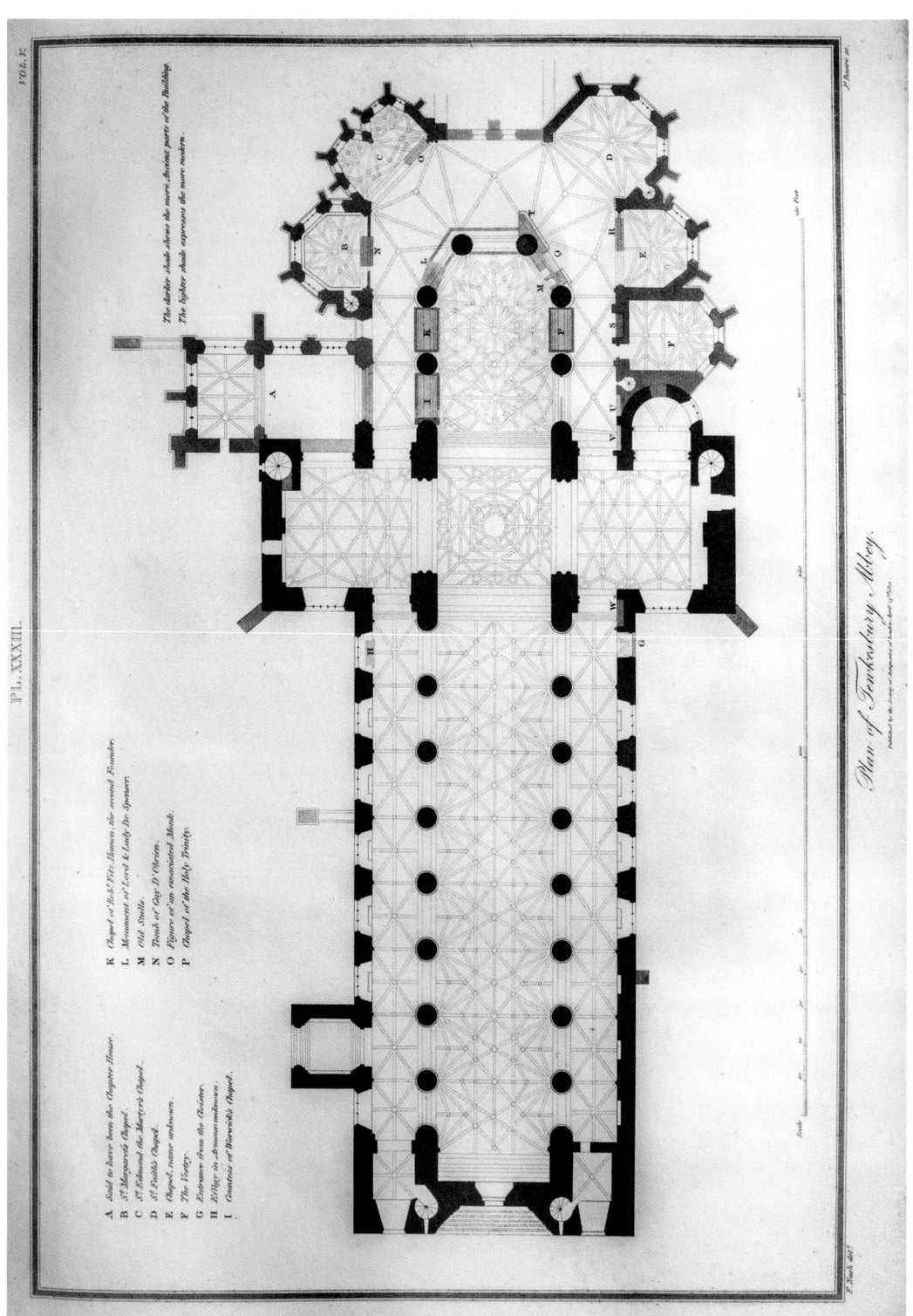

Plan (dated c.1821) from the *Vetusta Monumenta*, published by the Society of Antiquaries between 1718 and 1906

CHAPTER ONE

Prologue: Before the Abbey

THE story of Tewkesbury Abbey is one of a great medieval church and community either affecting or being affected by key moments in Britain's national evolution and, occasionally, local situations. From Domesday Book to the reign of Queen Elizabeth II, Magna Carta to the two World Wars, the Dissolution of the Monasteries to the Great Flood of 2007, via the close interest of monarchs and powerful barons, civil wars, plague, unrest and crises, one of the most beautiful, magnificent and yet peacefully prayerful churches has come down to us. Today, it is served by a community that continues to bring the Gospel message to the town of Tewkesbury and the numerous visitors and pilgrims that enter the Abbey.

Although it has often been suggested that there was some form of Christian settlement at Tewkesbury as early as the seventh century, there is little accepted evidence to substantiate this. Medieval monks sought to suggest that their own monasteries were as venerable as anyone else's. This led to a 'pecking order' of monasteries, with those claiming roots going back to the earliest times being regarded as the most senior. Understandably, this led to a number elaborating their claims through pious fables that had little foundation in fact. The stories surrounding the monastery at Glastonbury, involving Joseph of Arimathea and possibly even a youthful Jesus of Nazareth, are perhaps the best known.

In Tewkesbury's case there were suggestions that a hermit variously called Theoc, Thecus or Theocus founded a cell or chapel near the present Abbey as early as AD 655. Sadly, no reference to a hermitage or similar feature has been found earlier than the sixteenth century and it is thought that the name of the hermit was deduced in the late Middle Ages from the name of the town.[1] Likewise, early stories concerning local lordly brothers Doddo and Oddo who are said to have established a Tewkesbury church in AD 715 are also open to serious question. There is no evidence for the existence of Doddo or Oddo, although the latter may well be confused with Odda, who does not appear factually for almost another 300 years. Odda was a thegn, later an eorl (earl) who is not recorded in any situation of importance until 1015. Thereafter Odda, who seems to have been a virtuous man, is gradually given greater responsibilities, until by 1051 he is not only earl over Devon, Somerset, Dorset and the Welsh but is also responsible for key naval defences. His name appears in *The Anglo Saxon Chronicle*. Aelfric or Elfric, Odda's brother, is thought to have died in 1053 and was buried at Pershore. Odda himself died in 1056 and was also buried at Pershore, having founded the chapel

1

that bears his name at Deerhurst.[2]

Another candidate as a possible founder of the original Tewkesbury church was Briohtric, King of Wessex, 786–802. There is a tradition that he founded a church at Tewkesbury and that Hugh, a lord of the manor of Tewkesbury, arranged for Briohtric's burial in the church. The weight of evidence points to Briohtric being buried at Wareham instead.[3]

However, it would appear that a minster church had evolved at Tewkesbury, possibly during the eighth or ninth centuries, but more probably in the tenth century. The parishes that it covered had almost certainly been previously looked after by Deerhurst minster, which had covered a huge area. The mid tenth century was a period of reform in the Anglo-Saxon Church, particularly of the Benedictine Rule, under Dunstan, Archbishop of Canterbury, 959–88. He was joined by Aethelwold, bishop of Winchester, 963–84, at a time when Winchester was England's capital city, and also by Oswald, bishop of Worcester, 961–92, who was also archbishop of York from 971–92.[4] Oswald's double appointment was severely practical, as the archbishopric of York was both struggling financially after the ruinous and sustained attentions of the Vikings and was somewhat isolated. Conversely, the Worcester bishopric was not only comparatively rich but also offered a southern base from which Oswald could more easily attend meetings at Winchester and Canterbury.[5] The three senior bishops were also enthusiastically supported in their reforms by Edgar the Peaceful, king of England 959–75. The idea of the reforms was uniformly to improve the discipline, spirituality, scholarship and learning within English Benedictine monasteries. Along with the reforms, the *Regularis Concordia* was approved by the Council of Winchester in 973. This was a rule book, written by Bishop Aethelwold, to instruct English Benedictines on how to live their monastic lives. However, it was also written with an eye to how 'secular' clergy might live their lives. It was hoped that the result of the reforms would be that the quality of 'secular' priests, who were usually trained in monasteries, would improve. They would be sent out in ever-growing numbers to minsters and parishes, possibly occasionally assisted by monks who were not quite as tied to monasteries as Norman monks were later required to be.

It certainly appears probable that there was an Anglo-Saxon minster at Tewkesbury by the latter half of the tenth century, as it may have been attacked by Vikings c.980, according to one authority. During the Viking raids, the church or minster at Tewkesbury was said to have been 'several times plundered, and twice consumed by fire'.[6] However, it is evident that by the time of the Norman Conquest in 1066, the minster church seems to have largely recovered and, as the Domesday survey shows, had its own daughter church or cell at Stanway,

The Foundation dates of local Abbeys

c.965	Malmesbury, Wiltshire
c.972	Pershore, Worcestershire
c.972	Winchcombe, Gloucestershire
c.989	Evesham, Worcestershire
c.1075	Great Malvern Priory, dependent on Westminster Abbey
c.1084	Worcester Cathedral (re-founded)
1100	St Peter's, Gloucester (rebuilt and re-founded, dedicated)
1102	Tewkesbury Abbey (re-founded)

Tewkesbury Abbey as seen from Cleeve Hill to the south-east

Gloucestershire. Tewkesbury minster, which might have had up to three clergy, held land in seven villages and in total owned nearly 3,000 acres.[7] It seems to have owned 35 people described as slaves. Tewkesbury minster does not appear to have been subservient to any other church or monastery (it would have been noted in the Domesday survey if that had been the case).[8] There is a tradition that states that a late Saxon lord of the manor, Haylward Snow (also called Aethelweard Meow) placed Tewkesbury minster under the monastery at Cranborne, Dorset in about 980. The taking over by a monastery of a 'secular' minster would have been most unlikely. It may well have been thought a good idea to suggest that, in order to create the impression that the monastery at Tewkesbury was of greater antiquity than was actually the case.[9]

Where the Anglo-Saxon Tewkesbury minster was originally situated remains a matter of some debate. There are hints that it might have been near or on the Mythe, just outside the present town at the top of a hill on the way to Twyning. Some have maintained that it could have been in the St Mary's Lane area to the north of the east end of the present Abbey. However, most authorities feel that it was very probably close to, or on the actual site of, the present Abbey. The discovery of an apparently pre-Romanesque wall under the south transept of the present Abbey may or may not suggest where the old monastery could have been.[10]

PROLOGUE: BEFORE THE ABBEY   3

View of the Abbey from the Ham

There are three further indicators suggesting that Tewkesbury Abbey may have been built more or less on the site of the old Anglo-Saxon minster. The first is that when the Normans came to rebuild a church, they preferred to build on a site that had been consecrated already, if they possibly could. They did not like to abandon a site already given over to the worship of God. Second, the Normans preferred to keep the patronage of the saint of the old church and incorporate it into the new. They would have been particularly happy with the Blessed Virgin Mary, who is the patron saint of Tewkesbury Abbey. Such a dedication was very popular in the tenth century during the Benedictine reform, so maybe this represents a further 'straw in the wind' that indicates a tenth-century Anglo-Saxon origin for the foundation, and pointing to it being on the Abbey's present site.[11] Finally, the monks who came to build the new Abbey itself in 1102 would have been most anxious to continue the *Opus Dei* – the 'Work of God' or monastic offices – day by day while building was ongoing. It would have been far easier to have managed this if the original Anglo-Saxon building was nearby, or possibly even within the walls of Tewkesbury Abbey, to be knocked down when the east end, the quire and the first stage of the tower were complete.

In the first half of the eleventh century, the lordship of the huge manor of Tewkesbury belonged to Beotric (sometimes Brictric, Berthric, Brihtric or Beorhtric). It was thought that he was probably the wealthiest thegn or lord in southern England below the rank of earl.

The son of Aelfgar, Beotric possessed estates in Gloucestershire and Worcestershire as well as in and around Cranborne, Dorset and Dawlish in Devon.[12] If it hadn't been for the Norman invasion in 1066, he might well have become an earl himself, enjoying an almost semi-royal status. As it was, he was probably descended from the royal family of Wessex. He centred himself on Tewkesbury where he had a residence or hall, with another residence at Oxenton, also in Gloucestershire. Patronage of Tewkesbury Church was vested in him as lord of the manor. It has been said that prior to the Norman invasion, Beotric had been 'Ambassador beyond [the] Sea', and as such there was a report that he had come across a lady called Maud, sometimes Matilda, in Normandy, probably in the duke of Normandy's court. She wished to marry Beotric but he effectively spurned her. Subsequently, she married Duke William of Normandy. Recent research has strongly suggested that Beotric of Tewkesbury and Beotric the roving ambassador, possibly from Kent, were two separate Beotrics. However, it is evident that the Tewkesbury lord of the manor was unceremoniously deposed when King William wanted the Honour of Tewkesbury for his wife.[13] Queen Maud was granted much of Beotric's lands, including the lordship of Tewkesbury.[14] When she died in 1083, Tewkesbury Manor reverted to the Crown.

King William II (William Rufus) granted the manor to Robert Fitzhamon, soon after he came to the throne in 1087, possibly because of Fitzhamon's assistance against Robert, King William's brother, probably as a reward for supporting him when Odo, bishop of Bayeux, and half-brother of William the Conqueror, rebelled in 1088.[15] Moreover, Robert Fitzhamon appears to have been a favourite of William Rufus, and when Robert married he was given

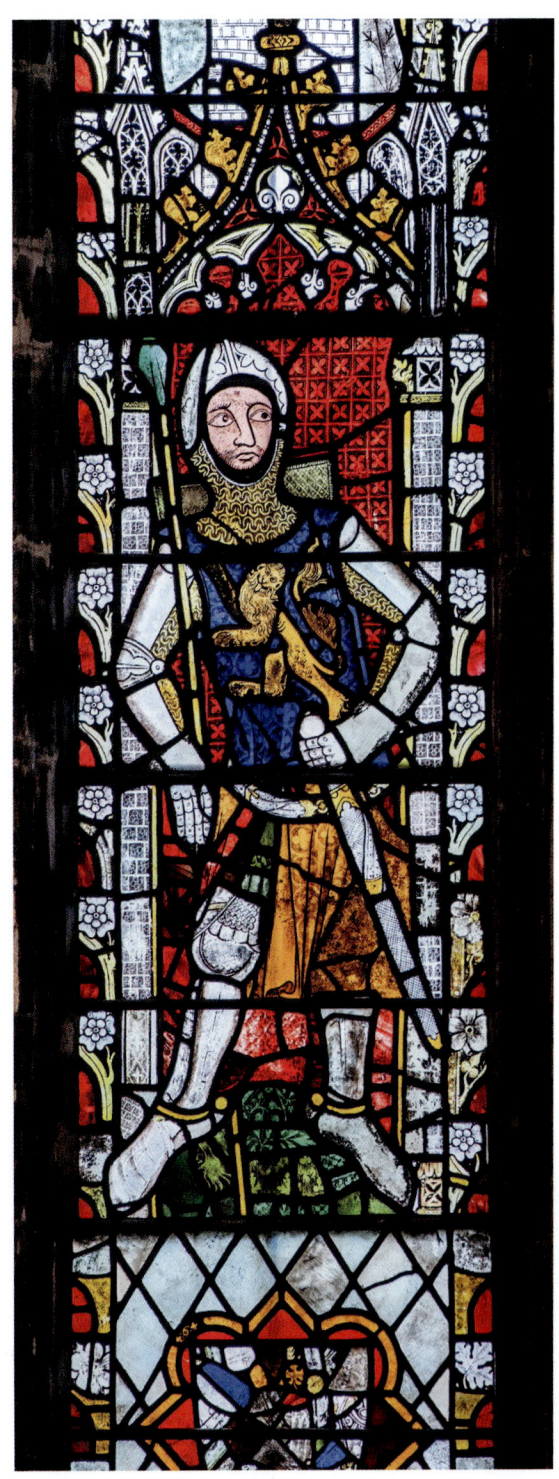

Robert Fitzhamon, founder of Tewkesbury Abbey, as depicted in a fourteenth-century window in the quire

PROLOGUE: BEFORE THE ABBEY 5

Robert Fitzhamon

Robert was the son of Hamo the Dapifer or senior (Royal) Steward, or possibly Sheriff, of Kent, who may also have had responsibilities in Essex. Born c.1050, it is said that Robert may have been the grandson of Hamo le Dentu, earl of Creully, near Bayeux, Normandy. This is problematic, for Hamo died at the Battle of Val es Dunes in 1047, fighting against Duke William of Normandy (later William I of England). His dates and perceived treachery make it unlikely that his son would have been given so responsible a position in England after the Conquest. Yet some authorities claim that Robert's father came over with the then Duke William as a kinsman. However, another possibility is that one of Hamo's brothers, Vital, an abbot of Bernay, was the actual grandfather at a time when abbots were still allowed to marry, although this cannot be proven.

Robert did not fight at the Battle of Hastings. Little is known of his career before 1087. He was loyal to King William II (Rufus) in 1088 when Bishop Odo of Bayeux rebelled. William II needed Robert's help in besieging Rochester Castle. Robert's loyalty was repaid when he was given the feudal barony of Gloucester, comprising over 200 manors in Gloucestershire and neighbouring counties, including the 'Honour of Tewkesbury'. Subsequently, he overcame Rhys ap Tewdwr, Prince of South Wales, in 1090, and Prince Iestyn ap Gwrgan (Justin), Prince of Glamorgan, in 1091. This gave Robert huge estates covering most of south Wales by right of conquest. He consolidated his grip by rebuilding the old Roman castle at Cardiff and building new castles at Newport and Kenfig (Cynffig), near Bridgend. Initially, the latter two may well have been wooden motte and bailey castles. Some authorities suggest that Robert now styled himself 'by the grace of God, Prince of Glamorgan, Earl of Corboile, Baron of Thorigny and Granville, Lord of (the Honours of) Gloucester, Tewkesbury and Cardiff and Conqueror of Wales.'[16] Others maintain that such titles were added later.[17]

Between 1088 and 1094, Robert married Sybil (Sibyl), fourth daughter of the earl of Shrewsbury. She was both beautiful and religious. By her, Robert had four daughters, two of whom became abbesses. Amicia, the youngest, married the earl of Brittany. Mabel, heir to Robert's vast estates, married Robert, the first earl of Gloucester, illegitimate son of King Henry I.

Robert was later also loyal to King Henry I, supporting him against his uncle, the then duke of Normandy, Robert (Curthose). Robert Fitzhamon was one of three barons who negotiated a truce in 1101. However, fighting occurred again later and Robert was captured. Released when King Henry came over to Normandy with a large force, Robert received a head wound at Falaise in 1105, living two more years but affected mentally. He died on 10 March 1107. He was buried in the chapter house at Tewkesbury Abbey but was later reburied in Tewkesbury Abbey itself in a place of great honour to the left of the high altar in 1241, over which the Founder's Chantry was erected in 1397.[18]

further lands which, together with the lands given to him earlier, created the extensive manor that became known as the 'Honour of Tewkesbury', as well as further vast estates.[19]

Robert Fitzhamon's estates were a great prize. However, the Domesday survey suggests that Tewkesbury had been 'destroyed and dismembered', possibly harking back to Viking invasions, or conceivably as a result of an abortive revolt in the area under Roger, earl of Hereford, against William I in 1075.[20] Robert Fitzhamon was now not only the lord of that manor, too, but was also patron of Cranborne Abbey. Subsequent conquests in south Wales gave Robert considerably more land.

It was at this point, or perhaps a little earlier, that the idea of founding a major Benedictine monastery at Tewkesbury, worthy of the patronage of so great a lord, came to Robert or possibly his wife, Sybil, with her deep Christian faith. With the estates that he now had, Robert had the resources available to think seriously about such a huge enterprise. In the Normans' culture, the Church 'was integrated with society, which it formed and moulded ... [it] provided not only motivation but also unity, identity and inspiration'.[21] From the mid tenth century onwards, Norman lords subscribed to 'the almost universal respect held by civilised contemporaries for monasticism as a vital social function and a superior way of life'.[22] Moreover, 'Not merely protection and patronage of the Church, therefore, but a liberal patronage of monks was thus an essential part of lordship and the princely office'.[23] Robert could well have seen it as his duty, especially as a comparatively recent entrant to the upper echelons of society, to be the founder of a substantial abbey church and monastic community. He would also have been aware of the building of the Norman (Romanesque) St Peter's Abbey, Gloucester, later to become the cathedral, that began in the 1070s. However, part of the driving force for what was the Tewkesbury Abbey enterprise was to appear in the shape of Gerald (Giraldus) of Avranches, abbot of Cranborne, Dorset, who may have been the key to the whole idea in the first place.

Pre-Dissolution Abbots of Tewkesbury

1102–9	Gerald (Geraldus)
1110–23	Robert (former chaplain to Robert Fitzhamon)
1124–37	Benedict
1137–61	Roger (sometimes called Robert)
1162–78	Fromund
	∼ *Interregnum* ∼
1182–83	Robert
	∼ *Interregnum* ∼
1186–1202	Alan, (former prior of Canterbury; first abbot buried in the Abbey)
1203–14	Walter (former sacrist of the Abbey)
1214–15	Hugh (sometimes Hugo; former prior of the Abbey)
1215–31	Peter (former monk of Worcester)
1232–54	Robert (of Forthampton; former prior of the Abbey)
1255–75	Thomas (de Stoke, or Stokes; former prior of St James, Bristol)
1276–82	Richard (de Norton)
1282–1328	Thomas (de Kemsey or Kempsey)
1328–47	John Cotes
1347–61	Thomas Legh (or de Legh)
1361–89	Thomas Chesterton (former Abbey cellarer)
1390–1420	Thomas Parker (or Pakare)
1421–42	William (de Bristol or Bristow)
1443–?1467	John Abington (or de Abingdon) Possibly also known as John de Salys
1468–81	John (de Strensham or de Streynsham)
1481–1509	Richard Cheltenham
1509–34	Henry (Beoly or Beeley)
1534–40	John (Wakeman, earlier Wick, Wicke or Wyth; former prior of the Abbey; first bishop of Gloucester diocese, 1541–49)

CHAPTER TWO

1090–1121: The Building, Consecration and Dedication of the Abbey

PART I: THE BUILDING

As abbot of Cranborne, whose lord was Robert Fitzhamon, Abbot Gerald (Giraldus) must have had various occasions to visit Tewkesbury and its church. Indeed, *The Founders' Book* suggests that he stayed at the (old) Tewkesbury minster for some time before Robert Fitzhamon became lord of the manor, leaving the monks at Cranborne largely to their own devices.[1] If that is true, it would have been within the years 1087–89. When Robert Fitzhamon took over his vast estates, he would have come to Tewkesbury from time to time when he wasn't in Bristol or Cardiff where he had built a castle.

Abbot Gerald found the position of Tewkesbury and its church 'preferable to Cranborne'. The ground was more fertile, with the advantage of 'a fine, navigable river' nearby.[2] At Tewkesbury, Abbot Gerald would also have been close to one of Robert Fitzhamon's key residences. When Robert was actively considering enlarging the personnel at the then Tewkesbury minster by 15 monks, thereby possibly making it an abbey, the abbot apparently felt that the 'old' Saxon church at Tewkesbury was 'insufficient' and enthused about building a magnificent new abbey to his lord.[3] Robert's wife, Sybil, supported the idea. It is not known whether Robert decided to build out of a sense of gratitude to God for being so blessed, or out of *noblesse oblige* and duty, or because of the pious blandishments of his wife and Abbot Gerald. It may have been a mix of all these, coupled with the fact that, as yet, he had no heir and wanted one. He may well have felt that the commitment to a fine abbey, generously endowed, would be rewarded by God. A massive enterprise like building a major abbey and monastery was not to be undertaken lightly, and it seems that there was a council made up of nobles and knights who discussed and subsequently backed the project.[4]

Some time in the 1090s, work evidently began on adding enough accommodation to cater for all the monks and almost certainly servants, too, who would be arriving from Cranborne.[5] In 1102, 57 monks transferred to Tewkesbury from Cranborne. The latter became a priory consisting of a prior and two monks dependant on Tewkesbury, which was formally constituted an abbey with Abbot Gerald as its first abbot that year. Abbot Gerald received the confirming, official benediction for an abbot from the Norman Bishop Sampson of Worcester.[6] Tewkesbury may be said to be the last of the major Norman monasteries to be founded or re-founded in this area. However, what it may have lacked in antiquity it more than made up for in generous endowments from Robert Fitzhamon who gave to the monastery gifts of lands and manors. Indeed, later on the chronicler William of Malmesbury observed, soon after the Abbey's dedication *c*.1125, that:

Abbot Gerald (*Giraldus, Girald*)

Gerald was a well-connected Norman monk of Winchester who became chaplain to Hugh, earl of Chester, sometimes referred to as being 'of Avranches'. If this is true, he originally came from a southern Normandy port.[7] Although elected abbot of Cranborne in 1086, it was evidently Robert Fitzhamon's wish that he become the first abbot of Tewkesbury Abbey. With the abbot of Gloucester, Gerald visited Bishop Wulfstan, the last Saxon bishop of Worcester, later consecrated as a saint, on his death-bed in 1095 and received absolution.

In 1102, Gerald received the benediction as abbot of Tewkesbury from the Norman Bishop Sampson of Worcester, Gerald's diocesan bishop.[8] As abbot, Gerald appears to have been a gifted administrator, quickly establishing a major monastery while pushing ahead with the construction of the Abbey. After the death of Robert Fitzhamon in 1107, the building work continued under the patronage of Robert, lord of the manor of Tewkesbury and later earl of Gloucester. In 1109, as a result of the offence he gave to the avaricious King Henry I in resisting to pay additional dues on some property, Abbot Gerald was compelled to resign, returning to his original monastery in Winchester where he died the following year.[9]

It cannot be easily reported how highly Robert Fitzhamon exalted this monastery, wherein the beauty of the buildings ravished the eyes, and the charity of the monks allured the hearts of such folk as used to come thither.[10]

Building the Abbey commenced in 1102 under the direction of a monk named Alfred, who was one of the first monks to come across to Tewkesbury from Cranbourne.[11]

Building almost certainly began at the east end with a two-bay sanctuary and quire that had north and south aisles, much as today, although looking rather different, having rounded arches.[12] However, the ambulatory – the processional way around the east end beyond the high altar – probably had three chapels leading from it: one to the east, another to the north-east and a third to the south-east, rather than the more numerous, later, Gothic chapels seen today. It may have been much as the east end of Gloucester Cathedral is now in its layout.

Painting on the ceiling of the chapel above the apse in the south transept that forms part of the present Lady Chapel

The seven Decorated-style windows, so much a part of the quire and sanctuary now, would not have been in place. Instead there would have been a triforium (a first floor) and above it a clerestorey (or clear storey – to let in light). The Norman pillars would then have been of the same massive height as the pillars in the nave today, while the triforium would have been a continuation of the 'chapel' above the apse in the current Lady Chapel in the south transept. There would have been chapels on the triforium floor, too, in the quire, though not many – perhaps two on each side.

The stone used was comparatively local Cotswold stone, perhaps from Stanway, where the Abbey owned the manor, and where there was a quarry. There were possibly quarries on Bredon Hill. Painswick stone was not used until much later, while the only Caen stone in the Abbey is the early twentieth-century effigy of Archdeacon Hemming Robeson.[13]

The quire having been completed, the builders would have moved on to the crossing area, and the two transepts, each of which had two bays but no aisles. There is evidence to show that the builders were prepared to reuse pre-existing stonework thought suitable. For example, on the west exterior wall of the north transept, about two-thirds of the way up, a carved panel can be seen that was probably originally Romano-British.[14] Each transept had a two-storey chapel with an apse on the east side. The south transept's chapel is still there as the current Lady Chapel with a second-storey chapel above it, said to be the only example of its type still left in an English parish church. The equivalent on the east side of the north transept was replaced in the thirteenth century. The first storey of the tower was begun, and was open to the ground until the fourteenth century.

Romano-British stone panel in the exterior wall on the north transept's west side

It is reasonable to suppose that at least the first two sets of nave arches were completed before the dedication, if for no other reason than that they needed to be in place to supply proper support for the central tower, the first stage of which would have been completed. It would have looked different from today. The ceiling of the nave would have been wooden and barrel-vaulted, not unlike an enlarged version of the ceiling of the north porch as it is now. The richly decorated stone vaulting that we now see in the nave would not have been constructed until the fourteenth century. The vaulting of the original wooden ceiling would have extended down on either side to just above what is today the nave triforium. There was no nave clerestorey at that time.

The north porch itself may or may not have been completed before the Abbey's consecration and dedication but it is a larger version of the entrance porch to Cranbourne Church, which was built *c*.1120.[15] The only difference, apart from size, is that at the Abbey the entrance has a carving of the Blessed Virgin Mary and

1090–1121: THE BUILDING OF THE ABBEY   11

Above the north porch: Mother and Child statue by Darsie Rawlins, of 1959, which replaced a medieval statue of similar style

Child centrally placed over the entrance – a 1959 replacement by Darsie Rawlins of the medieval original – whereas at Cranbourne it is a figure of Christ.[16] The other six arches of the nave may well have been begun but it is a matter of speculation as to whether the whole west end was completed by 1121. Either then or a little later, a stone screen was constructed across the whole of the nave, probably connecting to the two pillars at the east end of the nave. The second pair of pillars, heading west, would have had suspended between them a wooden Rood, much like the one which is above the current quire screen, though possibly a little larger. The stone screen or pulpitum was there to separate off the nave end of the church, which was to be used by the town as a parish church, while east of the stone screen was for the monks only.

There are two strands of evidence that suggest that the west end may not have been completed in time for the Abbey's consecration in 1121.

Masons' marks may be seen on the stonework, such as on the pillars in the nave

The first is a string course some five feet off the ground, that may be found on the north-west corner of the Abbey, where there remains a possible Consecration Cross scored into the stonework. This suggests that the walls may have been built no higher until after the dedication service. However, the Consecration Cross by itself does not tell us whether or not that part of the Abbey was complete. This is not seen on the south side as the monastic buildings would have already been in place. The second strand of evidence is the amount of time that elapsed between work beginning on the Abbey church in 1102, and its dedication some 19 years later. By medieval monastic standards, this represents a remarkably quick build for a large abbey building. Most medieval churches of the size of Tewkesbury Abbey seem to have taken at least 30 years, if not longer, to be built. However, this evidence is by no means conclusive, as the original Bristol Cathedral and the Romaneseque rebuilding of Romsey Abbey were also completed in a similar – or even quicker – time frame to that of Tewkesbury.[17]

The west end itself is imposing, especially when viewed from the outside. Originally, there were seven arches around and above the western entrance, which were later reduced to six each side of what has been called a 'triumphal' arch.[18] Near the top of the arch, on either side, are two rows of 'blind' arches or arcading with two turrets with conical pinnacles above. It is evident – notably from the inside – that originally there was an intention to build two west towers, rather in the manner of Durham, Lincoln and, much later, Bristol Cathedral. However, the scheme was abandoned, perhaps in order for the Abbey to be as near completion as possible by 1121, conceivably because the cost was becoming unsustainable. The baluster-shaped shafts seen in the apertures in the upper part of the two turrets look Saxon. However, when they were inspected during the 2002 restoration, the stonework was found to date from the early eighteenth-century restoration. There is no way of knowing whether or not the original stonework was Anglo-Saxon,

The Abbey tower showing both Norman/ Romanesque stages, the first belonging to the original building of c.1120 finishing at the string course just above the clock; the second added during the time of Robert Fitzroy, c.1145

incorporated into the Norman church.[19]

Robert Fitzhamon himself died in 1107. A measure of the respect in which he was held is reflected in that he was initially buried in the Abbey chapter house, which was considered a great honour. Later, in 1241 the body of the Abbey founder was brought into the Abbey itself and put in the position of highest honour: on the north side of the high altar.[20]

Robert Fitzhamon died leaving no male heir, but three, or possibly four, daughters. Henry I arranged for Robert Fitzroy, his illegitimate son, to marry Mabel, the eldest daughter available for marriage, the others having gone to nunneries. In so marrying, Robert inherited the vast Fitzhamon lands at a stroke, effectively for the benefit of the extended royal family. The King created Robert the first earl of Gloucester in 1122.[21]

Robert Fitzroy's lordship lasted until 1147. He is credited with building the second stage of the great central tower of the Abbey, still Romanesque in style and date but rather more ornate, with blind arcade decoration. The idea, suggested by the early nineteenth-century Tewkesbury historian James Bennett, that Robert also put a steeple on the top of the tower, is unlikely. The steeple occurred later, although exactly when is not clear.

Meanwhile, Abbot Gerald had fallen out with the King. The latter had apparently wanted to extract more in taxes from the Abbey than the abbot felt was reasonable. The result was that in 1109 the abbot was dismissed. He returned to his original monastery at Winchester, where he died a year later in 1110. He was succeeded as abbot by one Robert, a former chaplain to Robert Fitzhamon, himself also a Norman.[22] He was to remain in post through the dedication of the Abbey in 1121, dying in 1124.[23]

Robert Fitzroy, first earl of Gloucester, as depicted in a fourteenth-century window in the quire

Robert Fitzroy

Robert was the illegitimate son of Henry I and possibly a Welsh Princess named Nesta, daughter of one of the Welsh princes slain by Robert Fitzhamon, and was born in 1090, well before his father's accession to the throne in 1100.[24] He was known as Robert Fitzroy of Caen. His father, the King, was apparently the instigator of Robert's marriage with Robert Fitzhamon's daughter, Mabel (two other sisters having gone into nunneries). This was because the estates that Robert Fitzhamon had acquired were vast, and the King was keen to ensure that such lands were kept close to his family and did not become the power-base of a potential rival. According to the chroniclers Robert of Gloucester and Peter Langtoft, when she heard of the King's suggestion, Mabel protested that Robert merely had his name but no title, whereupon the King said that he would create Robert the first earl of Gloucester. Satisfied, Mabel consented to the match and she and Robert took over her father's entire estates. However, perhaps Henry I was a little slow to keep his word, for Robert was not created earl of Gloucester until 1122.

Robert built Bristol Castle, which he seems to have made his main base. However, he was more than a military man. He was also something of a politician, said to have been second only to Stephen, the King's nephew, at the end of the reign of Henry I. Although he initially supported Stephen to be the next king, he was to fall out with him, and later backed his rival, 'Empress' Matilda. Robert was said to be 'cultured, literate, militarily adept and politically astute'.[25] He so impressed the chronicler William of Malmesbury that he dedicated his 'Deeds of the Kings' to him. William is reported to have said to Robert:

> Your munificence and disregard of money is amply shown by the monastery at Tewkesbury, from which, as I hear, you not only do not extort presents, but even return its voluntary offerings.

Robert is also credited with inviting the abbot of Tewkesbury and 12 monks to dine with him every Sunday. This is unlikely to have been entirely true as he was often in Bristol, but it seems evident that he was a very hospitable man.

Robert was Lord of Tewkesbury when its Abbey was dedicated in 1121, and inhabited what Florence of Worcester called a 'magnificent house' that either he or Robert Fitzhamon built at Tewkesbury. Robert also founded the priory of St James, originally near but now almost in the centre of Bristol, which was a cell of Tewkesbury Abbey. The priory church survives today and its west front is original. Robert was buried there when he died in 1147. He also founded abbeys at Neath and Margam.[26]

PART II: CONSECRATION AND DEDICATION

THE Abbey was consecrated to the service of Almighty God on 23 October 1121 and dedicated to the Blessed Virgin Mary. There have been suggestions that the consecration was in 1123 but this is unlikely as the presiding bishop on the occasion, Bishop Theulf of Worcester, died on 20 October 1123, three days before it would have taken place. Three other bishops assisted: Bishop Richard de Capella of Hereford, Bishop Urban of Llandaff and Bishop Grene or Gregory, the then recently consecrated bishop of Dublin, later to be elevated to archbishop.[27]

The service and, up to a point, the rubric (that is the directions for the service's conduct) for the consecration may have been taken from a document such as the *Samson Pontifical* which had been written roughly 100 years previously, probably in Winchester.[28] It is named after the Norman Bishop Samson, Bishop Theulf's immediate predecessor as bishop of Worcester from 1096 to 1112. Alternatively, it has been suggested that the *Magdalen Pontifical* may have been used. However, its provenance appears to suggest that it may be a little late for use on this occasion. There is no clear evidence for which Pontifical would have been used.[29] A 'Pontifical' is a volume containing all the services in which

Reconstruction of how the nave may have looked c.1125. Note the barrel-vaulted ceiling and the absence of the clerestorey. Note, too, the pulpitum at the end of the nave and the paintings on the flanking pillars (*see also the illustration on p. 38*)

16   A HISTORY OF TEWKESBURY ABBEY

a bishop or someone of equivalent ecclesiastical status, such as a mitred abbot, presided.[30]

Other than for the presiding bishop, there would have been no 'Orders of Service' detailing words used, in what order, who would say them and what the rubric was. In any case, few could read. While many would have known the form of the Mass (Holy Communion) in medieval Latin by heart (even though many would probably not have understood it), nothing would have prepared them for the complexities of this service. However, only the bishops, clergy, monks and possibly the social elite among the laity, such as Robert Fitzroy and his wife, Mabel, née Fitzhamon, would have been allowed into the consecration service. Also present would have been abbots and perhaps senior colleagues from other monasteries, such as St Peter's, Gloucester (later the cathedral) and from Evesham. However, when the Dedication just before the Mass was reached, everyone would have been allowed in.[31] At the top of each page in the *Pontifical* (*see overleaf*), the rubrics were set out, each line alternately in red and green, making it fairly easy for the officiating bishop to follow. In larger script underneath, but in black, were set out the prayers, which were usually intoned, although some were offered in silence. Smaller script was used for the chants for the cantor and those singing. In the illustrations, a basic form of notation can be faintly seen.[32]

View of the nave as it is today, looking east. Note the clerestorey, the opening up of the nave's length and the fourteenth-century lierne-vaulted ceiling with painted ceiling bosses

Bened herbarū cēra dolores. Itē at. At. At. At.
Benedictē sup unguentū. t medicinā. Itē at.
Bened panis. Itē at. xcii. Bened arborū.
Bened pomorū. xciii. Bened uuę t fabę
Bened uini. xcvi. Bened ceruisę uasorūque eius
Bened ceruisę si mus aut inmundū qd in ea mergit̄
Bened fontis in q̄ aliqua neglegentia contigerit.

Hec sunt quę ante dedicationē p̄paranda sunt. Duodeci crucī
pictę foris. xii. intꝰ. Crux. Candelabra. xxiiii. cerei. Duodeci
foris. xii. intꝰ. Vasa conuenientia ad sacrandū & ad deferē
dā aquā. Duo maiores cęrei ad candelabra. xxiiii. claui. qb; c
infigant̄. Oleū scm & crisma. ysopū. Sabulū. t cineres. Vinū. Sa
Maiora grā incensi. Panni altaris. Tapetū. Bacinē. Manutgia

Ds q̄ sacrandorū tibi. MISSA P EDIFICANTE ECCL
auctor es munerū. ad scificationē loci p̄piti ad
dignare. ut q̄ hęc in bonorē nominis tui condideri
ptectorē tē habere monibꝫ mereant̄ atq; custodē
Ds q̄ loca nomini tuo dicata scificas. et benedictioni
bꝫ tuis dicanda precediſ. presta q̄s. ut qd beato ap
tuo. ill. famis tuiuſ. ill. b in edificio deputauit. dign
Votorū nr̄orū mun q̄s dr̄e ppi. SECR Preparet offi
tiaꝰ assume. ut talibꝫ sacrificiis exoratus. et nr̄ıs ue
delictis imptiaris. et huī tabernaculi exte scificati
Sc̄ificati dr̄e salutari mysterio p cōmulatore exau
q̄s ut p nob non desit oratio. quoꝝ nos donasti pat
nio gubernari. P HEC MISSA CANAT̄ P MISSĀ DICATE

INCIPIT ORDO AD DOMU DI CONSECRANDAM
PRIMITUS CU INDUTUS FUERIT EPS DICAT HANC
ORATIONE IN LOCO UBI SE INDUERIT

DS·QUI·PATERNA·MA

state ignea claustra disrupisti infer_
noru. et sanguine tuo populu tibi adquisisti sem_
piternu. indue nos armis spiritalibus uirtutu. et
inuicta sce crucis potentia. ut contra diabolu pu_
gnaturi. te in auxiliu habeamus. quatinus heredi_
tate tibi de iniquo spolio diaboli adquiramus. et
qui in domu zachei quonda miseratus descendisti.
ad domu qua scificaturi sumus uenire dignare. et
populu qui ad cuis dedicatione confluxerunt. spi_
tali gaudio remunera. saluator mundi dne ihu xpe.
qui cu patre et spu sco uiuis et regnas ds. p om a scta.
Post hec ueniant ante ostiu eccle que dedicanda
est cantando sonoriter hanc antiphonam.

Zachee festinans descende quia hodie in domu tua oportet me manere at
ille festinans descendit et suscepit illum gaudens in domu suam hodie huic
domui salus a domino facta est alleluia. ORATIO

Actiones nras qs dne et aspirando preueni et adiuuan_
do psequere. ut interueniente beata et glosa sem_
pque uirgine di genitrice maria cuncta nra opa_
tio et a te semp incipiat et pte cepta finiatur.
Ds qui nos pastores in poplo uocari uoluisti. presta
qs. ut hoc qd humano ore dicim. in tuis ocul. ee uale

Two pages from the manuscript known as the *Samson Pontifical* (after Samson, bishop of Worcester 1096–1112). The main part of the manuscript was created in Winchester in the early eleventh century, but had been taken to Worcester by the second half of the eleventh century, where it was altered and variously added to. The red and green lines of text are for the presiding bishop to say; the larger black text are prayers and the smaller black text with lines and dots show a form of plainsong with early notation. (MS 146 Copyright © Corpus Christi College, Cambridge)

Bishop Samson of Worcester (1096–1112)

This worldly, rich, generous Norman bishop was previously a royal chaplain, canon and treasurer of Bordeaux in France. He managed to combine these posts without being ordained. However, on his preferment in 1096, he was ordained deacon and priested on 7 June 1096, and consecrated a bishop the following day. This elevation did not prevent him from fathering a daughter, Isabelle of Douvres, who is supposed to have had an affair with Robert, the first earl of Gloucester. Bishop Samson's brother was, at one time, archbishop of York while his two sons, Richard and Thomas, both became bishops. He gave Abbot Giraldus benediction, thereby confirming the latter's appointment at Tewkesbury Abbey in 1102.[33]

The inside of the Abbey would have been dark and candle-lit. The great west window that is seen today would not have been there as the cost of glass was then ruinously expensive. There were probably three round-headed, plain lancet windows with a small round window on top called an oculus (*see p. 80*).[34] The windows now seen down the north and south nave aisles would have been much smaller – probably just a single, round-headed lancet – and possibly full of plain glass. The misericords now found in the quire would come some years later. Probably the only seats would have been three or four sedilia (priests' seats) for the clergy taking key parts in the service, plus possibly seats for visiting bishops. Otherwise, people had to stand.

Proceedings began outside the Abbey. The arrival of Bishop Theulf and other bishops, together with a number of visiting monks and clergy – possibly from Worcester – who would have known the consecration rite by heart, would have signalled a singing of the *Te Deum*, a Christian hymn of praise to God dating back to at least the fifth century.[35]

In the Anglo-Saxon rite from which the *Samson Pontifical* largely comes, there would have been three processions around the outside of the Abbey, during which a litany, invoking the intercessions of the saints, was chanted. While this was happening, the deacon would have slipped into the Abbey and shut the great west doors.

On the first two circuits of the Abbey, Bishop Theulf, enacting the end of Psalm 24, would have been refused permission to enter by the deacon. At the end of the third circuit, to the question the psalmist poses, 'Who is the King of Glory?' the response would be given: 'Even the Lord of Hosts, He is the King of Glory,' upon which the Abbey doors would have been opened and the bishop declared, 'Peace be to this House and to all that shall dwell therein. Blessing be unto them in their coming in and their going out.' He would then have led the procession into the Abbey itself, although at this point the laity would have been left outside.[36]

Once inside, the bishop would have proceeded to 'Blessing the Pavement', but not before the procession had made its way to the high altar, before which the clergy would have been prostrated for a second litany. Movement around the Abbey would have been affected by whether the pulpitum had already been erected. It would certainly have been more convenient on this occasion to have built it immediately after the consecration and dedication. Before and during each part of the service, antiphons – a set of responses based on scripture – would be sung. Initially, the focus was on the Old Testament but the antiphons switched to the New Testament once the various rites of purification had been completed. Often the antiphons would be followed by an appropriate psalm, which the monks should have known by heart anyway.

Whatever the situation, after the second litany the bishop stood in the middle of the Abbey in the nave, in order to establish, by prayer, the link between the Church and the Tabernacle on Mount Moriah, which was the site of Abraham's attempted sacrifice of Isaac and of Jacob's vision of a ladder to Heaven. The Bishop traced two alphabets, in ashes, diagonally across the floor with his crozier.[37] The first alphabet, from north-east to south-west, would be the Greek letters; the second, from south-east to the north-west, in Latin: the two universal languages of cultured people at the time. The two diagonal lines would form a cross. This was to signify that the divine revelation was for everyone, regardless of race or culture, in whatever language they spoke. The antiphon used, *Fundamenta eius*, from Psalm 87 verse 1, associated the floor on which the Abbey was built with Christ, the foundation stone of the Church and here its founder. It has been observed that 'The initial focus on the pavement and the intensity of the prayers used at this point are striking evidence for the symbolic importance of medieval church floors which pews and modern paving obscure'.[38]

The pavement blessing over, the church would then be 'baptised' by being washed with holy water, blessed in the Abbey font once salt and ashes had been added. Then further additions of wine and oil of Chrism would be included.[39] The altar was 'Lustrated' first by the bishop (that

> **Bishop Theulf of Worcester (1115–23)**
>
> The Norman bishop was a royal chaplain and canon of Bayeux Cathedral. He was appointed as bishop on 28 December 1113 but did not become a bishop until 27 January 1115 when he was consecrated by Archbishop Ralph d'Escures of Canterbury, Bishop Richard of London and five other bishops. He dedicated Tewkesbury Abbey on 23 October 1121 and died on 20 October 1123. William of Malmesbury asserts that, on his death bed, Bishop Theulf confessed to having purchased the bishopric.[40]

is 'to purify by ceremonially washing'). Some authorities suggest 'asperging' instead, that is sprinkling holy water. The presiding bishop would do this, circling and asperging the altar seven times. Then he would process around the walls inside the Abbey, asperging as he went, beginning in the north-eastern extremity. This he would repeat three times. There would also be some external asperging on the walls and even occasionally possibly on the roof, though probably not on this occasion. This part of the dedication concluded with holy water being poured on the floor – east to west, north to south – in the shape of a cross, 'echoing but not obscuring the earlier crossed alphabets' as one scholar has put it.[41]

It was at this point that the relics would be brought to the altar and placed in an unsealed cavity. The altar itself would be marked with five crosses with oil twice over, and the third time with the oil of Chrism.[42]

As in baptism, so in the consecration of a church. Having been 'immersed' in water, the church was now 'anointed' with holy oil. The altar already anointed, the bishop would do the same 12 times to the walls, both interior and then exterior. There are two exterior crosses still visible at Tewkesbury: one by the great north door, and another at the northernmost point of the west wall, about five feet off the ground.

As the bishop completed the external 'anointing' and returned to the Abbey interior, so he would have been followed by the laity allowed into the Abbey for the first time during the service.[43]

At the conclusion of that act of purification, the bishop would have returned to the altar, and there made the sign of the Cross over it with incense. This was to signify that the Abbey had been purified and that not only was the Holy Spirit now present but that the focus of what was happening had moved from the centre of the Abbey to the altar where the remainder of the rite would occur. No longer was the focus the Old Testament but the New.

The relics of saints already in an altar cavity would be briefly removed while the cavity was censed, and they were then returned and the cavity sealed with mortar, symbolising the reality of the continuity of the Church and its mission as well as the sacrifices of Christians in the spread of the Gospel. The altar linen, vessels and ornaments would then be blessed and the altar dressed.[44]

There then followed the prayer of Dedication of the church to the named saint – in the Abbey's case St Mary, mother of Jesus Christ – followed by commendations of the church to the Holy Cross and the Holy Trinity.

Following the Dedication, the bishop, accompanied by clergy, would have left the Abbey so that he could take off his soiled vestments, wash his hands of oil and mortar and vest for the Mass.[45]

The Bishop would re-enter in solemn procession with clergy, best vestments, crosses, Gospel books and including 12 monks or servers bearing lit processional candles. Three of the candles would go in each corner of the Abbey. They would be symbolising the *Book of Revelation*, chapter 21 verse 14.[46] Mass would begin with the introit:

> Full of awe is this place.
> It is the house of God
> and the Gate of Heaven.
> It will be called the court of God ...
> *Genesis* 28, v17

The conclusion of the Mass would signal the end of an unforgettable occasion for those who had witnessed it or any part of it.

It is very difficult to estimate how long the full service would have taken. In a small church, possibly two to three hours. In a church the size of Tewkesbury Abbey possibly as long as four hours in total.

CHAPTER THREE

1122–1215: From Dedication to the signing of Magna Carta

Having conducted Tewkesbury Abbey's dedication service, Bishop Theulf of Worcester departed and died shortly after, in October 1123.

The Abbey may have been newly dedicated, but the monastery itself had been firmly established and organised by its first abbot, Gerald, who was followed in 1109 by Abbot Robert who died in 1124. By the end of that year Abbot Benedict was in charge.

The most senior monk under an abbot, who assumed command if the abbot was absent or ill, was the prior. Abbot Gerald had five other senior monks called *obedentiaries* who had particular departmental responsibilities at Tewkesbury. The cellarer was responsible for most house-keeping matters, including all food and catering. The chamberlain was in charge of the monks' clothing, footwear, laundry and bedding. The sacrist together with the precentor were responsible between them for the services, including music, vestments, lights, liturgy and such service books or manuscripts that were used. Finally, there was the almoner, concerned with the pastoral work of the Abbey. He was also responsible for distributing money to the poor and needy. Later, it seems that other monks were also made *obedentiaries*. These included the infirmarian, who ran the monastery's hospital and the guest-master, who looked after visitors, some little better off than beggars all the way up the social scale to royalty. The novice-master supervised and trained those wishing or sent to become monks, from young boys through to adult men.[1]

The *Opus Dei* (The work of God) – the monastic offices – were held eight times every 24 hours, together with Mass (Holy Communion), which was also daily. This involved monks rising from their beds at night, and coming down the night stairs that emerged in the present Lady Chapel. The doorway can still be seen. All these offices were usually carried out with great care and devotion at this time, not least under Abbot Benedict (abbot 1124–37) who was known for his piety.[2] The offices were interspersed with periods set aside for manual work, study, meals, relaxation and private devotion (*see overleaf*).

Meanwhile Robert Fitzroy, earl of Gloucester and lord of Tewkesbury, was supporting his half-sister, Empress Matilda (Queen Maud), in her bid for the English Crown after the death of their father, King Henry I, in 1135.[3] Her rival, a cousin, Stephen, had had himself crowned the same year.

Earl Robert landed in England, having fetched Matilda from France in 1139, before returning to his main power-base at Bristol. The earl sponsored an attack on one of Stephen's main supporters, Waleran, earl of Worcester, at his main base of Worcester. Gloucester garrison, probably organised by Miles, constable of Gloucester (a close ally of Earl Robert) attacked Worcester on 7 November 1139, burning part of it, sacking it and kidnapping some citizens to be ransomed.[4] Earl Waleran retaliated by first attacking Sudeley Castle, where he 'ravaged the country around it' and then Tewkesbury 'savagely' the following year. In the latter attack, the Abbey was apparently burned. This almost certainly refers to the monastic buildings rather than the Abbey itself, as Abbot Roger, sometimes called Robert, and the monks 'succeeded in persuading him [Earl Waleran] not to burn the Abbey Church'. In another report the whole Abbey community was spared.[5]

In between raids, battles and advising his half-sister, Earl Robert founded the chapel of St James at Bristol, apparently *c*.1129, although

The Daily Offices for medieval Benedictine monks

Mattins (or Matins): From the Latin *matutinus* meaning 'of morning'. Originally at midnight, the Benedictines changed it to 2 am. It was called Nocturns for many centuries, as each part was called a Nocturn. A Nocturn consisted of three psalms and their antiphons, versicle, Lord's Prayer, another prayer and three lessons as well as benedictions or blessings. On a Sunday or a major feast-day there would be three complete nocturns, not just one as on an ordinary weekday.

Lauds: This short office, sung at dawn, included a number of psalms that always included Psalms 148 to 150, sometimes called the Laudes because the word, meaning 'Praise Ye', is often used.

Prime: (The First hour) Also sung early in the morning. It included a canticle, a short lesson, psalms and a hymn.

Terce: (The Third hour): It was also sung in the morning. It included a hymn, three psalms with antiphons, a reading, the lesser litany, Lord's Prayer, versicles and Collect. It might be preceded or followed by a celebration of Mass.

Sext: (The Sixth hour) This occurred about midday and might occur immediately after Mass. Similar to Terce and None and this usually included the singing of Psalm 69.

None: (The Ninth hour) This was the office for the mid-afternoon and was short. It included a hymn, followed by a psalm, a short reading, response and closing prayer.

Vespers: This early evening office included a hymn, two psalms, a New Testament canticle, a short lesson, responsary, the Magnificat and prayers. It is seen with Lauds as the two most important of the Day Offices.

Compline: This short office is designed for those about to go to bed. It includes a responsary, a hymn, a psalm, the *Nunc Dimittis* and prayers, entrusting oneself, body and soul, to God

The upper part of the central tower, added by Earl Robert c.1140

1137 has also been suggested. He turned it into a cell or priory belonging to Tewkesbury.[6] It was completed *c*.1170 and is today said to be the oldest surviving building in Bristol.

Earl Robert added the upper part of the central tower at Tewkesbury *c*.1140, up to but not including the present battlements.[7] It continued to be a 'lantern' tower, its windows giving a little additional natural light to the monks worshipping in the quire below it. This was just after the death of Abbot Benedict and the election of Abbot Roger, who was to oversee the community for over 20 years until 1161. He was succeeded by Abbot Fromund.[8]

On 31 October 1147, aged 57, Earl Robert died and was buried in his chapel in Bristol.[9]

Earl Robert was succeeded as earl of Gloucester and lord of Tewkesbury by his eldest son, William, the first earl of Gloucester to be born in Tewkesbury. The latter came under suspicion regarding his loyalty to Matilda's son, now King Henry II, and subsequently

The south transept of the Abbey, showing where monastic buildings were attached to the Abbey. The red colouring of some of the stonework here is as a result of the great fire of 1178

surrendered the burgeoning port and city of Bristol to the King in 1175. The consequence of this was that the great lordship of Tewkesbury, important before, now became a central part of the earl's estates. The earl confirmed and extended rights and privileges to the townsmen of Tewkesbury, including making it a 'free burgh' originally given by his father in a great charter.[10] William married Hawise de Beaumont, daughter of the earl of Leicester, and the couple had a son and three daughters. Sadly the boy,

Robert, predeceased his father, dying in 1166. When William died, he was buried at Keynsham Abbey, Somerset, which he had founded in memory of his son.

Only too aware that he had no son and heir, William (sometimes known as Fitzcount) came to an agreement with King Henry II in 1176 that the King's favourite and youngest son, Prince John (Count of Mortain, also known as Lackland), then earl of Cornwall, should also be made heir to the earldom of Gloucester on the understanding that he marry one of Earl William's daughters, Isabel (Isabelle) even though they were third cousins.[11] Earl William died in 1183, with his estates income calculated to have been in excess of £580 per annum. This was a huge sum when compared to that of a manual labourer who might receive a silver penny for a day's work (roughly £1 25p per annum if, unusually, in full paid employment all the year round).[12] Prince John duly married Isabel in 1189, thereby acquiring not only vast English lands but also Glamorgan in Wales.

Prince John, both before and after his succession to the earldom of Gloucester and even before his marriage to Isabel (Isabelle), seems to have enjoyed coming to Tewkesbury. He was a mere youth when the abbot and monks of the Abbey 'sumptuously entertained' him in 1178.[13] It was the same year that the Abbey suffered a terrible fire, traces of which may still be seen by the redness of parts of the stonework, both internal and external, in the south wall of the south transept. It is not clear whether it was the strain of entertaining a royal prince or problems regarding the Abbey fire, but Abbot Fromund died the same year.[14] His successor, Abbot Robert, did not receive his Benediction until September 1182, four years after his predecessor's death – but only lived a further year before dying himself. There was a further interregnum. Yet, among these sad events, Tewkesbury Abbey was gradually becoming more influential through those who presented churches – and therefore their incomes – to the monastery. Between 1163 and 1183, for example, Nicholas ap Gurgant gave St Mary, Cardiff, the Castle Chapel and 'a great number' of other churches to Tewkesbury Abbey. Gilbert Foliot, bishop of London, presented the monastery with the parish of All Saints, London.[15]

The new abbot, Alan, formerly a scholarly prior of Christchurch, Canterbury, was appointed in 1186, receiving his abbot's Benediction the following year. He edited a collection of letters of the former Archbishop of Canterbury, St Thomas Becket.[16] St Thomas' martyrdom was the result of ill-judged remarks by King Henry II in December 1170. Alan became a monk in Canterbury in 1174 and was appointed prior in 1179. In 1186, Archbishop Baldwin had him elected abbot of Tewkesbury. He was to oversee the Abbey as abbot until his death in 1202.[17] His simple tomb is in the south quire aisle near the sacristy. It was probably during his time or possibly earlier that the abbot provided for 13 almsmen or bedesmen belonging to the town and parish of Tewkesbury, known as the founder's almsmen. Successive abbots continued to provide money for food, clothing and rent right up to the Dissolution of the Monasteries in 1540.[18]

In the meantime, Earl John was developing a deer park covering much of the land between what is now Tewkesbury Park and Deerhurst, as well as the construction of a bridge over the River Avon. It is known that even after he became King in 1199, he still came to Tewkesbury and to the Abbey at least four times during his reign (1199–1216), including one Christmas (1204), and granted two charters to the Abbey.[19] However, just before becoming King, John had his childless marriage with Isabel annulled on consanguineous grounds (that they were too closely related). Subsequently, Isabel was married to Geoffrey Mandeville, earl of Essex, who thus became the fourth earl of Gloucester and lord of Tewkesbury with the vast lands involved – for which he is said to have paid the King 20,000 marks (a mark being two-thirds of a pound sterling).[20] However, King John kept Glamorgan, as he had discovered that there

Abbot Alan of Tewkesbury

Abbot Alan's birth details are obscure. Some suggest he was possibly born in Tewkesbury; others in Kent around 1140. He may have had something to do with the Christchurch Monastery, Canterbury while still a child. Subsequently, he attended the Schools in Paris, forerunners of the university. In 1174 he was a canon of Benevento Cathedral in southern Italy when he decided to enter Christchurch, Canterbury as a novice monk. Less than four years earlier, in December 1170, Archbishop Thomas Becket of Canterbury had been murdered in his own cathedral. John of Salisbury, an archbishop's clerk, began the massive task of collecting and editing the archbishop's letters. However, John became bishop of Chartres and Alan, already seen as a scholar, was asked to complete a task barely begun. This he did with meticulous care, putting all 600 letters in as near chronological order as was possible, with appropriate notes. A copy – possibly the master copy – is held by the British Library.

When the ageing Prior Herlewin of Christchurch resigned in August 1179, Alan was elected as his successor. Seven years later, Archbishop Baldwin, who was embarking upon ecclesiastical building schemes that might threaten the well-being of some Canterbury poor, found Alan a doughty opponent. In 1186, the archbishop's solution was to send the troublesome Alan miles away by having him elected abbot of Tewkesbury.

Initially lonely in his new surroundings, Abbot Alan found that he was welcomed and his judgement and learning respected. He was asked to act judicially in both ecclesiastical and state matters, and in 1200 he was hearing cases on behalf of King John, who respected him a great deal.

Abbot Alan was said to be sympathetic, understanding and supportive to those who had problems. He was also outspoken about those who failed to live up to their high calling, such as Roger Norreys, abbot of Evesham, who apparently lived an extravagant and licentious life.

Abbot Alan died in May 1202. His tomb lies close to the door to the sacristy.[21]

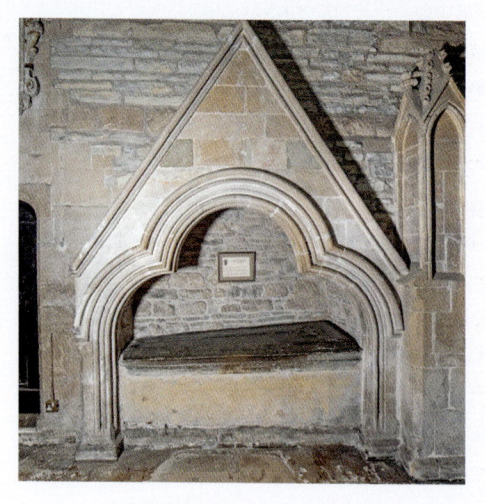

Abbot Alan of Canterbury's tomb in the south quire aisle

seemed to be an almost inexhaustible supply of useful mercenary soldiers to be found there.[22]

Abbot Alan, who died in 1202, was followed by Abbot Walter, who had been sacrist at the Abbey. As such, he would have been responsible for ensuring the liturgy, robes, sacred vessels and books or manuscripts were appropriate and well looked after for each service. He found that the Abbey was owing 700 marks, but soon discharged the debt and subsequently ensured that the monastery kept solvent. However, this was of comparatively small consequence compared to the national situation that was about to engulf the Abbey.

The crisis concerned the appointment of an Archbishop of Canterbury. In brief, King John refused to recognise as the new archbishop Simon Langton, Pope Innocent III's nominee. After much wrangling, the Pope issued an Interdict, effective from 23 March 1208, which meant that in general all services and rites in churches, including Tewkesbury Abbey, were suspended. This meant that people could not receive Holy Communion, be given a Christian burial, be married, baptised or 'churched' (thanksgiving for childbirth), although some of the latter were apparently carried out in church porches. Sermons could only be preached on Sundays in churchyards.[23] It is not clear how stringently these rules were applied at Tewkesbury Abbey, although it certainly appears that the Abbey was closed for services for six years.[24]

John refused to yield, so in November 1209 the Pope excommunicated him. This had a greater effect on the King than the Interdict in that it began to isolate him, for in meeting or associating with an excommunicate, a person risked being excommunicated themselves. King John now turned on the Church and plundered it. By 1211, the treasury was receiving at least £24,000 a year in revenue taken from churches.[25] Yet there is no record of John robbing Tewkesbury Abbey.

Eventually, in 1214, the King was effectively forced to give way to the Pope.[26] Stephen Langton became archbishop; the excommunication and Interdict were both lifted and Tewkesbury Abbey and all the other churches could return to normal religious life.

In the meantime, either in 1213 or 1214, Abbot Walter died, to be succeeded by the Abbey's own prior, Hugh, who was elected and consecrated as abbot in 1214. Sadly, he died within a year or so of taking office.[27] On his death, Bernard, one of the Tewkesbury monks, was elected by his fellows – but the appointment did not meet with the approval of the bishop of Worcester. Instead Peter, a monk of Worcester, was elected and received benediction as abbot in April 1216.[28]

Relations between some barons and the King had reached a point where Stephen Langton, as Archbishop of Canterbury, had to intervene to try to find a pragmatic compromise. The result was Magna Carta, the final version with the King's and 25 barons' seals affixed at Runnymede by the River Thames on 19 June 1215. The then earl of Gloucester and therefore lord of Tewkesbury, Geoffrey de Mandeville, was present, as well as two of the de Clare family, soon successively to be earls of Gloucester themselves.[29] A copy of Magna Carta was sent to Tewkesbury Abbey, which appears to have been lost possibly during the early eighteenth century, it having been seen and remarked upon by Sir Matthew Hale, the distinguished seventeenth-century judge and jurist, a man of unimpeachable integrity, during a visit to the Abbey before 1713.[30]

Magna Carta, securing important legal rights for barons and freemen (although very few for serfs), has been seen as an important landmark in Britain's history. However, within two years of its approval many of those present, who also had an interest in Tewkesbury and its Abbey, were dead. King John, a former earl of Gloucester, together with Geoffrey de Mandeville, then earl of Gloucester, both died in 1216. Richard de Clare, who was also present at Runnymede, held the earldom and lordship of Tewkesbury for a few months only before himself dying in 1217. Only Richard de Clare's son, Gilbert, who was also present at the agreement, survived to become earl of Gloucester and lord of Tewkesbury in 1221.[31]

It is to the impact that the de Clare family had on Tewkesbury Abbey that attention is now turned.

CHAPTER FOUR

1216–1314: The Age of the de Clare family, the building of a Lady Chapel

WILLIAM Fitzcount, the second earl of Gloucester, patron of Tewkesbury Abbey, had three daughters who married: Mabel, the eldest, married Amaury (Amauri) v de Montfort, count of Evreux (Eureux), Normandy.[1] Her husband died comparatively young, *c*.1191, leaving her a son, who died in childhood.

William Fitzcount's second daughter, Isabel (Isabella), through the intervention of the King, Henry II, inherited virtually the entire estates of the earldom of Gloucester, including the Honour of Tewkesbury, to make her an attractive match for her husband.[2] She married Prince John, youngest and favourite son of Henry II, eventually King himself. After ten childless years together, the marriage was annulled in 1199 on consanguinity grounds, so that John, as he ascended the throne, could marry Isabella of Angoulême. Isabel of Gloucester subsequently married Geoffrey de Mandeville, earl of Essex, in 1214, apparently reluctantly, for which he paid 20,000 marks to King John for her hand and vast estates. However, John hung on to Glamorgan and other areas, notably the port of Bristol, for a time.[3] The new marriage also produced no surviving children.[4] Earl Geoffrey died in a London tournament in February 1216.[5] Isabel may have been a little old to bear children at the age of 43 when, as a very rich widow, and now countess of Gloucester and Essex in her own right, she married thirdly Hubert de Burgh. At this point Hugh was Lord Warden of the Cinque Ports, Constable of Dover Castle, Chief Justiciar of the Kingdom and later earl of Kent, one of England's most senior and powerful nobles. Sadly, within two months of the wedding, she had died in October 1217.[6]

However, William Fitzcount's third daughter, Amice, married Richard I de Clare, earl of Hertford, who, through his wife, was briefly earl of Gloucester (after Countess Isabel's death) before dying himself in December 1218. Their son, Gilbert I de Clare survived as earl of Gloucester after his father's death, founding a dynasty through his marriage to Isabel Marshal that was to be synonymous with the earldom of Gloucester and the patronage of Tewkesbury Abbey for decades to come.[7]

Tewkesbury Abbey's abbot was now Abbot Peter (1216–32). He had come from Worcester Monastery before his election.[8] In 1218 the monks' dormitory roof collapsed as monks returned from an early service. One monk, Gilbert, was said to have had a broken thigh and head wound. Apparently others, including the prior, Gunfrey, escaped unhurt.[9]

Abbot Peter proved more aggressive than predecessors in protecting the Abbey's interests, even though initially deciding in 1224 to sell land the Abbey owned in both Ireland and Wales because of disturbances in both places. He fell out with William of Blois, bishop of Worcester 1218–37, over issues concerning property and episcopal visitations, together with 'excessive expenses' incurred when ordinations and synods were carried out at Tewkesbury Abbey.[10]

Abbot Peter felt so strongly that in 1224 he journeyed to Rome, apparently successfully making representations to the Pope, returning in 1226 much respected by the monks. While the dispute continued, Abbot Peter was caught up in other matters. In October 1230 Earl Gilbert I de Clare died. He had been supporting King Henry III, in a campaign in France. Gilbert left special directions for burial in Tewkesbury Abbey where no de Clare had been buried before. His body was interred before the high altar by Abbot Peter, assisted by the abbots of Tintern, Flaxley, Dureford and Keynsham. The only former patron buried within the monastery at that time – but not yet within the Abbey itself – was its founder, Robert Fitzhamon. Yet from Gilbert I de Clare's burial onwards, patrons of the Abbey were interred within its walls for the next 250 years.[11] The bishop excommunicated both abbot and monastery for further wrangling over the appropriation of Fairford parish church, during which, in 1232, Abbot Peter died.

Nothing significant had happened to the Abbey architecturally since the addition of the upper part of the crossing tower in the 1140s. Now, in about 1220, a large chapel was added to the north side of the north transept. Its original chancel is now the Camera Cantorum for choirs. The original nave outline can be partially traced in the external stonework on the north side of the north transept. The evidence – not least its considerable stone mouldings and decoration generally – suggests that it was probably the Abbey's first Lady Chapel.[12] This would tie in with increasing veneration of the Blessed Virgin Mary, seen in the late twelfth and thirteenth centuries, particularly in monasteries including Benedictine houses. The chapel's style was a lavish version of Early English Gothic, complete with Purbeck marble shafts that place it sometime after 1200; probably c.1220, when similar chapels were being built elsewhere, such as at Bristol Cathedral and Westminster Abbey.[13] At its east end the Abbey almost certainly had three or possibly five lancet windows, later replaced by the Decorated-style fourteenth-century east window. The chapel was probably free-standing before other chapels were added.[14] Entry was gained from the north end of the north transept through an archway. There may have been an external door to the chapel nave opposite the internal one. This would have been almost exactly where the present passageway steps and almshouses are now.[15] In keeping with the rest of the Abbey at that time, the chapel roof was probably wooden, to be replaced with stone – and the de Clare and Despenser heraldry on the bosses – in the fourteenth century.[16] The greater weight accounts for the support of buttresses that were also added at this time.

The bigger chapel space – now entirely occupied by the Abbey shop – was a double-chapel created c.1237 by the demolition of the north transept Norman apsidal chapel. It had been similar to the present-day Lady Chapel in the south transept. Saved stone was reused in the new construction. The pushing out of the east wall made additional space. The double-chapel thus created was dedicated to St Nicholas and St James – the latter presumably being the dedication of the former first-floor chapel that now no longer existed.[17] This followed a

The north end of the north transept, showing the site of the destroyed nave and the separate original chancel of what was probably the Abbey's first Lady Chapel, now the Camera Cantorum

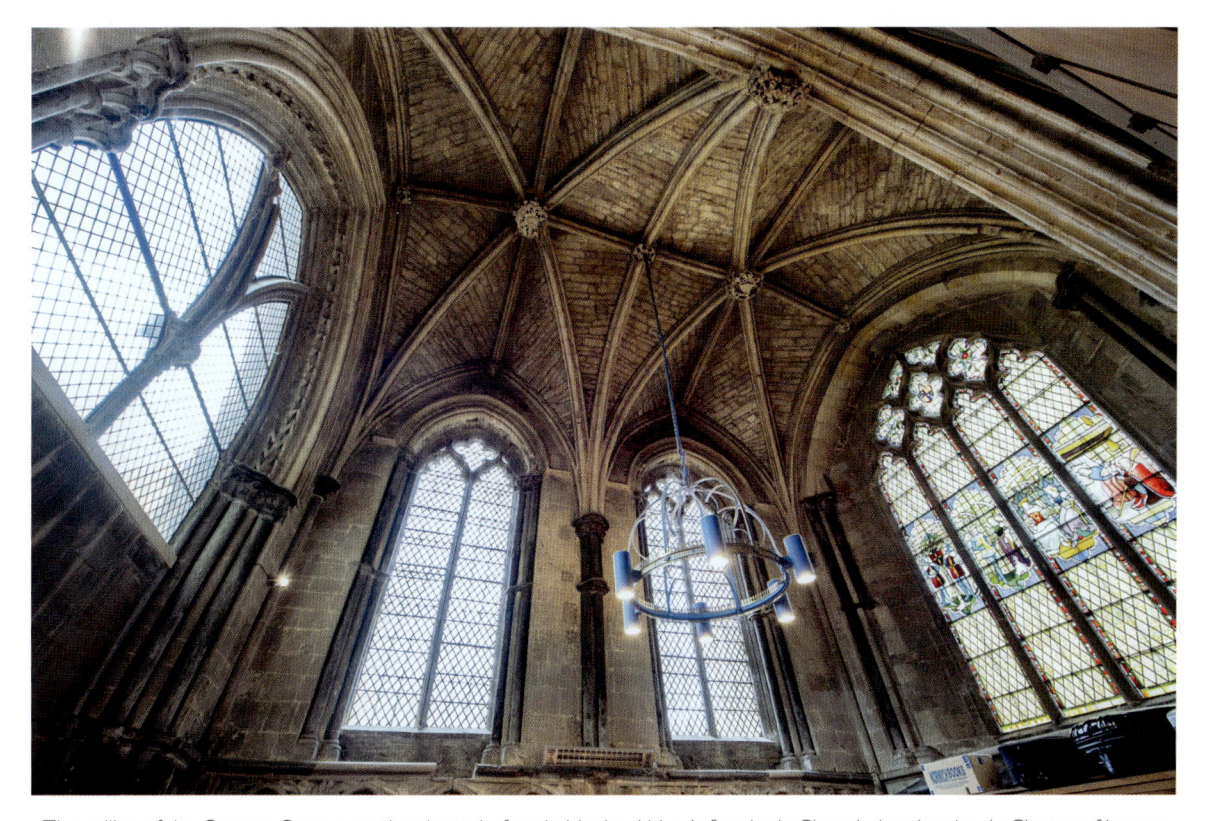

The ceiling of the Camera Cantorum, the chancel of probably the Abbey's first Lady Chapel, showing the de Clare roof bosses

developing trend in other abbeys and cathedrals to have all chapels on the ground floor. Prior Henry de Sipton saw this project through to its dedication in 1238.[18] Following a precedent set at Canterbury by Archbishop Anselm, rebuilding or improving an abbey or cathedral was largely left in the hands of the priors. This allowed the abbots – in Tewkesbury's case, Abbot Robert Forthington, himself a former prior of the Abbey – to concentrate on other matters.

Abbot Robert had been elected abbot by a 'free vote' of the monks in 1232. This had been granted by Hubert de Burgh, who had briefly married Isabel, countess of Gloucester. Hubert did so as guardian of Richard II de Clare, patron of the Abbey, who was still a minor.[19] Hubert paid King Henry III 7,000 marks (£4,666) for being guardian, as it allowed him access to the de Clare estates during Richard's minority.[20] Guardianship also brought responsibilities. Whereas today, being patron of anything is largely symbolic and ceremonial, in the thirteenth century, being patron of an important monastery was to be its secular protector, and such patrons often took a lively interest in that monastery's life.

Abbot Robert was said to be saintly. He was also 'an able and vigorous abbot, bent on maintaining the rights of the monastery against both episcopal [Church] and lay encroachments'.[21] He continued the tussle with the bishop of Worcester, William of Blois, that had resulted in the excommunication of his predecessor, Abbot Peter of Worcester and, for a short time, the entire monastery. The bishop had even initially taken exception to Abbot Peter's body being buried in the Abbey. It took the good offices of the patron's guardian, Hubert de Burgh, to resolve matters equitably.[22] This must have been a relief to the abbot who, in 1234, had endured a fire that burned down the principal gate of the monastery – roughly where the Crescent Abbey grounds entrance is today – together with two stables. The fire was such that it is said to have 'threatened the Abbey.'[23]

Abbot Robert is thought to have paid the re-roofing cost of the monks' dormitory from money set aside for his household maintenance. Barely a year into his new appointment, in May or June, 1233, Abbot Robert found himself receiving Queen Eleanor at the Abbey, and possibly her husband, King Henry III, too. Certainly, both visited the Abbey during that decade and it is thought that the Queen visited the Abbey on several occasions.[24] Moreover, Abbot Robert was already being credited with effecting miracles. Over 40 were mentioned as occurring within his first year as abbot: a man recovering his speech, a girl her sight, paralytics being cured, and so on.[25] In 1235, Isabel of Gloucester, widow of Gilbert I de Clare, who had died in 1230, presented a collection of relics 'of great sanctity' to the Abbey.[26] These included a stone said to have come from Calvary and even what was said to be the stake or base into which the Cross of Christ had been fixed. There were relics of St Thomas of Canterbury and St Wulfstan of Worcester. Pilgrims had tended to be a drain on income rather than augmenting Abbey funds.[27] Robert had noted that no king or saint was buried at the Abbey, and so pilgrims – and their offerings – were not attracted to it. Now Abbot Robert instituted a 'Feast of The Holy Relics' every 2 July.[28] From then on, pilgrims were more frequent, especially when further apparent miracles were recorded in 1252 and 1255. The last year was seen as being particularly remarkable, as Abbot Robert had died the year before and his prayers were perceived as assisting miracles still said to be taking place.[29]

Monarchs who have visited Tewkesbury Abbey

King John – Both as Prince John, earl of Cornwall (1178) and as King, he was at Tewkesbury for Christmas 1204 as well as on other occasions.[30]

King Henry III – In 1233, possibly also 1236 and/or 1258. His wife, Queen Eleanor, is said to have visited several times.[31]

King Edward I – Came to Tewkesbury with his court in 1265 on two occasions; also in Tewkesbury in 1278.[32]

King Richard II – Stayed 'some time' in Tewkesbury in 1378 when there was a Parliament in Gloucester.[33]

King Edward IV – Certainly came in May 1471 and had a Mass held in the Abbey to mark his victory at the Battle of Tewkesbury over the House of Lancaster.[34]

King Richard III – As duke of Gloucester and the king's brother, he was with King Edward IV when he was victorious at the battle of Tewkesbury in 1471, and would have been with him for the service marking the victory.

Queen Mary Tudor – Who, as Princess Mary, Princess of Wales, spent Christmas in Tewkesbury in 1525.[35]

King Henry VIII – Visited and stayed at Tewkesbury Abbey or possibly Forthampton Court, 23–27 July 1535.[36]

King George III and Queen Charlotte – Visited the Abbey in 1788.[37]

(**Queen Mary, wife of King George V** – Visited the Abbey as Princess Mary of Teck in 1891, and as Queen in 1937).[38]

Queen Elizabeth II – Distributed the Royal Maundy at the Abbey in 1971, the 850th year of the Abbey's consecration. Apart from Selby Abbey, Tewkesbury is the only greater church to be so honoured. All the other Royal Maundy services have been in cathedrals, Westminster Abbey or St George's Chapel, Windsor.[39]

(**HRH Prince Charles, Prince of Wales** – Visited in 2002).

In 1236, Abbot Robert must have been partly drawn in to a row between Hubert de Burgh and King Henry III. Young Earl Richard de Clare, patron of the Abbey, was fast approaching marriageable age. As he was about to be head of arguably the greatest noble family in England in the thirteenth century, the King, Henry III, stood to make a great deal of money as marriage broker. For a price of 5,000 marks, he was about to allow a marriage between Richard and Maud de Lacy, the earl of Lincoln's daughter. However, Hubert de Burgh's second wife, Margaret, secretly had Richard marry her daughter, Margaret, better known as Meggota. When this was discovered in 1236, the King was understandably furious. Hubert de Burgh, no longer Richard de Clare's guardian, was accused of *maritagium* (a portion given with a daughter in marriage) but as he was the King's temporary prisoner in Devizes Castle at the time of the marriage, he argued that he neither knew of it nor sanctioned it, although this is unlikely. A large gift of money to the King also helped. Eventually the King relented. Richard de Clare and Meggota, who may well have been kept apart anyway, were separated and the King planned to have the marriage annulled. However, very conveniently, Meggota died in 1237. Richard de Clare was duly married to Maud de Lacy, the earl of Lincoln's daughter, on 26 January 1238.[40]

Richard de Clare's mother, Isabel of Gloucester and now of Cornwall, died in January 1240 aged 39 during childbirth. She had requested burial with her first husband, Gilbert de Clare, with whom she had apparently enjoyed a happy marriage before his death in 1230, in Tewkesbury Abbey. Her second husband, Richard, earl of Cornwall, refused, requiring her burial in Beaulieu Abbey which had belonged to his father, King John. However, Prior Henry de Sipton of Tewkesbury, present at Isabel's death, reasoned with him. Richard partly relented, allowing her heart in a silver casket to be buried next to her first husband at Tewkesbury, conveyed to the Abbey by Prior Henry. Isabel left much to Tewkesbury Abbey – silver-bound service books, copes, chalices, money and land. She also left a bottle in which there was a collection of relics sent to her by the Pope, purporting to include hairs from St Elizabeth the Virgin, part of a linen garment of St Agnes as well as relics from St Cornelius, St Basil and at least a dozen further saints and martyrs. It is not recorded what Prior Henry did with them.[41]

Abbot Robert was still in office when Bishop William Blois of Worcester died, and welcomed his successor, Bishop Walter Cantilupe, a person of significant personal integrity. The latter visited Tewkesbury Abbey to dedicate the high altar and the Abbey to the Virgin Mary in June 1239.[42] This probably refers to the high altar slab of Purbeck marble that is currently there, possibly the longest surviving in England.[43] It is not known for sure what happened to the original altar that was said to be Norman. There is a monument that looks rather like a very worn table-top tomb

The Purbeck marble high altar mensa, consecrated by Bishop Walter de Cantilupe of Worcester in 1239

A detail of the surface of the high altar mensa. Note the Consecration Cross in the middle. The filled-in crack on either side of the Cross was a result of the mensa being cut in two in the early part of the seventeenth century. The other cracks above and below occurred accidentally during the reordering of the Abbey in the late nineteenth century. (The mensa was finally returned as high altar in 1879)

in the main churchyard that some credit with being the original altar, but there is no evidence for this.[44]

In 1241, two new bells having been consecrated a couple of months before, Abbot Robert had Robert Fitzhamon's body moved from the Chapter House. It was interred in a place of particular honour, the north side of the sanctuary, on 25 October, the Feast of Saints Crispin and Crispinian.[45]

It is evident that Abbot Robert was efficient. Bishop Cantilupe conscientiously held a visitation to Tewkesbury Abbey in 1251 and again in 1253 but could find nothing to criticise, even though each monk was interviewed.

In 1254, Abbot Robert died. Probably in 1255, he was succeeded by Abbot Thomas de Stokes, previously prior of St James, Bristol, a priory belonging to Tewkesbury Abbey. He remained abbot until his death in 1275. During his Abbacy, there was another fire in 1256, which destroyed some of the service buildings. However, there were more joyful times, such as when Earl Richard spent Christmas at Tewkesbury, which he is said to have done on more than one occasion.[46] In 1262, Earl Richard II de Clare died, possibly after being poisoned, having first been reconciled to the monks of the Abbey with whom he had had a dispute in 1258. He was buried to the right of his father before Tewkesbury Abbey's high altar.[47]

Earl Richard II's son, Gilbert II, known as the 'Red Earl', succeeded to the titles, estates and the patronage of the Abbey. In 1265 he commanded royal troops when they defeated Simon de Montfort at the Battle of Evesham, although earlier, in 1263, he had been de Montfort's ally.

Earl Gilbert II's marriage to Isobel of Luisgnan, a kinswoman of the King, produced only daughters. This was eventually to lead to divorce. Earl Gilbert married his second wife, Joan of Acre, a daughter of King Edward I. One of the four children they produced was the longed-for heir, Gilbert III, born in 1290 or possibly 1291 at Tewkesbury. One of Gilbert III's younger sisters, Margaret, later married Piers Gaveston, King Edward II's favourite.[48]

In 1265, Abbot Thomas de Stokes was summoned to attend Parliament, thus effectively becoming a mitred abbot.[49] It was a mixed blessing that required time away from the monastery on state affairs which, while enhancing the abbot's standing, might have been a real distraction from possibly pressing affairs at the abbot's monastery.[50] Abbots of Tewkesbury were summoned to attend Parliament during the reigns of King Edward I, II and III, Richard II and Henry VIII and possibly at other times, too. Abbot Thomas died either in 1275 or 1276, and was succeeded in 1276 by Abbot Richard de Norton.[51]

Within two years of becoming abbot, Richard de Norton received King Edward I, who was staying in Tewkesbury when King Alexander of Scotland arrived to do him homage as King of Scotland.[52] Late in 1278 and into 1279, the abbot was severely criticised by Godfrey Giffard, bishop of Worcester, who ordered the Abbot and the *obedientiaries*, the 'middle managers', to take greater care over their duties. There was too much waste. Worst of all was the monks' gluttony and drunkenness – a sad contrast to 25 years before when the monastery was apparently without fault. Bishop Gifford commented that monks should 'eat to live and not live to eat'. Abbot Richard did not survive long, dying in 1282.[53] However, his successor, Abbot Thomas de Kemsey, had to endure Visitations by Bishop Gifford in 1284, 1287 and 1290, who still found things to criticise.[54] When the bishop died

38

in 1302, the prior of the monastic Worcester Cathedral demanded the right of Visitation during the bishopric vacancy. He found the Tewkesbury Abbey gates shut against him when he arrived. The ensuing dispute involved the Archbishop of Canterbury, the Court of Arches and the temporary excommunication of the abbot and senior monks. The abbot of Tewkesbury was found guilty of 'contumacy' – wilful disobedience or insubordination – but eventually a compromise was reached.[55]

Furthermore, there was a fire in the belltower in 1292, and in 1295 Earl Gilbert II, the 'Red Earl', died. He was buried next to Earl Gilbert I, his grandfather, before the high altar at Tewkesbury.[56] Now his son, Gilbert III, a young boy, was earl of Gloucester and Hertford and patron of Tewkesbury Abbey. His grandfather, King Edward I, granted a Charter to Tewkesbury in 1300.[57] Presently, Gilbert III was married to Maud de Burgh, daughter of the powerful earl of Ulster, on 29 September 1308. This made him a brother-in-law of Robert the Bruce of Scotland, married to Maud's sister, Elizabeth, in 1302.[58] Earl Gilbert III, although young, was unusually moderate, wise and loyal to the King. In 1311 he acted as Regent of England for King Edward II when the latter was fighting the Scots, and again in 1313, when still only 21, when the King was in France.[59] Out of loyalty to the King, he later

An attempt to imaginatively reconstruct how the Rood and pulpitum may have looked. Note that the figure of Christ is seen in Judgement; St Mary and St John are much smaller than later Roods. Although there is no direct evidence for them, the pillars are shown supporting what must have been at least a 40-foot beam. The height of the pulpitum is gauged from the stone steps that were once in one of the south nave pillars and may have led to the top of the pulpitum. However, it is just possible that the steps were eighteenth-century

1216–1314: THE AGE OF THE DE CLARE FAMILY, THE BUILDING OF A LADY CHAPEL

appeared with his men at Bannockburn in 1314. The legend is that he was accused of 'treachery and deceit' by his King. This incensed him to such a degree that, possibly alone, he charged the massed Scottish forces and was killed.

Robert the Bruce had Gilbert III's body looked after and sent back to Tewkesbury Abbey, where it was buried to the left of his father.[60]

There were no more de Clare male heirs to be earls of Gloucester and Hertford. Matilda, Gilbert III's wife, survived six years after her husband's death before joining him in the quire of Tewkesbury Abbey. Hers is the only gravestone set in the floor to have survived, albeit defaced. The Despenser family were about to take over.

CHAPTER FIVE

1315–1470: The Despensers, Lady Eleanor and major changes

In 1321, Eleanor de Clare, Earl Gilbert de Clare III's eldest sister, married Hugh II Despenser. Gilbert had been killed at the Battle of Bannockburn in 1314 (*see previous chapter*). There being no other male heirs, the lordship of Tewkesbury had passed to Eleanor, as well as much of the wealth of one of England's richest families.[1] However, now that Eleanor was married, the de Clare lands and fortune belonged to her new husband, Hugh. He had already acquired position and wealth in his own right by his father's and his own devotion to the then King, Edward II.[2] Over many years, the King needlessly alienated his nobility through his behaviour, policies and shameless preference of favourites, of whom the Despensers were two. Hugh and his father became 'marked men'. Hugh Despenser senior was hanged in Bristol, while his son, Eleanor's husband, was hanged, drawn and quartered in Hereford in 1326.[3]

Gilbert III, Eleanor's brother, had been buried in Tewkesbury Abbey quire in 1314.[4] Eleanor's husband's mutilated body would soon join him, being placed in the ambulatory, at the back of the sedilia.

Earlier, Tewkesbury Abbey monks had become aware of the 'ruinous' condition of the nave. Between 1271 and 1275, Abbot Thomas de Stokes and the monastery successfully petitioned Pope Gregory X to appropriate Fairford Church, Gloucestershire, to help pay for repairs. Yet monks were also aware of building and architectural advances, the improvements in glass manufacture and the consequent development of the Decorated style of church architecture. They were almost certainly considering the expensive possibility of redesigning and rebuilding the east end of the Abbey. Abbot Thomas de Kemsey (abbot 1282–1328) even journeyed to Rome to see the Pope in 1316, where he again successfully pleaded to appropriate Fairford Church, so that its income could be used to finance building work, even though no action up until that point had been taken. His tomb – sometimes referred to as the 'Forthington tomb' – is set into a recess in the sacristy wall facing the ambulatory.[5] Eventually, in 1332, Pope John XXII agreed to send an instruction to Bishop Orleton of Worcester, and the Papal Licence was acted on a year later, a mere 60 years after it had been initially issued.[6]

As far as the building of the quire, sanctuary and chevet of chapels of the Abbey is concerned, it is not known who suggested what to whom and when. There is no record of their commissioning and building. On the one hand, the monks were probably seeking to extend, modernise and beautify the east

External view of the Abbey's east end in snow, showing a number of the fourteenth-century chapels

end of the Abbey. On the other hand, in one commentator's words, Eleanor wished 'to convert the old Norman structure into a Decorated casket for her family memorials.'7 Relatives from her great-great grandfather, Gilbert I de Clare, down to her brother Gilbert III de Clare, first husband, Hugh II Despenser and other relatives, were all buried near the high altar. Immensely wealthy, she wanted a resting place for them all that she felt was fitting. Clearly, Eleanor was either very much the main contributor to, or else the entire benefactor of, the rebuilding of much if not almost all of the east end of the Abbey as now seen, including the quire, the chapels and the seven great windows above the quire and sanctuary. Eleanor's objectives and those of the monks, although different, happened to coincide. The end result was to lift the east end of the Abbey from being a majestic but rather sombre piece of Norman architecture to a lighter, more beautiful, gloriously awe-inspiring high point of the Abbey.

The seven quire windows and the sanctuary ceiling, both envisaged by Eleanor de Clare in the 1320s. She married Hugh II Despenser and after his death married William, Lord de la Zouch. The windows and ceiling were only completed in the early 1340s. The theme of the east window is the Last Judgement

The project had probably been begun by 1321, when Eleanor married Hugh II Despenser, and was certainly taking place by the time of her second marriage to William de Mortimer, Lord la Zouche, a veteran of the Battle of Falkirk (1298) and briefly Keeper of the Tower of London (1328–29) in January 1329. The abbot who oversaw most of the building in Eleanor's time was Abbot John Cotes (1328–47). His tomb is found behind the sedilia in the ambulatory.

It is thought that the old Romanesque chapels at the east end – like Gloucester Cathedral, possibly no more than three – were knocked down during the 1320s and new, more numerous chapels erected as is seen today. This move allowed the ambulatory to be widened. The two chapels on the north side were dedicated to British saints St Margaret of Scotland and St Edmund, king and martyr, the latter being a double-chapel. The chapel in the south-east corner was dedicated to St Faith. The initial dedication of the next chapel is not known, but much later became St Catherine's. St John the Baptist was added to the dedication in the twentieth century. It is evident that the biggest and finest chapel was the easternmost, some 72 feet long, which was the new Lady Chapel. Its original size and shape may be judged by looking at the stone markings seen externally. The other chapels are anything but uniform and reflect the skills of various craftsmen.

The sacristy and the room above for the sacrist were built at the same time as the chapels. The sacristy was used for vestry and storage purposes. Items of value would have been kept in the sacristy and it was possible for the sacrist to observe what was happening in the sacristy by using a squint placed on the stairs to his room.

During the 1340s the great Norman pillars around the high altar were drastically shortened, and from these the Decorated-style arches now spring. All of the Romanesque superstructure east of the crossing was removed apart from the pillars. The quire itself, with its seven windows above it, was built, together with its stone vaulting.

The windows themselves represent some of the finest examples in existence of mid fourteenth-century English stained glass.[8] The two westernmost windows depict early lords of the manor including the founder, Robert Fitzhamon. The next two windows on either side show various prophets and kings, while the central, seventh window shows the Last Judgement and Coronation of the Virgin.[9] Points of particular interest include, at the top of the 'rose window', God seated in Majesty in the centre and a tiny crowned Virgin Mary being received into Heaven by Christ. Christ himself displays his wounds, except the wound in his side, which has been replaced by green glass by an unknown restorer. To Christ's left is the Archangel Michael, Christ's standard-bearer, holding a shield with the instruments of Christ's passion, the *Arma Christi*. However, these instruments are now just fragments as a result of restoration work.[10] The *Arma Christi* was a fairly new concept in medieval art and this depiction is thought to be the earliest surviving example in stained glass.[11] At the bottom right, a naked female figure, possibly Lady Eleanor herself, is praying to Christ. However, she does not look entirely 'at home' there, and it has been suggested that this light may come from somewhere else in the Abbey.[12] There are also shields of arms at the bottom of the window.[13] The sacristy has a 'museum window' that consists of fragments from the seven windows of the quire. In over 650 years since the windows were created, numerous restorations of variable quality have resulted in apparent surplus pieces being put together to form this window.

Eleanor Despenser (née de Clare) is seen without clothing or possession, humbly seeking God's mercy

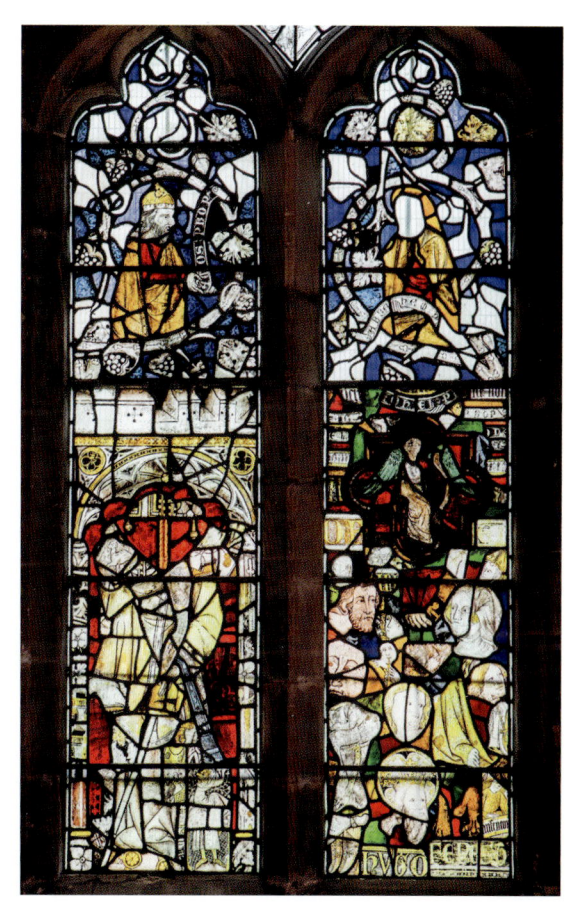

This window was created between 1924 and 1925 out of fragments from the seven quire windows, that resulted from a restoration project to make good sixteenth-, seventeenth- and eighteenth-century work in these windows

The original choir stalls and misericords were carved between roughly 1335 and 1350. They would have extended further than as seen today, probably to the first bay of the nave. All would probably have had canopies rather than just those on the north side. Almost all the misericords are to be found on the north side. Most are of grotesques, mythical beasts, animals or birds.[14]

Eleanor herself, born a de Clare – who married into the ill-fated Despensers and subsequently married Lord la Zouche – eventually died on 29 June 1337, after the death of her second husband. She would have seen much of her scheme come to fruition but it is very doubtful whether she saw the completed quire. This is given greater credibility when it is remembered that she herself was buried with her second husband in the east end Lady Chapel, completed earlier and probably pulled down at the Dissolution of the Monasteries, rather than in the quire. Although imprisoned on at least one occasion, she managed to preserve much of the Despenser estates as countess of Gloucester, including the lordship of Tewkesbury and the patronage of the Abbey. These now devolved upon her son, Hugh III Despenser, who died in 1349. He and his nephew, Eleanor's grandson, Lord

1315–1470: THE DESPENSERS, LADY ELEANOR AND MAJOR CHANGES   45

Edward Despenser, KG, who lived until 1375 – the 'kneeling knight' on his chantry chapel of the Holy Trinity – were around long enough to both finance and see the ideas of their mother and grandmother completed.[15]

During the 1340s, the nave vaulting was changed, removing the original barrel-vaulted wooden ceiling and replacing it with the present stone vault.[16] This was yet another generous Despenser benefaction. The effect was to lighten the nave, because of the incorporation of a clerestorey whose windows let in additional light. However, the impact of the Black Death (1348–49) was such that building skills used towards the west end of the nave may have slipped in quality. It is noteworthy that in the nave, at triforium height, in bay seven, parallel to the north entrance, there is a cross painted, not easily seen from the ground. One wonders whether it was put there by craftsmen seeking deliverance and blessing on themselves and their work as the Black Death swirled about them.[17] In the monastery itself, the number of monks sank to 20, with six at Bristol and three at Cranbourne.[18] Along the centre of the nave vault, from west to east, a series of 15 roundels of stone, called bosses, depicting in order the Life, Death and Resurrection of Jesus Christ, were added, together with lesser bosses on either side, showing angels either playing a variety of musical instruments or being shown with sacred emblems. There were also bosses with floral designs and human faces that could be portraits of fourteenth-century worthies. At the east end Despenser heraldry is also to be found among the bosses. Altogether, there are 237 bosses in the nave.

Finally, in the 1350s, a new lierne vault was introduced in the crossing tower which had been a Romanesque lantern tower. While it is evident that the Despensers helped financially here, too, there was another benefactor, Sir Guy de Brien, KG (Lord Bryan). His monument is at the entrance to St Margaret's Chapel, and his heraldry may be seen on the vault itself.[19] This was because Hugh Despenser III, Eleanor's son, had married Elizabeth Montacute; but as he had subsequently died in 1349, Elizabeth had remarried, choosing the distinguished soldier and diplomat Lord Bryan. He had been King Edward III's standard bearer at the Battle of Crécy, later an admiral and also an ambassador. On his monument, the arms of his Despenser wife impaling de Bryan on either side of his own arms are visible. He died in 1390 at the remarkably old age in those days of 79. He was buried at Slapton, south Devon where his family had been benefactors for some time.[20]

In 1397, Abbot Thomas Parker (abbot 1389–1421) had the Founder's Chantry erected over the founder's tomb, just north of the high altar.[21] It attempted to underline the importance of the founder, not only given the Despensers' massive contribution to the beauty of the Abbey as a whole, but to complement the chantry chapels that had been built at the behest of the Despenser family. The floor tiles are still those belonging to the late fourteenth century. The overall effect enhanced the prestige of major benefactors. The Holy Trinity Chantry on the south side was such a chapel, built roughly 15 years' earlier.

Opposite, above: The vault below the crossing tower, c.1350–60. The Sun in Splendour, badge of the House of York, together with bosses with the arms of Despenser, de Bryan and Montacute impaling de Bryan. The central 'sun' and the surrounding stars date from Scott's restoration

Opposite, below: The central tower above the Despenser vault, showing the arcading that would have been seen from the ground for the first 200 years of the Abbey's existence

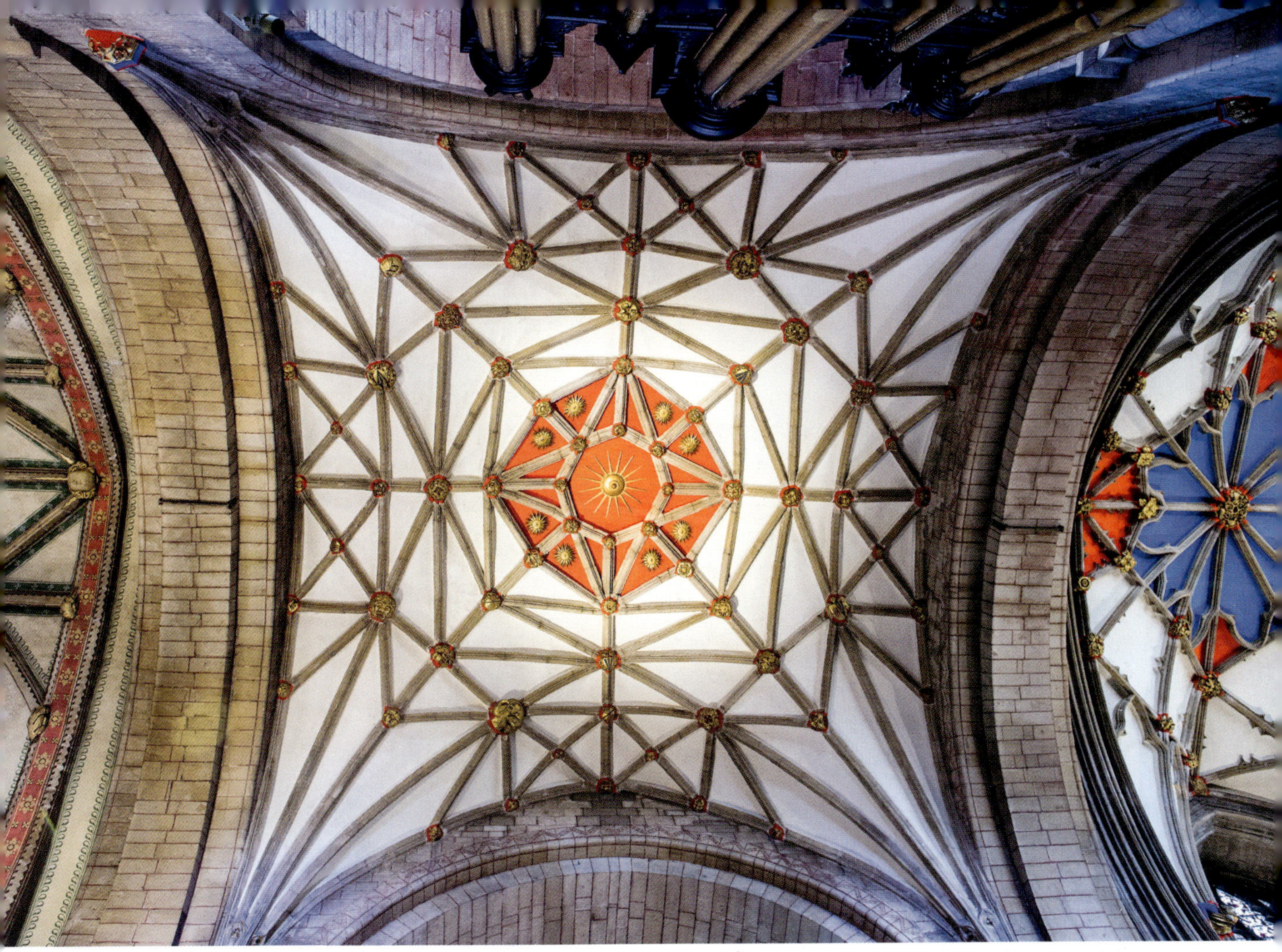

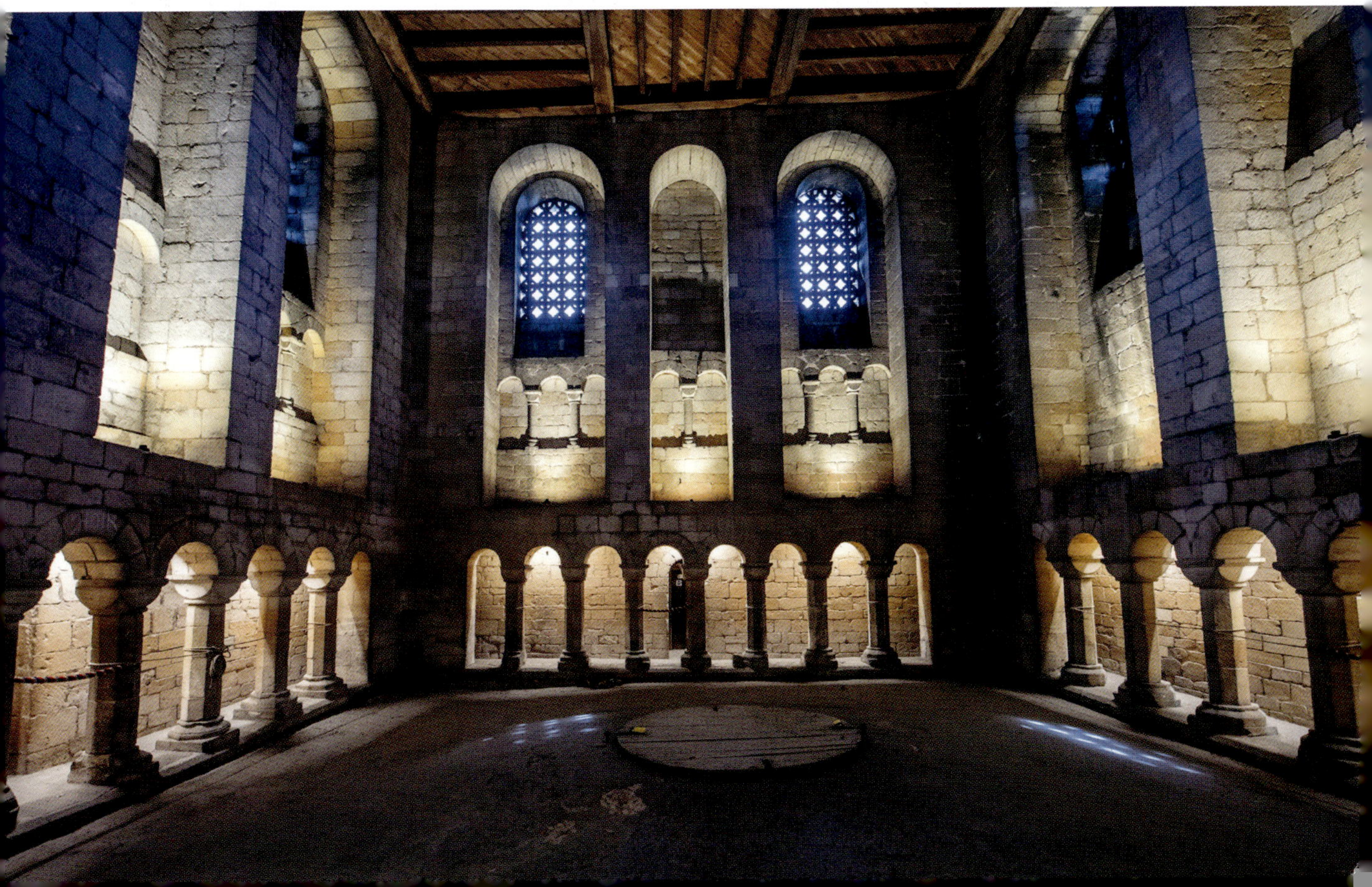

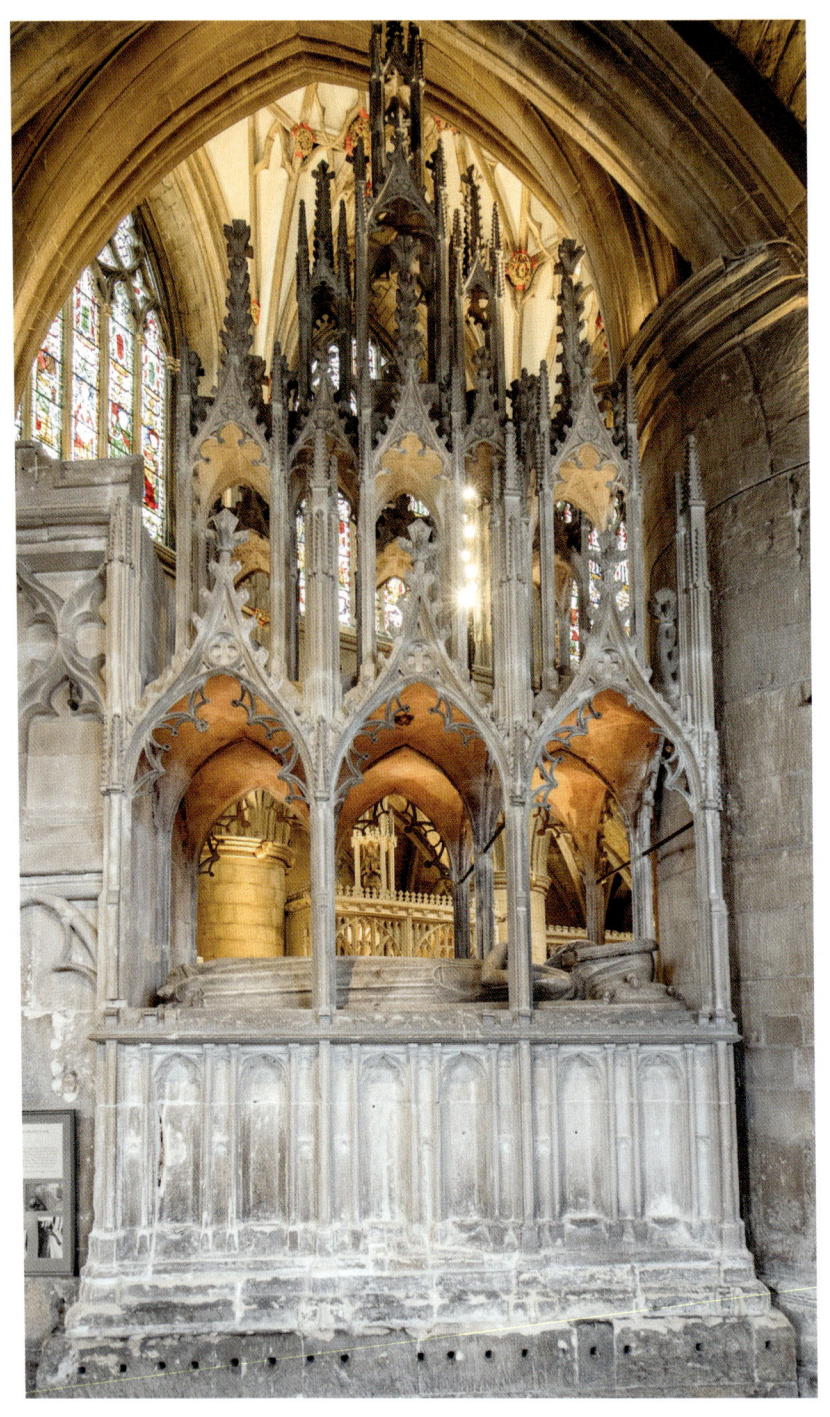

The tomb of Hugh III Despenser and Elizabeth Montacute, in a place of honour just to the north of the high altar. It is one of the most ambitious of its period (the 1350s) and has been compared with that of King Edward II at Gloucester Cathedral. Henry was with King Edward III at the Battles of Sluys (1340) and Crécy (1346). After Henry's death in 1348, Elizabeth married Sir Guy de Brien. She died in 1359

1. Originally, the Abbey founder, Robert Fitzhamon, was buried in the Chapter House when he died in 1107, and his body was subsequently translated to the presbytery in 1241. Abbot Parker had the chantry chapel built for the founder in 1397, thereby arguably giving him a higher status in late fourteenth-century eyes

2. The kneeling knight is Lord Edward Despenser, veteran of the Battle of Poitiers (1356). He was invested as a Knight of the Garter in 1361. Holy Trinity chantry chapel was erected in his honour c.1380 by his widow, Elizabeth de Burghersh, after his death in 1375

3. The interior of the Holy Trinity chantry chapel. Note the wall painting at the east end, depicting the Holy Trinity, and the partially destroyed panel at the right-hand side, representing the Coronation of the Virgin. Note also the early fan vault

4. Isabella Despenser married Richard Beauchamp IV, earl of Worcester, who died in 1422. Isobel had the chantry built in his memory, consecrated in honour of St Mary Magdalene, St Barbara and St Leonard. The chapel was dedicated in July 1433. Isobel subsequently married Richard Beauchamp V, Earl Warwick. She died in December 1439, and was buried in Tewkesbury Abbey

49

The Abbey's Green Men

The term 'green man' (or men) seems to have first been used in the 1930s. It was thought then, and immediately post-War, that in churches they were relics of pagan nature worship (including possibly deriving from the *Derg Corra*, the 'man in the tree' of Celtic mythology, or the Celtic deity *Cernunnos*). Green Man public houses may also have suggested the name, though the pub names derived from leaf-clad figures of folk custom rather than heads from which leaves grow.

'Green men' did not exist in England prior to Christianity. Their popularity in western Europe grew with the spread of the faith. However, with the Reformation, they fell out of favour. They may be interpreted as a symbol of rebirth, representing the cycle of new growth that occurs every spring. Occasionally, the leaves that appear in conjunction with 'Green men' are vine leaves, suggesting a possible Christian reference (the vine as symbolising wine, thus the blood of Christ, in Christian iconography).

In Tewkesbury Abbey they appear in the fourteenth-century rebuild of the east end, when the concept was popular. They may be seen in St Catherine and St John the Baptist's Chapel, St Faith's Chapel, the ambulatory, the sacristy and the frieze of the Trinity Chantry Chapel.[22] One also appears on the street side of the Gage Gates, a 1959 replacement of the one on the original gate of 1712.

Examples of fourteenth-century 'Green Man' stone carvings found at the east end of the Abbey

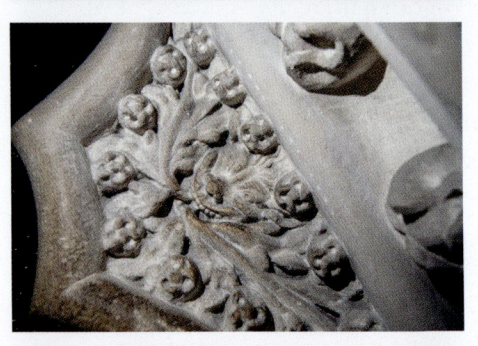

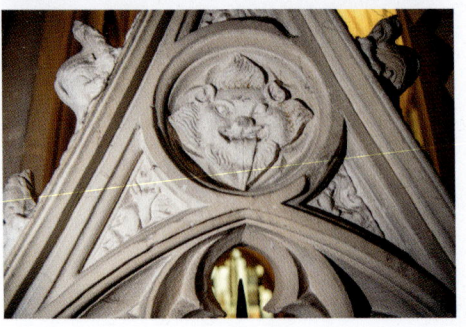

It was commissioned by Lord Edward Despenser's widow, Elizabeth Burghersh, her husband having died in 1375. He is the 'kneeling knight' on the roof of the chantry chapel, facing the high altar.[23] On the altar wall of the chantry, Edward and Elizabeth are pictured adoring the Holy Trinity. Elizabeth survived until 1409.

Another later family chapel is the Beauchamp or Warwick Chantry on the north side of the quire, commissioned by Lady Isabella Despenser, in memory of her first husband, Richard Beauchamp, fourth earl of Warwick and earl of Abergavenny, who had been mortally wounded in 1421. Lady Isabella was a granddaughter of Lord Edward Despenser, the 'kneeling knight', and widow of Richard Beauchamp, fourth earl of Warwick, who was mortally wounded in 1421. It has been said of the Beauchamp/ Warwick Chantry that 'its exaggerated four-centred arches and rows of canopied niches [makes the] latter a ground-breaking example of the refinement of Perpendicular style in the fifteenth century'. The saints in its dedication include St Mary Magdalene, St Barbara and St Leonard.[24] It bears the rose of York, the chevrons of the de Clares and the earl's own Beauchamp arms with the crescent on the fess, showing that he was of the younger branch of the family. This chantry chapel was probably built in 1423, the year Isabel married another Richard Beauchamp, this time the fifth earl of Warwick.[25] Killed at Rouen in 1439, his body was returned to Warwick. Lady Isabella died a few months later, in December 1439, and is buried in the Abbey.[26] Only two years later, Abbot Thomas Parker, who had ruled the monastery for 32 years, also died. One of his last acts was to accept King Henry VI's gift of Goldcliff Priory to be attached to the Abbey.[27]

Earlier, in 1424, Lady Isabella, as countess of Warwick, had given birth to Lord Henry. He grew, becoming a tall man and a favourite of the King, Henry VI. By the time the young lord died in June 1446, just 22 years old, he had either been created or had inherited the titles of King of the Isle of Wight, Guernsey and Jersey (in 1444) – the only person ever to be given that title – duke of Warwick, First Earl of England, Lord Despenser and Abergavenny and lord of Bristol Castle as well as lord of the manor of Tewkesbury. He gave the church at Shuston to the Abbey. He was said to have been buried 'in the quire'. Between 1875–79, during the huge restoration of that period, a stone-walled grave was uncovered under the tower containing the bones of 'a man of unusual size', conjectured to be those of Henry, duke of Warwick. Both statements become possible when it is realised that in 1446 the quire extended out to the nave side of the tower, and not as it is today.[28]

Lady Isabella also had a daughter, Lady Anne, who 'married' Richard Neville, sixth earl of Warwick, while both were still children. Through their marriage, Richard, also known as the 'king-maker', eventually inherited the lordship of Tewkesbury in 1449 on the death of Duke Henry's infant daughter, confusingly also Lady Anne Beauchamp, after a legal tussle.[29]

Generally, the period from 1445 to 1468, under Abbot John Abington (also possibly known as John de Salys) represented years of consolidation for the Abbey community. To the north of the Abbey precinct the monks built shops with living accommodation, now numbers 41–48 Church Street. They also began the 'first phase' of the current Abbey House, and improved their hold on Goldcliffe Priory. In 1469, Bishop John Carpenter of Worcester confirmed that Deerhurst Priory also now belonged to Tewkesbury Abbey.[30] It seemed that all was well with Tewkesbury Abbey and its monastery. Appearances, however, were to prove deceptive.

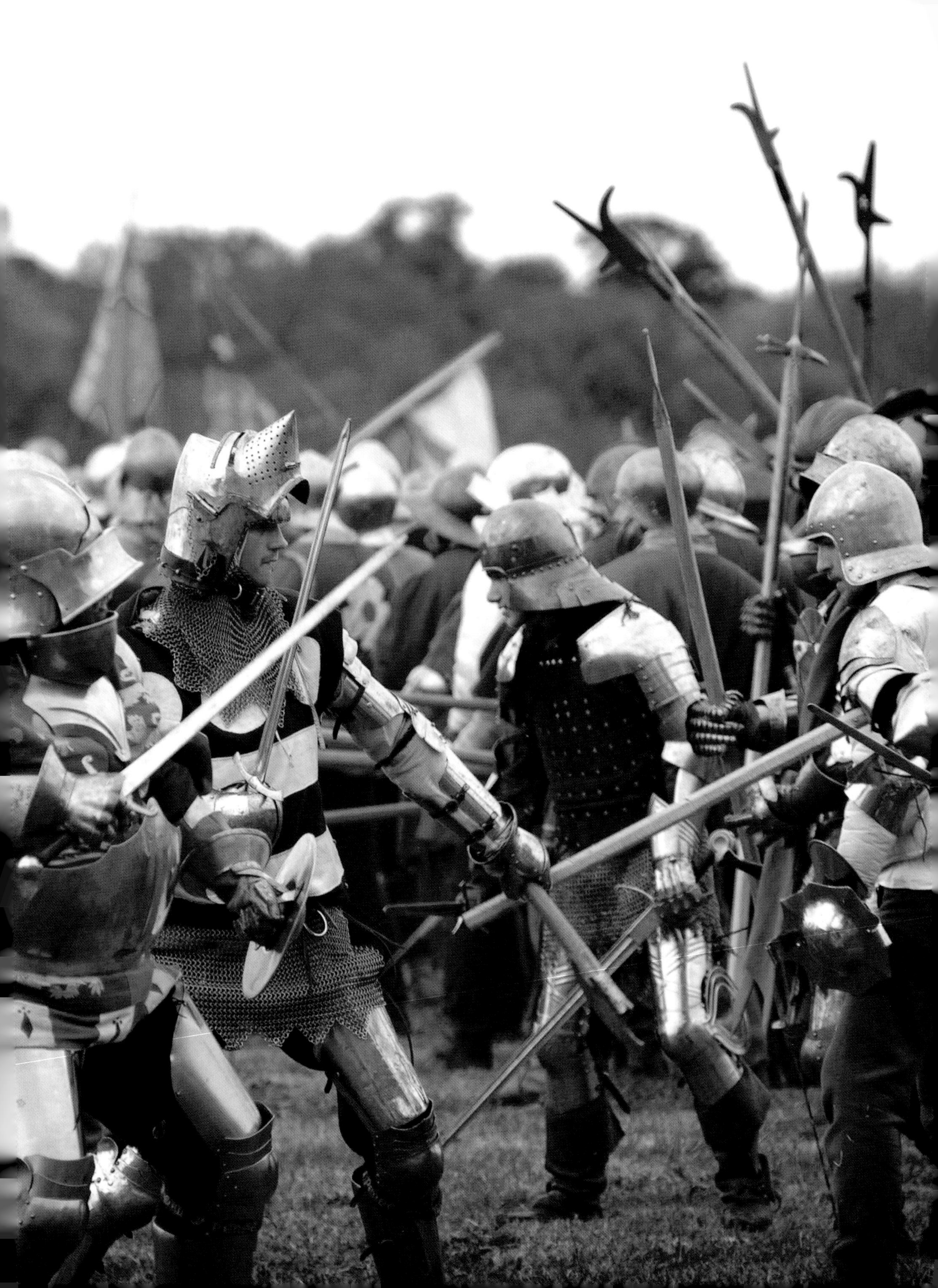

CHAPTER SIX

1471–1540: The Battle of Tewkesbury, Henry VIII and the Abbey's Dissolution

Into the purposeful development of the Abbey's life and growing resources, the Wars of the Roses intervened. First, in April 1471, the then lord of the manor of Tewkesbury, Richard Neville, earl of Warwick, was killed at the Battle of Barnet. All his estates were confiscated by the Crown but were later shared between his two daughters, Isabelle and Anne.[1] Isabelle was now lord of the manor but on her marriage to George, duke of Clarence, the lordship went to him. He was the brother of the Yorkist Richard, duke of Gloucester, the future King Richard III.

Second, and of far greater immediate impact, the Battle of Tewkesbury was fought on Saturday 4 May 1471, between Lancastrian and Yorkist armies on the south-west side of Tewkesbury. The forces of Queen Margaret, wife of King Henry VI, were drawn up on high ground near Gupshill manor, having probably spent the previous night on the Gaston, a large field close by. Her army commander was Edmund Beaufort, duke of Somerset. The pursuing Yorkist army, under King Edward IV, had probably spent the night at Tredington, a nearby village. The King knew Tewkesbury slightly, having visited it in February 1464.[2] When they felt ready, the Yorkists marched towards their opponents. The armies were both said to be about 6,000 strong.

Queen Margaret herself may have watched the battle from what is now called Queen Margaret's Camp, opposite the present Gupshill public house. The Yorkists, unlike the Lancastrians, seem to have had some cannon, which they fired at the Lancastrian lines. Some of the latter, possibly goaded into action by seeing men killed in their lines without being able to respond, left their comparatively good position to attack the Yorkists, but were forced to retreat, some men breaking and fleeing. The retreat became a rout. Many tried to reach the River Severn. However, a band of possibly two hundred mounted Yorkists, concealed by a high hedge on the edge of what is now Tewkesbury Park, fell on the fleeing Lancastrians. As they tried to reach the Lower Lode to cross the river, they were cut down in what is now called the Bloody Meadow. Others are said to have drowned in the mill pond; still more sought sanctuary in the Abbey. They were pursued by the Yorkists and accounts differ as to what extent sacrilege was committed by the slaughter of Lancastrians within the Abbey. Abbot Strensham succeeded in persuading the Yorkists to leave the Abbey, taking their luckless Lancastrian prisoners with them. Some 15 Lancastrian nobles, knights and others would be executed. The Lancastrian Prince of Wales was dead, and he and a number

A re-enactment near or on the site of the Battle of Tewkesbury, 1471 (*and p. 52*)

The possible, although unlikely, site in the Abbey quire where Edward of Lancaster, Prince of Wales, was buried after the Battle of Tewkesbury in 1471. No-one knows the exact location of the burial, although some circumstantial evidence suggests that it might have been near the foot of a pillar north-west of the tower. It is probable that the original tomb was of marble with inlaid brass

of his nobles and knights were buried within the Abbey. Edward IV celebrated in the Abbey with a *Te Deum*, or song of praise to God, his victory complete. Queen Margaret slipped away, across the Lower Lode. There is a local legend that she spent the night at Payne's Place, a house built in about 1450, in Bushley, a nearby village. Thomas Payne, a merchant, would have been a sympathiser. The next day she continued to Little Malvern Priory, where she was discovered by the Yorkists. She was sent to a nunnery.[3]

The victorious Yorkists inserted a 'Sun in Splendour' over the central spot where the Lancastrian Edward, Prince of Wales' plaque is in the floor.[4] This was presumably with the blessing of Duke George, now lord of the manor.

54   A HISTORY OF TEWKESBURY ABBEY

Burials of Lancastrian notables in Tewkesbury Abbey, 1471

Conjectural notes of the original sites of graves

Following the Battle of Tewkesbury and the subsequent executions of surviving Lancastrian notables, there is evidence to suggest that the following were buried in the Abbey as follows:

† Edward, Prince of Wales
   (*the quire*)
† Edmund, duke of Somerset; † John, marquis of Somerset; † Thomas John, earl of Devon;
† Sir Humphrey Audley; † Sir Thomas Tresham
   (*St James' Chapel, now the Abbey shop*)
† Master Henry Wrottesley
   (*St John the Baptist's Chapel*)
† Sir William Newburgh
   (*by the font, at that time halfway down the nave*)
† Sir Edmund Hampden; † Sir W. Robert Whittingham; † Sir William Vaux; † Sir John Lewknor
   (*St George's Chapel, probably the north nave aisle*)
† Master Henry Baron
   (*St John's Chapel, probably the south nave aisle*)

NOTES:
1. The burial of Edward, Prince of Wales, in the quire, a privilege hitherto confined to members of the families of the patrons of the Abbey, may have been granted to him because he was betrothed to Anne, a co-heiress of Richard, earl of Warwick, (arranged July 1470) and thus could claim a family connection at the time of his death.
2. Sir John Delves and his son were possibly buried in St John's Chapel in the nave, but it is thought that their bodies were taken back to Delves Hall near Uttoxeter and buried locally.
3. The body of the prior of St John of Jerusalem was buried in his own priory at Clerkenwell.
4. A monument at the east end of the south aisle, mistakenly thought by some to be John, Lord Wenlock, (*see below*) may be that of Sir Thomas Morley, son-in-law of Lord Edward Despenser (the 'kneeling knight').
5. John, Lord Wenlock, killed in the battle, was thought possibly buried in the Abbey, but there is no supporting evidence. He had had a chantry chapel founded in Luton, Bedfordshire. There is no evidence that he was buried there, either. At present, his burial place remains a mystery.[5]

As a result of the bloodshed inside the Abbey, it was polluted and therefore shut for all worship until it had been 'cleansed'. It was reconsecrated on 30 May, over three weeks after the battle, by the bishop of Down and Connor, acting as suffragan for the bishop of Worcester.[6] Apart from the burials that occurred in the Abbey of those slain or executed as a result of the battle, it is thought that some horse armour or possibly the metal surrounding the wheels of the Lancastrian army's camp followers' discarded carts, was used to strengthen the security of the door to the sacristy (*see overleaf*).[7]

In December 1476, Isabelle, duchess of Clarence, passed away. Anne, her mother, was a Beauchamp, whose father and grandfather were Despensers. She was followed within months by George, her husband, who had been executed (some would say murdered) by Edward IV, in February 1478 for several acts of disloyalty.

Sacristy door: The metal on this door has been variously identified as from either armour or horse armour from the Battle of Tewkesbury. Experts from the Royal Armouries Museum, Leeds, identified the strips of metal as the latter. Another suggestion is that the metal strips came from the wheels of the carts of the Lancastrian camp followers

The legend that he was dispatched through the judicious use of a butt of Malmsey wine is open to question. Both the duke and duchess were buried in the Clarence Vault, just to the east of the Abbey's high altar.[8] The lordship of Tewkesbury manor now belonged to Edward, son of George, duke of Clarence, but he too was executed in 1499, this time by King Henry VII, first Tudor king.[9] The lordship of Tewkesbury was in the Crown's hands until 1547 when it briefly came into the possession of Sir Thomas, Lord Seymour of Sudeley, until his own execution in 1549. It was passed back to the Crown where it remained under Royal patronage until sold to Tewkesbury Council in 1609 for £2,453.[10]

Meanwhile, in 1488, King Henry VII obtained an Act of Parliament restoring the Despenser and Warwick lands to the Dowager Countess of Warwick. She was the widow of Richard Neville, the 'King-Maker', mother of the Duchess Isabel and therefore grandmother of the Clarence children. This was no generous act as the King forced her to surrender all her possessions by deed to himself and his children. The Dowager Countess was left with one small manor in Warwickshire and an inadequate pension. Thus were the former de Clare, Despenser and Warwick lands, acquired over centuries, lost to an all-powerful monarch.[11]

The monastery, too, was suffering a little, with a census in 1494 showing just 33 monks at the Abbey.[12] An inspection or 'Visitation' of the monastery in 1498 found no serious faults, although there was no inventory of 'goods, chattels and jewels'. The abbot, Richard Cheltenham, did not keep a sufficiently rigorous eye on maintenance, for by 1500 the cloister and the bell tower were in 'a ruinous' condition.

Yet the King had his own tragedy. In 1502, Abbot Richard assisted in the funeral at Worcester of Prince Arthur, the King's eldest son. The King's second son was now Crown Prince, becoming Prince of Wales in February 1504, and in 1509 King Henry VIII on his father's death.[13] In the same year, Abbot Richard also died (abbot 1481–1509). His tomb marks the boundary of the St Catherine and St John the Baptist Chapels with the south-eastern part of the ambulatory.

By the year 1512, the new Abbot, Henry Beeley (1509–31) was already making a mark in Parliament, being recorded as 'leading the procession' to the House of Lords. In 1518 he enjoyed 'conferral of parliamentary status' that meant formal admission to the House of Lords. If he had not had 'mitred abbot' status before, Abbot Beeley certainly had it now. It is said that from 1518 to the Dissolution of the Monasteries 'the Abbot of Tewkesbury Abbey was regularly summoned to sit in the House of Lords'.[14] His influence was rising. In 1522, he became Visitor of the Black Monks (i.e. the Benedictine Order) in Worcester Diocese, the same year that extensive re-roofing of the nave was undertaken, and a year after the north transept had also been re-roofed.[15] At about the same time, William Tyndale, originally a Gloucestershire man from near Dursley, made his momentous decision to translate the Bible into English, which he achieved on the Continent 1524–25. His brother, Edward, was a wealthy and influential man, having been a receiver to the lands of Lord Berkeley at one point, and at another being Steward of all Tewkesbury Abbey lands. He even leased the manors of Pull Court (Worcestershire), now a part of Bushley, a village near Tewkesbury, as well as Burnett (Somerset) from the Abbey.[16]

In 1525, Princess Mary (Princess of Wales and the future Queen) kept Christmas at Tewkesbury and Cardinal Wolsey was consulted 'as to her state and entertainment'.[17] Five years later, in 1530, Abbot Beeley was one of 21 abbots who unsuccessfully petitioned the Pope to grant King Henry VIII a divorce from his first wife, Catherine of Aragon.[18]

Protestant ideas, developed since the start of the Reformation a few years earlier, began to surface in Gloucestershire. They had to be countered. It was probably Abbot Richard Cheltenham who, in agreement with the abbot of

Detail of the Oriel window on the north side of Abbey House. Beneath the window can be faintly seen 'HB', for Henry Beely, the penultimate abbot of Tewkesbury

St Peter's Abbey, Gloucester, began to send one or two young monks to Gloucester College, now Worcester College, Oxford University, where the monastery kept rooms. One monk, Robert Cisseter (or Cirencester), later prior of St James, Bristol, graduated from Oxford after several years in 1523, having studied logic and philosophy as well as theology; John Beeley studied for eight years, returning to Tewkesbury to be the last prior.[19] There were others, too, not least John Wych (or Wakeman), who held the degree of Bachelor of Divinity, the penultimate prior of Tewkesbury, its last abbot and later first bishop of the new Gloucester Diocese.

At this point there were comparatively few with Protestant views, but those that did were sometimes key people locally. Among the most outstanding was William Tracy, an influential Sheriff of Gloucestershire, who lived at Toddington near Tewkesbury and whose Will was particularly radical. He suggested that there was only one Mediator between God and Man, namely Jesus Christ, and accepted no other, thereby effectively challenging the validity of clergy and the Church's authority. Archbishop Warham of Canterbury declared Tracy a heretic.[20] Thomas Cromwell, the King's Chief Minister, thought otherwise, and in 1532 brought pressure on Abbot Beeley to allow Richard Tracy, William's son, to lease the manor of Stanway. This manor, one of two – the other being Forthampton – were the favourite, personal manors of Tewkesbury abbots. In the meantime, Tracy's Will, duly published, had raised a sufficient outcry that it was refused probate. Such was the feeling that it is said that in 1532 his body was exhumed and burned.[21] Abbot Beeley attempted to soften Thomas Cromwell by sending him in July the same year 'a cast of Lanners' – hawks used in falconry – a favourite sport of Cromwell's.[22]

Abbot Beeley was ailing. The ever-scheming Cromwell sent two of his commissioners, John Tregonwell and Thomas Bayard, to the Abbey in 1533 to find the 'most amenable' monk to become the next abbot. They reported back later that they had ensured the election of the then prior, John Wych or Wakeman, who had been in post since about 1530 – possibly 1531 – and would fill the post as Cromwell would wish. Sir William Kingston, Tewkesbury's Crown Steward, also intrigued on John Wakeman's behalf.[23] Cromwell's desired result was achieved by simply threatening to bring in an abbot from outside the monastery if intended voting did not meet with his approval. In March 1534, the old abbot died. In June, Wakeman was installed as abbot (*see panel*). Barely two months later, in August, Abbot Wakeman led the Abbey's by now 38 monks in each signing his support for the Act of Supremacy that confirmed King Henry VIII's position as 'Supreme Head' of the Church of England.[24]

Abbot Wakeman's support for the King and his Chief Minister was rewarded. The next year, between 23 and 27 July, 1535, the monastery had the honour – and expense – of hosting the King, Queen Anne Boleyn and the King's Chief Minister and Principal Secretary, Thomas Cromwell, who was also Chancellor of the Exchequer. Henry and Anne were not as close as formerly and the King was already showing interest in Jane Seymour, yet Queen Anne was still referred to as the King's 'most dear and entirely beloved lawful wife'.[25]

Cromwell had just become the 'Visitor-General of Monasteries', together with his other new appointment of 'Vice-Gerent in Spirituals'. These appointments made him the King's administrative deputy in all matters spiritual, and gave him precedence over both archbishops in the newly-formed Church of England, through the Act of Supremacy.

The Royal couple with Thomas Cromwell arrived at Tewkesbury Abbey, together with 'a large number of courtiers'. This would have presented huge problems in accommodating so many guests to what was felt an appropriate standard. While it is likely that the Royal couple stayed in the abbot's lodgings (as at Reading and Abingdon Abbeys) there is evidence to suggest that Henry VIII and Anne Boleyn may have actually stayed at Forthampton Court, the abbot's personal manor, just across the River Severn from the Abbey itself. The Royal party had just come from Winchcombe where the King and Queen had lodged at Sudely Castle. Thomas Cromwell, who had only joined the party on 23 July, had stayed at Winchcombe Abbey.[26] The four to five days of the visit to Tewkesbury would have given ample opportunity for the King and Queen to explore in detail both the Abbey and its monastery on more than one occasion.

It has to be remembered that it was from Winchcombe, probably also on 23 July, that Thomas Cromwell sent out his agents, called 'Visitors'. As 'Vice-Gerent in Spirituals', Cromwell usurped the ancient tradition that bishops had of 'Visitations' to each monastery. His agents' Visitations were to be rather different from what had gone before.

Cromwell sent his Visitors to each abbey and monastery looking into their wealth, property, income, expenses and administration. They had much to say about Tewkesbury Abbey, now the wealthiest monastery in Gloucestershire and said to be the eleventh wealthiest in the country with an annual income of £1,598 per annum, equivalent to nearly £1.5 million per annum in 2020 terms.[27] However, Tewkesbury Abbey, like other monasteries, was almost certainly much richer than it appeared to be. This was because instead of raising the rents – which were recorded – as the land value increased, great fines were exacted from tenants upon the renewal of leases – which was not recorded. It is thought that the real income of religious houses might be as much as double the amount of their stated rental. This would put Tewkesbury Abbey's income approaching £3 million a year in 2020 terms.[28] This made it richer than St Peter's Abbey, Gloucester – later Gloucester Cathedral – and also Worcester Cathedral Priory. It was also noted that the abbot was also cellarer, too, as at Winchcombe, thereby enhancing his standard of living still more.

Another group of 'Visitors' was sent out to search for wrong-doing in the monasteries – particularly on two counts: the sexual failings of monks and the discovery of false miracles and relics. Inspections completed, each monastery, including Tewkesbury, was to be subjected to new rules entailing many previous customs and ceremonies being abandoned. Furthermore, pilgrims and others were no longer to see relics. The monastic rule, including that of 'enclosure' whereby monks stayed on the campus and went nowhere else, was to be strictly enforced. Richard Layton, later dean of York, who was sent to inspect Tewkesbury Abbey, found no fault at all, even though he had found plenty elsewhere.[29]

These were the opening salvoes in what eventually became the Dissolution of the Monasteries, planned by Cromwell, agreed by the King and unreservedly supported by Queen Anne Boleyn. As far as is known, nothing was said to the abbot of Tewkesbury as to what was already beginning to happen elsewhere.[30]

Abbot Wakeman was delighted with the Royal visit to Tewkesbury. He showed his appreciation by sending Cromwell a horse and £5 with which to buy a saddle. In his letter to Cromwell, he wrote 'I thank you for your goodness at my preferment, and your loving commendation to the King when he was at Tewkesbury, as yet undeserved of me'.[31] He might have been less delighted if he had been aware how Protestant Queen Anne Boleyn was in her religious sympathies.[32] She had almost certainly read Simon Fish's bitterly critical – and therefore heretical – pamphlet *Supplication for the Beggars*, published in Antwerp but available in England from February 1529. It accused the monasteries and the clergy of the Roman Catholic Church in general of taxing rather than helping the poor, of holding half of England's wealth yet being only 0.25% of the whole population. As Queen Anne looked around the magnificent Tewkesbury Abbey with its painted walls and pillars, its beautiful stained glass, its wonderful, embossed nave ceiling, the sumptuous vestments of the clergy and the superb quality of the patens, chalices and other church plate, not to mention the sheer high standard of the hospitality, she might well have thought that Fish had made a good point. She would have found the same situation, to a greater or lesser extent, in other abbeys included in the 1535 progress.

1535 was also the year in which the reforming Hugh Latimer became bishop of Worcester, and for six years bishop with oversight of Tewkesbury Abbey until the establishment of the diocese of Gloucester in 1541. He and his licensed preachers actively promoted the new, Protestant approach to religion throughout the diocese. Although no record appears to exist on the point, one commentator has suggested that 'given the size of the parish [of Tewkesbury] and its prominence in the region, Bishop Latimer must surely have preached there at some time during his episcopate'.[33]

It was also at about this time that the antiquary John Leland, chaplain and librarian to King Henry VIII, visited the Abbey. He noted a number of books that were in the monastic library that subsequently disappeared at the Dissolution.[34]

In March 1535, the Dissolution of the Lesser Monasteries Act was passed. It would only be a matter of time before a similar fate befell the larger monasteries. There is a suggestion that as early as 1538 a possible purchase of Tewkesbury Abbey was being discussed by parish leaders.

The fate of Tewkesbury Abbey's monastic life was sealed with the Suppression of the Religious Houses Act passed in April 1539, otherwise known as the Act for the Dissolution of the Greater Monasteries, of which Tewkesbury Abbey was undoubtedly one of 552 larger monasteries now closed down. The Abbey held out for as long as possible, being the last in Gloucestershire to go, only finally surrendering on 9 January 1540 to the eight King's commissioners, although not all of them may have been present. Abbot Wakeman and 39 monks, including the priors of Cranbourne, Deerhurst and St James, Bristol, signed the deed transferring the house and all its possessions to the Crown in return for receiving pensions.

The abbot was well looked after, receiving a pension of 400 marks or £266 13s 4d per annum – a considerable sum – together with the manor house at Forthampton and the demesne, lands and tithes there, together with an appointment as Chaplain to the King. He was treated well because he made little fuss and his Abbey was relatively co-operative. The next monk in order was John Beoly (or Beeley), prior of Tewkesbury, Bachelor of Divinity of Oxford University, who received £16 6s per annum. The Priors of Deerhurst and St James, Bristol, received £13 6s 8d each; the prior of Cranbourne and another senior monk, Robert Cheltenham, BD, both received pensions of £10 a year. Two monks had to make do with £8 per year each; one with £7 per year. The ordinary monks, of which there were 27, were given pensions of £6 13s 4d a year each, exactly half of that given to the former priors of Deerhurst and St James, Bristol. For a rough comparison, it has been suggested that yeoman farmers at the time earned between £100 to £200 a year. Husbandmen – who probably had a little land and agricultural skills – earned about £10 per year while day labourers earned somewhat less. Thus the ordinary former monk's pension may have been as little as, or even smaller than, the income of the very poorest workers in society at the time. However, they were arguably not the worst off. The monastery had employed 144 servants at the time of its Dissolution. These servants were given what amounted to wages owing and severance pay;

Top: The eastern ambulatory looking north. The window on the right shows where the entrance to the fourteenth-century Lady Chapel was before being destroyed at the time of the Dissolution of the Monasteries in 1540.
Below: The eastern ambulatory looking south. The crypt that contained the duke and duchess of Clarence is in the foreground

The Tewkesbury Indenture

This document only came to light in the first few years of the present century. It was presented to the Abbey in May 2011 by Professor Peter Hancock, a former Tewkesbury resident. This agreement was between King Henry VII and Abbot Richard Cheltenham.

In return for the acquisition of the patronages of the parishes of Eastleach, Gloucestershire, and of Taynton, Oxfordshire, the abbot and convent of Tewkesbury were to:

1. Offer a daily Mass in St James' Chapel for the King, his Queen, Elizabeth, and for Prince Arthur, not forgetting the souls of Prince Edward, 'late son to King Henry VI', Edmund, earl of Richmond, father to the King; Edmund, duke of Somerset and also Lord John of Somerset;
2. On 4 May (the day of the Battle of Tewkesbury) every year to have a 'solemn dirge' (a song of grief or lamentation or, more likely, the office of the dead or possibly a sung funeral service) for the departed mentioned above;
3. On 5 May, a Solemn Requiem Mass to be sung 'for the souls aforesaid and all Christian souls'. All these services were to be in perpetuity;
4. The King was to give 'all manner of ornaments' to be used – and the abbot and Convent to look after them and pay for their repair at their expense when necessary;
5. If the dirges failed to be done, the monastery would be fined six shillings and eight pence. The same was the case if the Requiem Mass did not occur. Failure to make good the 'ornaments' would cost the monastery £3 8s 8d (six shillings and eight pence was roughly the equivalent of £351 in 2020 money. The fine for not making good the ornaments would be roughly £3,500 in 2020 money).

The agreement was signed on 17 March 1501.
Translation from the Abbey archives.

---

a grand total of £75 10s, which meant that, on average, just under 10 shillings and six pence went to each servant.[35]

There were many ornaments, jewels, goods and chattels that were sold, reportedly achieving a total of £194 8s in a sale, something of the order of £200,000 in 2020 money. This was not including the items that were 'reserved for the use of His Majesty,' such as two jewel-encrusted mitres, and hundreds of ounces of varying grades of silver.

Abbey land was sold; a fishery on the River Severn was leased. After a detailed survey, most of the monastery buildings were committed to the custody of Sir John Whittington; the keys to the receiver, Richard Paulet. Unfortunately, under the authority of these two, almost everything, from the buildings to the paperwork, was subsequently demolished or disappeared. This included the chapel on the north end of the north transept and also what had been the Lady Chapel at the east end of the Abbey. In the latter case there is a thus far unsubstantiated suggestion that the chapel had been demolished just before the Dissolution because it had been planned to build an even more glorious Lady Chapel.

However, the nave had effectively been the town's parish church. Earlier civic discussions bore fruit. The Abbey was to be saved for the town but Tewkesbury would have to find £483, that being the King's Court of Augmentation's valuation of the Abbey's bells, lead, glass and stone other than that in the nave. There had been a 'down payment' of £30 at the time of the Dissolution, probably to secure the later deal and to show that the town was serious in its desire to purchase the Abbey, but there would be a further £453 to follow. All this is set out in an official indenture, detailing the grant of the Abbey Church to the Parishioners of Tewkesbury, dated 4 June 1543. It was required that £200 was to be paid on the issuing of the indenture, the rest by Christmas 1544.[36]

What could have been a very difficult financial challenge for the town was helped considerably by the generosity of Alexander Pyrry, who died at this time, and was formerly Receiver of the abbot of Tewkesbury in the 1520s. He left a large bequest originally of £150 but possibly later adjusted to £115 to help pay for the purchase of the Abbey Church, together with a further £84 to go toward the cost of the 'lead and bells of the same', a total of £234. This meant that the town now had to find not £453 but £219 – still a very significant sum but one that Tewkesbury seems to have successfully raised.[37]

It would appear that the end of the Benedictine monks also signalled the end of a rector for the town who, according to one authority, was 'one of [the monks'] own fraternity' and funded by the Abbey community. Immediately after the monk's departure, the townspeople found that not only were they required to raise money to buy their Abbey but that they would also have to find money to fund a priest.

Benedictine monks had been a major part of not just the Abbey but the whole of Tewkesbury from 1102 and before through to 1540 – just over 430 years. It would take the Tewkesbury community time to readjust. It is evident that many in the town appeared to largely ignore what government and bishops said, as Wills from the period attest. Money was continuing to be left for such pre-Reformation practices as lights before altars and the provision of prayers for the dead. As one authority has put it, in Tewkesbury it seems that

> lay piety and traditional worship continued as long as possible according to customary practice. Apart from the use of the prescribed *Book of Common Prayer* in Edward VI's reign (the 1549 version and then the 1552 edition), traditional religion continued basically unchanged until the accession of Elizabeth I in 1558.[38]

External view of the east end, showing the fourteenth-century chapels, with the exception of the Lady Chapel, which was probably demolished soon after the Dissolution of the monastery in 1540, and whose footprint is indicated by the paved outline

CHAPTER SEVEN

1541–1660: The Abbey's Dissolution to the Restoration

THE closing of Tewkesbury Abbey's monastery in January 1540 had a significant impact on the town. While the numbers of monks had declined to over 30 from a medieval maximum of around 60, nevertheless supplying food, clothing and other items both for the Abbey and its guests meant significant local employment and trade. But the monastery's closure had an impact beyond Tewkesbury. Parishes that had their own chapels, subordinated to the Abbey – namely Ashchurch, Bushley, Forthampton, Oxenton, Tredington, Walton Cardiff and Deerhurst – suddenly found they were on their own. They were all part of the new diocese of Gloucester, except Bushley, which remained in Worcester Diocese.[1] In March 1540, within two months of Tewkesbury Abbey's 'closure', Deerhurst Priory and its lands were sold; St James' Priory at Bristol was sold, while the land around the Abbey was eventually sold to Thomas Stroud, Walter Erle and James Pagett.[2] In Gloucestershire, 'over half the county's land, more than in any other [county], had belonged to monasteries'.[3]

On 15 September 1541, John Wakeman, the compliant former mitred abbot of Tewkesbury, was consecrated the first bishop of Gloucester by Archbishop Cranmer of Canterbury, Bishop Bonner of London and Bishop Thurlby (the only ever Anglican Bishop of Westminster, later Bishop of Norwich and finally Ely).[4] It was evidently thought that John Wakeman would prove an equally compliant bishop. The new bishop must have realised ruefully that much of the expense of setting up and maintaining the new diocese would have been paid for, at least in part, by wealth that had originally belonged to Tewkesbury Abbey.

Meanwhile, in Tewkesbury, clergy support was uncertain for the town's congregation. There appeared to be no provision for either maintaining or paying them. Thomas Franklin earned a meagre stipend as a chantry priest of £4 7s 9d a year until 1547 when chantry foundations were suppressed and the funds financing them confiscated by the Crown. However, that money, together with £10 per annum, was eventually granted to the clergy at the Abbey for their ministry that might include an assistant.[5] From 1547 to 1549 Franklin was referred to as 'incumbent'.[6] Before him, John Sherewood in 1541–42, John Davis in 1543 and Robert Greene in 1545–47, all appear to have undertaken duties often undertaken by incumbents, including witnessing Wills, such as that of Edward Tyndale, a man of substance.[7] Greene was referred to as 'Curate'.

The King kept the right of appointing the incumbent or vicar. However, this he delegated, via his household, to leaders of Tewkesbury council. Already, as Tewkesbury had no Mayor, the two bailiffs of the council had the Abbey's churchwardens' accounts presented to them annually in the Abbey. For some time after, the person appointed to look after the Abbey was effectively a council nominee. Later – certainly from 1641 to 1660 – there were no bishops to institute and so such appointments could not correctly be said to be incumbent or vicar.[8] Today, the monarch still has an interest in who becomes vicar, as the Lord Chancellor, acting for the Crown, is a patron of the living.

In 1547, Henry VIII died and was succeeded by the nine-year-old Protestant King Edward VI. The earl of Hertford, the King's uncle, became Protector of the Realm and duke of Somerset. He awarded estates and titles to his brother, Sir Thomas Seymour. Apart from a peerage – Baron Seymour of Sudeley – Thomas gained the manor of Tewkesbury. He did not keep it long as he was found guilty of treason in 1549 and executed, with the manor reverting to the Crown.[9]

In December 1549, Bishop John Wakeman died. Archbishop Cranmer had thought him a scholar, making him responsible for the *Book of Revelation* in a revised translation of the Bible.[10] It is supposed that Bishop Wakeman died at Forthampton Court, although his burial site is unknown.

At the east end of the Abbey, between the Chapel of St Dunstan and the ambulatory, is a cadaver with an effigy of a decaying figure, usually taken to be that of Bishop Wakeman. Opinion is divided as to whether it is the bishop or an earlier abbot, possibly from another tomb. The carving, although dated *c*.1510, could just be late enough for Bishop Wakeman. Experts agree that the effigy is not in its original position and does not fit as it should. Indeed, such an effigy is normally found in a lower position. Moreover, the usual figure of an abbot or bishop in his robes, typically put above the present effigy, is missing.[11]

Elizabeth I's accession in 1558 (possibly during Thomas Nott's Abbey ministry) and the Queen's Protestant but pragmatic approach to religious faith questions, brought about the Elizabethan Settlement. This was a compromise that formed the basis on which the Church of England could function. The Second Act of Supremacy in 1559 made Elizabeth Supreme Governor of the Church, a position still held by the monarch. However, of more immediate concern to Tewkesbury Nonconformists was the new weekly requirement to attend the Church of England Abbey. Failure to attend might result in fines or even imprisonment. Clergy, who had been allowed to marry in 1547, but banned from doing so by Queen Mary, were given permission to marry under Elizabeth in 1559.[12]

The resident priest or minister from 1549–54 is unknown, although Richard Drake's name was mentioned as a possibility in 1552. Stephen Beard, styled at different times both 'incumbent' and 'vicar', was in post at Tewkesbury from 1554 to 1556. He arrived just after the Puritan Edward VI's reign (1547–53) and was at the Abbey for most of the Roman Catholic Queen Mary's reign (1553–58). As Princess, she had spent Christmas 1525 at the Abbey. In 1554 she re-founded the old Founder's Almsmen belonging to the town and parish, calling them Queen Mary's Almsmen.[13] She would have had little to complain about regarding Tewkesbury Abbey's attitude to worship. Litzenberger has put the point succinctly:

> The advent of Protestantism in England elicited a chilly response in Tewkesbury ... it appears that the parish leadership did not divest itself

The Wakeman cenotaph may or may not be of the last abbot, as the workmanship suggests that it may be slightly earlier in date (possibly c.1510–30) than 1549 when the former abbot, later bishop of Gloucester, died. Moreover, the cadaver does not appear to fit properly into the space allocated

of the trappings of traditional worship during the reign of King Edward VI as the Protestant Bishop of Gloucester, John Hooper, had ordered ... Apart from the use of the prescribed Book of Common Prayer in Edward VI's reign, traditional religion continued basically unchanged until the accession of Elizabeth I in November 1558.[14]

Even as late as 1585, over 25 years into Queen Elizabeth's reign, Tewkesbury Abbey was still reluctant to shed all vestiges of Catholic worship, and conformity was minimal. Somehow, the Abbey's liturgical resources still included 'The best cope of tinsel with red roses', three 'awles' or albs, an 'amyae' or amice (the linen cloth worn around the neck of the priest celebrating Mass or Holy Communion); and a bell, possibly a small altar bell, traditionally rung during the elevation of the consecrated elements. However, since the Act of Supremacy, the service would no longer have been in Latin.[15]

On Easter Day 1559, the wooden spire on top of the central tower collapsed during a service. Fortunately, no-one was injured. There is no firm date for its erection, although some believe it was built during Robert Fitzroy's time as lord of the manor, but this is unlikely.[16] It was not replaced.

The churchwardens' accounts of 1564–65 note three shillings and sixpence expended on 'a seat at the nether end of the church', mending the bellows of the organ and for nails for the same, showing that the Abbey already had an organ and must have had for a while.[17]

By 1570, the Abbey was still paying a low annual stipend of £10 to the minister and £8 to the assistant, then called 'the Secondary'. The Secondary also acted as chaplain of Tredington Chapel, a small village three or four miles from Tewkesbury. The money for their incomes, together with the costs of bread, wine, wax and incense 'were charged on tithes formerly belonging to the Abbey when the Crown leased the lands in 1569'.[18] Three years earlier, in 1566, a Mr Pert was the first 'commoner' to be buried in the church, having paid six shillings and eight pence for the privilege.[19] This proved a useful source of income. It joined others such as the occasional sale of lead, and also church ales – Tudor fundraising events rather like a fête or fair but with brewed ales available, first recorded at the Abbey in 1566. Further ways of raising funds included local taxation of the parish through rates and also 'pew rents', which included places in galleries.[20]

It is symptomatic of the unsettled religious times that Abbey clergy appear to have come and gone almost annually, but records are far from complete. Ministers tended to be of Protestant if not Puritan persuasion, owing their appointment to a sometimes Nonconformist-leaning Town Council.

The stone surfaces of the Abbey were lime-washed in 1571–72, taking over 22 hours. The chancel was again whitewashed between 1615 and 1618, and there was still more whitewashing between 1624 and 1627.[21]

In 1575, Tewkesbury was given a charter, therefore full legal and largely self-governing status as a borough, by Queen Elizabeth I.[22] A year later, a 'Free Grammar School' was founded, probably by William Ferrers, a London mercer, which continued to be active until around 1835.[23] It was housed in the Chapel of St James. A brick wall separated the school from the rest of the Abbey which was not restored fully until 1875.

Another Abbey building with a new role was the old campanile or bell-tower, which had stood to the north of the Abbey not far from what was now the Free Grammar School. When it was

Above: An illustration of the campanile or old belfry prior to the order being given for it to be turned into a prison or 'house of correction' in 1582, and the bells removed and rehung in the central tower of the Abbey

Left: The same view today, with the campanile gone

built and the bells installed are both unknown. However, in the early 1580s, the building was deemed sufficiently unsafe that the bells were moved back into the main tower of the Abbey. During Lent 1582, Bennett, among others, notes that, 'Her Majesty's Justices came to the town, and ordered the belfry tower to be covered and furnished for a house of correction for half the shire, and committed the building of it to the [Tewkesbury town] bailiffs'.[24]

It has probably been rightly suggested that, 'The Protestants finally gained control of both the town and the parish in the early 1580s but Tewkesbury's acceptance of established religious practices had been and would continue to be marked by local idiosyncrasies'.[25] The first incumbent who spent longer than a year or two in post was John Audrey (1591–97). He attempted to make sermons particularly important in his ministry. However, several parishioners, notably Henry Turner, responded with evident hostility.[26] Audrey appeared in an ecclesiastical court in 1591 for marrying three couples during the forbidden time of Septuagesima Sunday to Low Sunday without a Bishop's License.[27]

How and where the congregation sat also became an issue. One authority noted that, 'gender-segregated seating does not appear to have been a conscious policy [at the Abbey] much before 1595. But by that time it appears that women were sitting separate from men, and that the wives' seats were assigned to them through their husbands'.[28]

Meanwhile, the Abbey authorities had the long nave roof lowered in 1593–94 – the idea was probably to save on lead in future.[29] However, the work was mediocre, for in 1597 a storm blew off much of the nave roof which was not properly recapped until 1599.[30] This was all very expensive, and so, during John Audrey's incumbency, between 1594 and 1596, the churchwardens levied a church rate in Tewkesbury apparently for the first time.[31] It is also evident that, following Mr Pert's burial in the Abbey, others had the same idea. In 1596 there was an entry in the churchwardens' accounts noting the expense of carrying earth 'to fill graves sunk in the church …. the mason to laye the graves that sank with quarrell [stone from a quarry]'.

Clergy in charge of the Abbey from Dissolution to Post-Restoration 1542–1662 (* denotes status uncertain)

*John Sherwood	1542
John Davis	?1543–?1545
*Robert Greene	?1545–47
Thomas Franklyn	1547–49
*Richard Drake	1552–?54
Stephen Beard	1554–56
Thomas Nott	c.1557
*John Pyers	1561
*William Whitehead	1562
*John Williams	1563
*Nicholas Crondall	1567
*William Johnsons	c.1573
*'Parson' Banckes	c.1576
John Audrey	c.1591–97
Richard Curtis	1597–1602
Humphrey Fox	1602–08
William Blackwell	1608–11
Edward Lonsby (Losbie)	1612–23
*John Coxe	1623
John Geary (Geree)	1627–34
Samuel West	1634
Nathaniel Wight	1634–?1644
John Wells	1645–62
*Thomas Burroughs	1649–50

Audrey was followed by Richard Curtis (1597–1602), who restricted the use of bells, even though several parishioners protested. He was also prosecuted for failing to renew his license or possibly for a connection to the lucrative trade in clandestine marriages.

During Curtis' incumbency, new battlements were built on the tower which had not been properly repaired since the 1559 steeple crash. Enough money was raised, at least in part, by a festival of scriptural plays in the nave held over Whitsuntide in 1600. The festival apparently included beer, food and music as well as the plays. The Abbey community had held them before, in 1566 and in 1578 and 1584, and had kept a stock of costumes that they had rented or loaned out to nearby villages for their festivals since 1567 (for example twice in 1576).[32] However, Puritans were upset by two butts of ale made available by the churchwardens.[33] In future, licence requests would be refused by the council unless 'accustomed abuses' were reformed. There were no such requests and the tradition of plays in the nave died out.[34] A second, unforeseen cost was in 1599 when part of the north aisle wall collapsed, and 240 feet (73 metres) of stone had to be purchased. Men spent 300 days on its repair.[35] A parish rate was charged to help pay for it in 1601, but it was not enough and meantime the south side also required attention, so a second rate was charged. In all, about £31 was raised.[36]

Either at the very end of Richard Curtis' incumbency, or at the beginning of that of his successor, Humphrey Fox, in 1602 the monks' stalls, which had hitherto been situated 'under and west of the Tower', as Blunt puts it, were uprooted and put in the chancel or presbytery.[37]

Humphrey Fox (1602–08) was a Puritan cleric of independent means who rented 'the Great Abbey House', now Abbey House.[38] However,

Choir stalls, moved after the Dissolution of the monastery in 1540, seen in the north transept before their eventual return to the quire during the Victorian restoration and reordering by Thomas Collins in 1872 (engraving from William Beattie's *Castles and Abbeys of England, Volume the First*, 1842)

his sons, Hopewell and Help-on-High, were educated in Scotland. He took over briefly before he was suspended from the Tewkesbury living late in 1602 for Nonconformity (that is, he conducted services in a manner and/ or with words that were not authorised). In the Tewkesbury area, posture at the giving of Holy Communion became an extremely important sign of Nonconformist attitudes. Fox was prosecuted for 'administering communion without wearing the surplice and for administering the sacrament of the Lord's Supper to diverse parishioners sitting down, to the disturbance of the rest that were present of the congregation'. In 1606, Mrs Leight of Tewkesbury held 'conventicles', meaning 'unauthorised and possibly illegal acts of probably Nonconformist worship', in her house for Fox and his friends. He continued to conduct services in the Nonconformist style.[39]

He was refused a license in 1616 and suspended again in 1619 and in 1630. The authorities were sufficiently concerned about him as a leader of Nonconformity that in 1639 the Privy Council, supported by Bishop Goodman of Gloucester and William Hill, Town Clerk of Tewkesbury, ordered a search of Fox's study.[40] It is doubtful whether anything incriminating was found.[41]

Meanwhile, in 1603–4, the chancel roof was also rebuilt at a lower pitch but at the town's expense.[42] During Fox's incumbency a 'large, grey, marble stone' was discovered 'underground' in the Abbey in 1607 (exactly where is not known). It was 13 feet 8 inches long (4m), 3 feet, 6 inches broad (1m) and nearly a foot thick (28cm). It was placed in the middle of the quire lengthways and used as a Holy Communion table. Its five Consecration Crosses were still 'clearly discernible'.[43] It is almost certain that it was the Purbeck marble high altar stone dedicated in honour of the Blessed Virgin Mary by Walter de Cantilupe, bishop of Worcester, in 1239. It had been hidden away for safekeeping, presumably at the time of the Dissolution of Tewkesbury monastery, or possibly later when the stone altars were being removed c.1540.

William Blackwell (1608–11) was a Nonconformist curate of Beckford. He was frequently invited by Humphrey Fox to preach at Tewkesbury Abbey and became curate or incumbent in 1608.[44] Fox had moved on to Forthampton. During Blackwell's ministry, the authorised King James version of the Bible was published in 1611, apparently scarcely noticed in Tewkesbury. However, the Abbey churchwardens were careful to try, at least superficially, to keep on the right side of the authorities by having the King's Arms painted in the Abbey in 1610.[45] The manor of Tewkesbury had been sold to the Corporation the year before by the King for £2,453, although the King continued to retain rights regarding incumbent appointments.[46]

Just before William Blackwell's arrival, in 1607, the 'Blue Gallery' was built for parishioners 'in front of the high altar and containing 14 rows', followed by another in 1609.[47] By the end of the incumbency of Blackwell's successor, Edward Lonsby (or Losbie, also Lousby, Loosbee) (1612–23) there were at least three galleries – the 'new', the 'old' (presumably the 'Blue') and the 'scholars'. The last of those three was built in 1618 for up to 19 scholars of the free grammar school. Its cost was offset by a fair held in 1617[48] and places were rented out for sums ranging from one shilling (5p) to four shillings (20p) when 1p would be worth about £1.50 in 2020.[49] Around the same time but possibly a year or two later, elevated galleries were also built in the north and south transepts and in the north and south aisles 'as far as the stone screen'.[50]

Edward Lonsby was effectively incumbent 1612–23, being styled curate, preacher and minister at different points.[51] He was a Puritan, clearly not content with previous lime-washing of the Abbey's interior stone surfaces in 1571–72. The chancel was whitewashed again between 1615 and 1618.[52] Yet gifts were being given to the Abbey, such as a chalice and paten-cover by a Mr Whittington earlier in 1576, while another chalice and a paten were given by Edward Alley and Richard Dowdeswell respectively in 1618.[53]

After Edward Lonsby left in 1623, the next known incumbent was John Geary (or Geree) (1627–34) who was Puritan in outlook.[54] During his time, a sixth bell was added to the ring in 1632, a fifth having been added in 1612.[55]

In 1633, William Laud became Archbishop of Canterbury. He held views 'on church doctrine and church order that were diametrically opposed to those of the Puritans'. Laud wanted greater ceremonial and shorter sermons. He stressed the authority of sacred *objects*.[56] A special commission, appointed to conduct an archiepiscopal visitation to the Abbey in 1635, gave detailed instructions for the movement of the communion table. It was no longer to be in the 'body' of the chancel but its 'uppermost part'. It was 'fashioned from a large marble stone', and was to be placed in the traditional, Catholic 'north to south' position. This contrasted with the 'east to west position' of the Cranmer reforms of the early 1550s favoured by Puritans. Rails were placed around the altar, supposedly to keep out dogs and other 'noisome creatures'. Moreover, the commissioners noted other deficiencies within the Abbey. There was the 'Failure to display the proper symbols of authority in the Church interior. Churchwardens had neglected the Royal Arms, the Lord's Prayer, the Creed and the Ten Commandments'.[57] However, it is known that at least the Royal Arms had been painted inside the Abbey in 1610, and on a new gallery in 1616.[58]

Laud's commissioners gave instructions on keeping both Abbey and churchyard. The churchwardens had rented the churchyard out as pasture. That, together with selling the resulting manure, had raised important additional income for the Abbey for many years. This was no longer permissible. The Abbey's economy was disrupted. Churchwardens would be more dependant than before on parish rates. The diocesan authorities kept an eye on the Abbey – Bishop Goodman sent a member of his staff over to check that everything was as he felt it should be in 1636.[59]

Geary's Puritanism led to his suspension from the living in 1634 and he was never reinstated. Bishop Goodman only lifted the suspension once Geary finally undertook to leave the diocese in 1637. His successor, Samuel West, appears to have lasted less than a year before Nathaniel Wight became incumbent (1634–c.1644). He was more Conformist but even he was prosecuted by his own churchwardens in 1637 for allowing John Geary to preach in the Abbey. Abbey churchwardens had already prosecuted 30 Tewkesbury people for Nonconformity in 1635, the majority being skilled craftsmen such as carpenters, tailors, weavers and cutlers. There were no gentlemen and no leaders of the Corporation. There was a rapid recantation by the prosecuted but a resentment of the church hierarchy resulted.[60]

A combination of Archbishop Laud's policies and the prosecution of people at a local level had the effect of 'cultural fragmentation' – the idea of Christianity being expressed in one state church was being challenged.[61] In 1639 Tewkesbury Council voted to bar Roman Catholics from holding any office in the town.[62] The position of those in other denominations was challenged in the descriptions of the Anglican Sunday procession of the burgesses escorting the bailiffs to Abbey services, with special seats reserved for 'Bailiffs, Burgesses and their assistants' taking up seven rows of the best seats. Another six seats nearby were for the guild masters. Yet the situation was so fluid that in the same year of 1639, an avowed Nonconformist, Nicholas Mearson, was elected churchwarden. He had been prosecuted in 1635 for 'sitting at the time of Divine Service'. The following year, the other churchwarden became William Haines who, also in 1635, was prosecuted for his refusal to kneel to receive the Sacrament.[63] They were elected by a rather shadowy body, the Parish Assembly, consisting of the bailiffs, the justices of the Corporation 'and diverse others of the parish'.

How this body was convened has never been established. The formal Vestry, forerunner of the Parochial Church Council, took over in 1660.

Although 450 Tewkesbury men signed the Protestation or covenant to defend the Protestant religion in 1641, which represented 'perhaps half the male population of the town'.[64] Abbey churchwardens had the right, regardless of people's affiliations, to charge church rates of everyone. Religious matters nationally were in a state of flux. In 1642, an Act removing bishops from the House of Lords became law. The following year bishops, deans and cathedral chapters were abolished and Parliament established the Westminster Assembly. This consisted of representatives of both Houses, some English divines and eight Scottish commissioners. It was to deliberate on liturgy, discipline and government of the Church of England. It nudged matters towards the unfulfilled possibility of establishing Presbyterianism as the national religion.[65]

Terms such as 'Protestantism', 'Puritanism', 'Presbyterianism', 'Independents' and 'Baptists' reflected a variety of views about faith – and each chapel might see various theological points differently to its neighbour. This might not have mattered had everyone been prepared to listen to and accept, at least in part, the views of others. However, this tended not to be the case, resulting in the Abbey, as a central place of worship in the town, losing people to other, new congregations. Understanding, sympathy and Christian love were often in short supply.

Looking towards the Abbey from the River Swilgate direction, showing the area where all of the monastic buildings were to be found before their demolition at the Dissolution of the monastery in 1540

Tewkesbury Abbey, long Roman Catholic, found her worship to be not just Protestant but often veering towards a brand of Puritanism from which it was later to retreat.

One authority has noted that, nationally, at this time, 'the presentation process [of a clergyman to a living] remained decentralised and informal'.[66] In Tewkesbury, ever since the town had bought the Abbey from the Crown in 1543 – but especially since the Borough Council had bought the lordship of the manor from King James I in 1610 – the bailiffs and councillors had almost assumed it as their right to choose the Abbey parson or minister. As many councillors were of Nonconformist inclination, who was appointed might often depend on those wielding power and influence on the council at any particular time. They tended to disregard that the monarch, through his Lord Chancellor, still maintained the right to present a candidate to the living, but as most Lord Chancellors seemed less than interested, it was hardly surprising that the council tended to lead in such matters.

By 1645, John Wells was Abbey minister, a staunch Independent Cromwellian, with some Presbyterian inclinations.[67] He and his churchwardens had little time for those who did not pay church rates. That year, three soldiers were hired to collect church rates that were in arrears.[68] In 1647–48, the Abbey's great tenor bell cracked. It had to be recast at Gloucester. Its transport there and back – by water – and the work done on it came to £37 3d, a significant sum. Once again, the churchwardens raised the required money through an 'extraordinary' church rate which was unpopular in the town.[69]

For a while, Thomas Burroughs may have acted as 'Minister of Tewkesbury Abbey', probably between 1649–50, possibly in tandem with John Wells.[70] Burroughs, who had a reputation as a republican, did not stay for long. It is thought that during this period the heads were knocked off the figures round the Beauchamp Chantry.[71]

The north side of the Beauchamp/ Warwick Chantry Chapel, showing a number of statues that had been 'beheaded' – vandalism thought to be the work of seventeenth-century Puritans

During the Civil War itself, Tewkesbury was held at various times by both Royalist and Parliamentary forces. There is a persistent tradition, but no firm evidence, that at some point between 1640 and 1651, the Abbey nave was used to stable Parliamentary horses, and traces could be seen well into the eighteenth century.[72] What this does underline is that the nave was seldom if ever used for services. They took place in what is now the quire and the chancel. It is noteworthy that King Charles I's execution on 31 January 1649 is hardly mentioned at all in the Tewkesbury records, other than in Giles Geast's *Charity's Chronicle*.[73]

In 1646, it was realised that many ministers had been paid the same for many years. Oliver Cromwell and others decided to act, improving incomes by about £100 a year. In Tewkesbury's case, the better income was provided by sequestrations from other parishes.[74] In 1650, the bailiffs provided a new pulpit, placed in the newly repaired chancel, from which a minister was 'to preach twice every Lord's Day'. The bailiffs claimed that they had been paying a minister for more than 50 years.[75]

In the 1640s, though not during the occupation by Parliamentarians, the Abbey was perfumed with the scent of rosemary in preparation for Christmas. This practice was revived in 1661.

Bells were still being used as the best way of conveying a message or occasion quickly. Apart from 5 November and festivities surrounding deliverance from the Gunpowder Plot (1605), Bells were used to celebrate the Puritan 'Thanksgiving Days', of which there were perhaps ten a year. They had grown since the English Reformation, designed to drastically cut the 95 Holy Days (holidays) as well as 52 Sundays every year that the Roman Catholic Church had previously included. For example, one such Thanksgiving Day in the churchwardens' accounts, 'as per Master Bailiff's order' on 25 October 1651, was probably in thanksgiving for a successful harvest. The ringers were paid ten shillings, double what they were given for the annual ring on 5 November. On 24 December 1653, the bells pealed out again, this time proclaiming that Oliver Cromwell was now 'Lord Protector.'[76]

Also in 1653, marriages were secularised. Locally, notices about an intent to marry were displayed in Tewkesbury market place. The wedding ceremony itself would be carried out by local, unpaid magistrates called Justices of the Peace (JPs).[77]

That year included a 'public debate' in Winchcombe Parish Church. The question was 'whether it be lawful to minister and receive the holy sacrament in congregations called mixed or in our parish churches'. Clement Barksdale (Sudeley) and William Towers (Toddington), described as 'Orthodox Divines', defended the traditional church order and the administration of the Sacrament according to the then *Book of Common Prayer*. However, among others, John Wells (Tewkesbury Abbey) and Carnsew Helme (Winchcombe), described as Independents, were unhappy with what the *Book of Common Prayer* appeared to be saying. Traditionally, a person was a member of a particular congregation because of where he or she lived. Nonconformists felt that what mattered was whether an individual could be said to be 'Godly', and committed to the congregation of which they were a part.

Wells rejected calling churches 'houses of God' because 'the house built in the reign of popery and for the honour and adoration of saints was not built for the honour and service of God.' He responded violently when reminded of the traditional church calendar. 'At the mention of the word *Christmas*,' Barksdale observed, 'Wells was startled and cried 'popery!' To Barksdale's defence of the traditional episcopal church, Wells expressed contempt and hatred. 'We have enough of you already,' declared Wells, 'I would not go over to the door sill to dispute with one upon whose spirit I see so much of the pope.' Barksdale suggested Wells reflect on the book by John Geary (who was Wells' predecessor at Tewkesbury), entitled *Vindiciae Ecclesiae Anglicanae*. This, while arguing for allowing Nonconformity, was still vehemently opposed to separation from the Church of England.[78]

Another clash occurred in 1655, when George Fox, founder of the Society of Friends, the Quakers, came to Tewkesbury. Quakers were thought dangerous, as they relied on personal spiritual and mystic experience rather than scripture. Moreover, they acknowledged everyone as equals, accepting no authority from others. Therefore they were seen as a destabilising, antisocial force both to supporters of the *Book of Common Prayer* and to Presbyterians and Independents alike. Fox later recounted a night meeting he led in Tewkesbury in his journal. John Wells, still the minister, came to the meeting with others. Fox wrote that Wells 'boasted he would see whether he or [Fox] should have the victory'. Fox preached and 'turned the people to the divine light'. Fox seemed to deny the principle of hierarchy and subordination in society, which included religion. This was unacceptable to Independents and Wells reportedly 'began to rage against the light and denied it and so went away'.[79]

Politically, Quakers were not that important. The real conflict was between Presbyterians and Independents. Their divergent views often centred around different attitudes towards toleration and church structure.[80] The Independents eventually became Congregationalists, now often the United Reformed Church. However, some toleration was practised. An Ordinance of 1650 repealed former statutes imposing penalties for not attending a Church of England church on Sunday. There was still a requirement to attend some place of Christian worship.[81]

Meanwhile, at the Abbey there were always matters requiring the attention of churchwardens. In 1654, repairs to the west window were necessary. However, it was later evident that the repairs were inadequate.[82]

In 1655, a comparatively small organ, the Abbey's future Milton Organ, was transferred from its original site in Magdalen College, Oxford, to Hampden Court, London, so that Oliver Cromwell might hear it.[83] It was also the year in which major generals were appointed to cover every district to ensure that there was 'godliness and virtue' predominating in every community. Major generals were assisted by JPs.

Possibly the last Puritan act at the Abbey was the removal of the stone font in 1657 by the then two churchwardens, Richard Cooke and Thomas Smyth, the former putting it in his garden.[84] However, within four years and the Restoration, opinion had altered so much that it was decided that the same two men should be prosecuted.[85]

The font was removed from the Abbey in 1657. After the Restoration in 1660, it was returned. The present font and the elaborate cover date from between 1875 and 1879. However, the Purbeck marble base may be thirteenth-century, while the stem is probably fourteenth-century

1541–1660: THE ABBEY'S DISSOLUTION TO THE RESTORATION   77

In September 1658, Oliver Cromwell died, to be succeeded by his son, Richard, who abdicated as Lord Protector in May 1659. General Monk, Governor of Scotland, made overtures to King Charles I's son, also Charles, to return as a constitutional monarch. This idea was not universally acceptable in Tewkesbury, where some troopers from the nearby garrison went into Tewkesbury's taverns, trying to stir up trouble against General Monk's proposals.[86] However, Charles agreed to rule with Parliament and the Abbey ringers were paid 12 shillings to ring on the day Charles was proclaimed King, on 10 May 1660. The Restoration was marked by a proclamation requiring the display of the Royal Arms of Charles II in churches. Tewkesbury Abbey is one of many that still have theirs, sited just west of the present screen on the south side above the sedilia.[87] Parliament also promptly passed legislation making 29 May a public holiday, marking the King's birthday. Tewkesbury Abbey continued to ring bells on this Oak Apple or Royal Oak Day until it was formally abolished in 1859.

CHAPTER EIGHT

1660–1836: The Restoration to the end of the Regency

King Charles II was received as King in London on 29 May (Oak Apple Day) 1660. The coronation was on 23 April 1661 at Westminster Abbey. That day, Tewkesbury Abbey ringers received ten shillings for their labours and were also paid to ring when King Charles married Catherine of Braganza in 1662.

The Royal Arms of King Charles II is found over the sedilia to the south-west of the screen. A proclamation requiring churches to put up the Royal Arms was made immediately after the Restoration in 1660

In the Abbey itself, the condition of the west window was becoming alarming. This had been inadequately repaired in 1654, possibly because worshippers were reluctant to spend money outside where they normally worshipped. This was eastward from the two bays west of the crossing under the central tower, from roughly the point where the original medieval pulpitum had been. However, in February 1661 the window blew in, requiring urgent action. That same month, a parish meeting agreed to raise £82 from the town and parish, above and beyond the £30 they already had to 'rebuild the great window and repair the decays of the said church and leads'. Three years later they were still working to collect the money voted, showing a growing reluctance by the congregation and townspeople to support their Abbey.

In 1662, 26 Anglican bishops were reinstated in the House of Lords.[1] Episcopal power had returned. Henceforward, clergy could be instituted to their livings and be vicars – including Tewkesbury. A new version of the *Book of Common Prayer* was also published. It remained the Church of England prayer book until it was revised in 1928. Its importance to the Church is evident in that the year it was published, the Third Act of Uniformity was passed. This required those clergy who did not conform to the Prayer Book liturgy by St Bartholomew's Day (24 August) to be dismissed.[2]

A conjectural reconstruction of how the west front may have looked c.1140, at a time when glass was inordinately expensive. It is based on the Norman west end of the Priory at Bristol, built just after the Abbey was completed by Robert Fitzroy, first earl of Gloucester and Lord of the manor of Tewkesbury

Whether this is why John Wells resigned the Tewkesbury living or whether he was dismissed is not recorded. During that same year, a new incumbent took over. He was Robert Eaton, 'a godly man', son of a former incumbent, also called Robert Eaton.[3] Already, some old traditions were returning, such as 'dressing' the Abbey at Christmas with herbs like rosemary.[4] Bells were beginning to be rung on Saints' Days again, including St George's Day, though on fewer occasions.[5]

Another sign of a loosening Puritan grip was the Abbey font's return. It had been removed in 1657 by the then churchwardens Thomas Smith

The west front of the Abbey as it appears today. The window originally dated from 1686, after an earlier collapse of the west wall. The old glass had deteriorated and was replaced by the Revd Charles Grove in 1886 as a memorial to his wife, Frances Emily, who died in March of that year. Note that what should be seven great arches is now six

and Richard Cooke, the latter placing the stones in his 'backside' or garden, noted in the last chapter.[6] It was a further expression of the same suspicion of idolatry, perceived papist practices, even blasphemy, that had led to the destruction of Tewkesbury's ancient market cross in 1650 by the Presbyterian William Hill and the Independent John Bach, who were the two bailiffs at the time.[7] Religious perceptions had changed so much that the font, returned to the Abbey in 1664, was placed two or three pillars further up on the south side than its position today. The two churchwardens who had had it removed originally were recommended for prosecution by the parish

1661–1836: THE RESTORATION TO THE END OF THE REGENCY

Above: The stone vaulting replaced the ceiling of wood between 1330 and 1350. There are 237 bosses in all: 42 in the north aisle, 40 in the south aisle and 155 in the main vault. The centre bosses represent the Life of Christ, beginning at the west end. The centre boss in the third bay from the east end of the south aisle has the Despenser arms

Left: The top of the nave vault, with nave roof above

meeting of January 1661.[8] Thomas Boulter was paid £1 10s for organising the return of the font, while John Parrett supplied beer and John Jeemes was paid 8 shillings and sixpence for the font-cover.[9] In 1828, the font was removed from the nave and placed in the apse part of what is the Lady Chapel today.[10]

Probably in 1664, John Parrett mended the paving 'in the body of the church' after a flood. It was to be another century before flooding was as bad again.[11]

Religious and political uncertainties did not touch Tewkesbury in the 1670s. However, the duke of Monmouth's rebellion and subsequent defeat in 1685 was celebrated in the town. The ringers 'on news of the defeat of the rebels in the West at several times' were paid a handsome 15 shillings to publicise the government victory through ringing the bells.[12]

The Abbey fabric was again giving cause for concern. In 1686 it was the wall that held the west window and again the west window itself. There had probably been a fourteenth-century Decorated-style window previously. Now the window that is seen today was constructed, authorised by a parish meeting in April of that year, and suggested by some to be modelled on the 'Crécy' window in Gloucester Cathedral.[13] As if that wasn't enough, the same year 'the long roof over the nave' also required considerable attention. A rate of nine old pence in the pound was demanded of townspeople to cover the cost.[14]

In 1687, the minister, Robert Eaton, in post for five years, died in office, recorded in the register on 14 October 1687.[15] His gravestone may be found in the eastern ambulatory. There is also a memorial plaque in St Dunstan's Chapel.[16] He is not to be confused with another eighteenth-century Robert Eaton, incumbent of Bromsberrow.

James II's trial of seven bishops in 1688 contributed to his abdication later that year and the arrival of William and Mary, who were to rule jointly. John Matthews, recently appointed minister of Tewkesbury, while professing loyalty to James II, had nevertheless spoken out in support of the seven bishops. He was appalled when he realised that the King had abdicated, and horrified when William III invaded, visualising something of a blood-bath that never happened.[17] Such was the Tewkesbury Abbey minister's view of the Glorious Revolution.

However, the new monarchs and Parliament eased tensions in Tewkesbury and elsewhere by passing the Toleration Act of 1689, which allowed Nonconformists other than Unitarians freedom of worship. They were still excluded from public life unless they were prepared to take Anglican Holy Communion once a year.[18]

In Ireland, former Catholic king, James II, was defeated by his Protestant son-in-law, now King William III, at the Battle of the Boyne on 1 July 1690. The impact on Tewkesbury was immediate but brief. Drummers marked the victory around the town. The Abbey gave a wounded soldier tuppence ha'penny, and several apparent refugees from Ireland were also given a little money. When King William returned in early September, there was more drumming, Abbey bells were rung and a bonfire lit.[19] Again, in 1692, to celebrate a naval victory against the French, the Abbey ringers expressed the town's joy at Admiral Russell's victory.[20] A total of 13 seamen passed through the town in 1694, at least eight apparently former prisoners-of-war, newly released by the French, to whom the Abbey gave a little money.[21]

Matthews himself began as minister, but eventually became vicar – possibly in 1697. It would appear that he was marginally more High

Church than his predecessors. Evidence for this may be found in the Abbey Archives where there is a copy of one of Matthews' books of sermons that did not go, with so many others, to University College, London. This book had a 12-page section attached called *Ex Missale Romani* – 'From the Roman Missal', and seemed to comprise copies of Latin rubrics for various occasions. This might help to explain the uneasy relationship between him and the Town Clerk, Henry Collett, who was both Baptist and anti-Royalist.[22] Nevertheless, John Matthews was one of the longest serving incumbents, from 1688 to 1728.

The diocese kept a careful watch on Tewkesbury Abbey, the Archdeacon having a Visitation almost every year from 1663 to 1680, thereafter combining it with a Visitation to Deerhurst or Cheltenham.[23] Whereas the bailiffs of the town had had considerable power over what went on in the Abbey, especially immediately post-Dissolution, their power was increasingly being transferred to the churchwardens. This became apparent after a parish meeting in April 1682 when 'Mr Bailiff Dobins', who also happened to be a churchwarden, sought to concern himself with financial decisions being taken at the Abbey. Subsequently, the bishop of Gloucester, Robert Frampton, ordered Mr Bailiff Dobins 'not to concern himself in expense or otherwise of the church', appointing John Peyton as churchwarden in his stead. By this action, it became clear that immediate church decisions were no longer a council concern as previously. Decisions were to be left to the two churchwardens, James Simpson and John Peyton.[24]

The next significant expense for the Abbey was in 1696 when the six bells were cast into eight by A. Rudhall of Gloucester. Although there were problems with the recast bells until 1742, nevertheless 223 people contributed just over £68 towards the initial expense of £72 3s 3½d.

In March 1702 William III died, Queen Mary II having predeceased him in 1694. Interestingly, King William's passing was not apparently marked at the Abbey. Generally, he had been seen nationally as being both 'foreign' and rather cold. Yet the birthday in February of his sister-in-law, Princess Anne, and subsequent coronation as Queen Anne in April 1702 were both greeted with bells at the Abbey in celebration.[25]

For Tewkesbury Abbey itself, one recurring problem during Queen Anne's reign was its interior's use as a burial place, initially in the chancel. In 1702 – coronation year – the Parish Meeting agreed that 'no person shall be buried in or about the Chancel or the Aisles about unless the friends of any person so buried shall pay 28 shillings and eight pence',[26] (some £300 in 2020 money). Some people tried to circumvent this. Samuel Hawling, a Tewkesbury alderman, was buried in the Clarence vault in 1709, his wife similarly in 1729 and his son in 1753. They were reinterred elsewhere in 1829.[27]

Having remained incumbent throughout Queen Anne's reign, John Matthews continued through that of King George I (1714–27). The vicar and churchwardens faced more structural challenges with the Abbey. A particular problem was the nave roof, which by 1720 was being described as 'dilapidated'. Yet it had been repaired only just over a century earlier. There were difficulties funding further repairs. An appeal was made to the Lord Chancellor, then Thomas Parker, Lord Mansfield, who granted the Abbey a 'brief', dated 25 February 1720. Repairs were begun in 1723 and completed by 1726. Dendrochronological analysis has shown that although some of the nave roof timber dates to 1723, much of it was reused timber from 200 years earlier.[28]

Buttresses were added around 1720. One was built on the north-west angle of the north transept, with a corresponding support to the south transept – the latter possibly to compensate for the loss of support caused by the demolition of the cloisters and chapter house.[29] In 1723, a further flying buttress was added to the north nave aisle.[30]

The grave plots inside the Abbey were filling up. In 1724 Francis Smith, the Abbey surveyor, demanded that 'no new grave was to be cut within three feet of a wall or pillar'.[31] However, the Abbey authorities did allow the burial in the Abbey of an unknown army officer, killed in a duel in the High Street at the White Hart in 1725, next to The Swan coaching inn.[32]

The Pelican in her Piety formed part of the Doric high altarpiece of 1726, and is now in St Margaret's Chapel. Begun by John Copner of Tewkesbury, who died while working on it, it was completed by John Ricketts of Cheltenham

In a final act of Puritanism, the medieval altar stone that had been found post-Dissolution and, under Archbishop Laud, put as a high altar much as it is seen today, was removed and cut in two from end to end possibly in 1728, certainly by the end of 1730. The resulting two stones were placed in the north porch as seats for the next 100 years, and were not returned to their rightful position until 1879 in the Scott restoration.[33] There was now a smaller altar and a new Doric altarpiece, largely funded by the congregation. Part of that altarpiece, the Pelican in her Piety, is now in St Margaret's Chapel. In addition, there were the Lord's Prayer, Creed and Ten Commandments on marble slabs.[34] In order to accommodate the altarpiece, the sedilia on the south side of the present high altar was mutilated. John Copner of Haresfield began the work but he died of smallpox in Tewkesbury in 1726. The contract was completed by John Ricketts of Gloucester.[35] The floor before the altar was replaced with 100ft of blue and white stone in 1730.[36]

John Matthews finally resigned as vicar in 1728, dying the following year, aged 79.[37] A memorial to him was put in the south transept.[38] His successor, the Revd Henry Jones, originally a Cambridge Law graduate, sadly only lived a few months before dying in post. In turn, he was succeeded by his brother, the Revd Penry Jones who was vicar from 1729 to 1754. First the chancel in 1733 and then the rest of the Abbey in 1734 were whitewashed yet again, a small rate being charged 'not exceeding 2d in the £'.[39]

One of the main features of Penry Jones' incumbency was the advent of an Abbey organ. A decision in principle was made by the vicar, the two town bailiffs, Bailiff Kemble and Bailiff Hayward, and the parishioners, meeting in March 1735 – notwithstanding the bailiffs' lesser Abbey role than in the past.[40] A year later, in May

The organ screen, built in 1736–37, seen from the nave probably in the later nineteenth century. It was removed in 1875 as part of the reordering and restoration of the Abbey

1736, the parishioners agreed that an organ and organ gallery be built, 'in the void space at the east end of the church at the entrance into the chancel over the screen that separates the church from the said chancel not exceeding eight foot in depth and 24 foot in length'.[41] The churchwardens obtained a Faculty, that is formal permission from the diocese to alter the interior of the Abbey. The organ screen was erected roughly where the medieval rood-screen had been, at the second pair of pillars of the nave moving from the central crossing. It separated that part of the church which had pews from the empty part west of the new screen. The screen survived until the restoration of 1875–79.[42] Finally, in 1737, the Milton Organ was purchased from Magdalen College, Oxford. It was originally built for the College by Thomas Dallam in 1631.[43] It acquired its 'Milton' name when it was apparently heard and possibly played by the poet when it was transferred to Hampton Court between 1654 and 1660.[44] After the Commonwealth, it returned to Magdalen College in 1661 and was rebuilt by Robert Dallam and later enlarged by Renatus Harris in 1690.[45] It was paid for by Tewkesbury townspeople through an 'Organ Committee'.[46] However, the number of actual subscribers may not have been that many.[47] The organ was set up by Thomas Swarbrick, who not only ensured that the decorated Dallam organ front faced east, towards the crossing, but also constructed a 'second front' facing west into the nave. However, part of the instrument – the 'Chaire Organ' – did not come to the Abbey but went instead to St Nicholas' Church, Stanford-on-Avon (Northants).[48] Swarbrick went on to maintain the instrument until 1747.[49]

In the meantime, in April 1737, the Abbey Vestry resolved to employ an organist at £20 per year. James Cleavely of Gloucester was elected the first organist. He wrote to the Vestry, giving an undertaking that he would live in Tewkesbury and 'perform the office of an organist'.[50] The organ 'opened' on 2 June 1737, with its one manual, nine stops and no pedal organ. It would take over 250 years to evolve into the wonderful instrument it is today.

Tunes were also supplied from 1739 by a set of chimes, presumably sited in the bell chamber. However, these were deemed both 'old fashioned' and 'worn out', and were dispensed with by the end of the nineteenth century.[51]

Soon after, the approach to the main north door of the Abbey was altered. In 1750, the path from the street to the door was paved for the first time, and an avenue of trees planted.[52] The Gage Gates were given by Lord Gage – an MP for Tewkesbury since 1721 by virtue of being an Irish peer and so unable to sit in the House of Lords. The gates were not where they are now but situated on the external gateway of the north porch itself where traces of their former presence can still be seen.[53] Where the Gage Gates (*see overleaf*) currently stand were the Dowdeswell Gates, given by Tewkesbury's other MP at the time, William Dowdeswell.[54] His estate was at Pull Court in Bushley parish, where today the gates adorn Bredon School, which is largely housed in the rebuilt old estate house.

There had been a church clock certainly since Tudor times, and 1750 was also the year in which a new tower clock was put in, to be replaced in turn by the present Jubilee Clock of 1887.[55] Samuel Moore looked after the clock and chimes, for which he was paid £2 per year.[56] However, he was apparently not very efficient, for in 1755 he was replaced.[57]

Up until now, England had been using the Julian Calendar, whose year began on Lady Day (25 March). As most of Europe applied the

The Gage Gates, originally by the north door, were given in 1750 by Lord Gage, an Irish peer and one of Tewkesbury's two MPs at the time. They were made by William Edney of the Forest of Dean. Such a gift did Lord Gage little good as he was voted out in the 1754 election. Note the 'Green Man' in the centre near the top

Gregorian Calendar there was a certain amount of confusion, not least because the Gregorian system includes a 'leap' year every fourth year. England came into line as the result of 'The Calendar (New Style) Act' of 1750. For the first time the English year began on 1 January, in 1752. This also helps explain, for example, why the closure of the monastery at Tewkesbury on 9 January is sometimes put as being in 1539 – which is correct under the Julian Calendar – but is equally correct being 1540 if the Gregorian Calendar is used.

In 1754, Penry Jones died, having been incumbent for 25 years. He was succeeded by his nephew, the Revd Henry Jones the Younger (his father, also Henry, having been incumbent briefly in 1728). Henry Jones, a graduate like his father, was also simultaneously perpetual curate of Tredington (incumbent in all but name and freehold). His ministry at the Abbey was relatively peaceful, except for one parishioner, a footman called George Williams. He was a Unitarian, yet regularly attended Abbey services on Sundays. He invariably left his seat during parts of the service. When he returned, he always disturbed the congregation. In 1765, Williams went further, publishing a pamphlet against the doctrine of the Trinity and Church of England liturgy. Henry Jones was concerned and wrote to his bishop, William Warburton. The bishop supported Jones in admonishing Williams, saying that the next time Jones had cause to do it, it was to be in the bishop's name. Moreover, he asked Jones to present the bishop's compliments to Mrs Bromley, the footman's employer, and suggest to her that perhaps she ought to 'consult her own honour by turning him [Williams] away, and thereby free herself from all imputation of giving encouragement to so audacious insolence'. Subsequently, Williams left Tewkesbury and went to live in Overbury. Henry Jones, like his father and uncle before him, died in post. This was in 1769 when he was only 47 years old.[58]

Henry Jones' successor was the Revd Edward Evanson, another Cambridge graduate. He was presented to the living by Lord Chancellor Camden in 1769 on behalf of a Mr Dodd, then MP for Reading. Evanson also quickly acquired the living of Longdon, Worcestershire, and the perpetual curacy of Tredington. By this means he was able to pay for an assistant curate at the Abbey. He held unorthodox views, and in 1771 preached an Easter Day sermon that gave 'great offence' to many in his congregation. Moreover, he altered the Apostles' Creed and 'other parts of the service'. He was accused by some of being a Unitarian.[59] A prosecution against him took four years until, in 1775, he elected to leave Tewkesbury and move to Longdon, leaving his curate at the Abbey. He formally resigned the Tewkesbury living in 1777, whereupon the curate, the Revd James Tattersall, had the incumbency presented to him.[60]

During James Tattersall's time as vicar, King George III visited in 1788, accompanied by Queen Charlotte among others. The King wished to look at the Abbey, especially externally, as he was an interested student of church architecture. One of the King's party was Fanny Burney [Madame d'Arblay], one of the first women novelists. Gaining the Queen's permission, she and another member of the party, Miss Planta, returned to the Abbey. They looked around the interior, and Fanny Burney confided to her diary a description of what they found east of the wall near the head of the nave:

> The pews of the cathedral seem the most unsafe, strange and irregular that were ever constructed; they are mounted up, storey after storey, without any order, now large, now small, now projecting out wide, now almost indented in back, nearly to the very roof of the building. They look as if, ready made, they had been thrown up and stuck wherever they could, entirely by chance.[61]

Sadly, the vicar died in 1791, having been thrown from his horse. He had just visited his brother William, vicar of Wotton-under-Edge. He was buried at Wotton where a monument was erected to his memory. He was only 38 years old.[62]

The next vicar of Tewkesbury was the Revd Robert Knight, instituted in 1792. He was also rector of Baynton, Worcestershire, both Crown livings, presented by the same Lord Chancellor, Lord Eldon. Robert Knight was offered either by the Lord Chancellor but he indicated that neither by itself could support one clergyman sufficiently. To Knight's surprise, he was offered both. Knight held the two livings until early in 1818 when, with a later Lord Chancellor's permission, he effectively swapped the Tewkesbury living for that of Mickleton cum Ebrington in the same diocese, near Chipping Campden. He suffered from gout, and Tewkesbury was not seen as being a good place for a clergyman with his ailment. Knight himself, who had largely been an absentee vicar anyway, living in Newton, Glamorganshire, died the following year, aged 53.[63]

The Revd Charles White had been incumbent of Mickleton cum Ebrington in Gloucestershire,

The late medieval or very early Tudor north frontage of Abbey House, once part of the abbot's lodging. Note the Oriel window. In the carvings immediately beneath it, the initials HB for Henry Beeley, the penultimate abbot, can just be made out

but was now instituted to the Tewkesbury living in June 1818. He had no other living, so was presently given, in addition, the perpetual curacy of Deerhurst. Eventually, he also became rural dean of Winchcombe. When he became incumbent, Charles White had no vicarage. A voluntary subscription raised £852 – mostly through 'Queen Anne's Bounty' – with which land was purchased and a house erected and completed in 1827, apparently largely to Knight's own design. It still stands near the Abbey.[64]

In 1787, William Dyde had published the first guide to the Abbey. This was followed in 1795 by Samuel Lysons conducting the first recorded historical survey of the Abbey, including the opening of some tombs. Both these events underline a growing interest in the Abbey's history.[65]

During Knight's incumbency, from 1793 to 1794, the Abbey was visited and sketched –

Queen Anne's Bounty

This was a scheme started in 1704 initially to assist the incomes of the very poorest clergy. The money for it was derived from 'annates', or the first year's income of clergy new to their benefices, and also 'tenths' – the amount from the income of each priest that had to be paid to the Pope each year before the Reformation, when it was diverted to King Henry VIII. Later, Queen Anne's Bounty was also used to fund schemes designed to help clergy – in the case of Tewkesbury, help towards paying for a vicarage.

In 1947 the scheme was merged with the Ecclesiastical Commissioners to form the Church Commissioners.

including its old campanile or bell-tower, too, now the town jail – by J.M.W. Turner, the famous artist, who at one point was thought to own property in the town.[66]

In 1794, Edward Edgecombe, a local craftsman, was employed by the Abbey to re-pew the eastern end of the Abbey. Funds were raised, not least by a music festival possibly held in 1796–97.[67]

In 1796, the organ case was repaired and a swell organ put in at a cost of £186, and the manuals extended by John Holland of Bath. The pedal organ was not added until 1848.[68]

Meanwhile, back in the Abbey itself in 1822, pressure was building for the appointment of a verger to ensure that 'due decorum' was maintained during worship, pews were properly superintended and that strangers to the Abbey were looked after appropriately. An appointment was soon made and the verger paid £5 per annum. He was to wear a black gown and carry a wand of office, both of which were eventually given to him. However, disputes broke out between the parish clerk, the sexton and the verger of the 'who does what' variety. In October 1827 it was decided that the verger was to do what has already been mentioned and also 'prevent idle persons from loitering in the porch and in the Church during Divine Service'. He was also to attend upon the minister.

The parish clerk was to attend the minister in all offices connected with church services, and was to keep the church clean, as well as the Communion plate, the chandeliers, candlesticks and lamps. He was also to 'perform all such reasonable services demanded of him by the Vicar, Assistant Curate or Churchwardens'. For this he was paid £10 per annum. He also earned wedding fees at five shillings a time. If duties were refused or neglected, churchwardens were empowered to 'deduct £1 from his salary for every wilful neglect or gross act of disobedience'.

The sexton was to keep the churchyard free from 'the improper intrusion of children and others as well on Sundays as at all other times; to prevent clothes being hung therein to dry; to take care the grass be kept short and paved and gravelled paths be swept at least once a week', for which he was paid £1 6s annually. In addition, he was paid £1 6s for 'ringing the bell for Divine Worship and Parish Meetings, and ten shillings and sixpence for ringing the eight o'clock bell during the winter half-year'. He also earned £5 a year for daily winding up the clock and chimes in the tower. He received further fees for digging graves and tolling the bell at funerals.[69]

Meanwhile, another visitor to the Abbey was the Revd Francis E. Witts, JP, DL, rector of Upper Slaughter and vicar of Stanway, an active magistrate and diarist. His churchmanship has been described as 'broad'.[70] He records how, one Sunday in October 1823, he was invited to preach the anniversary sermon for the Tewkesbury dispensary in the Abbey. His reaction to the Abbey quire is interesting:

> The inner choir has been fitted up for divine service several years ago at considerable expense, and with judgement except as to the pulpit where the attempt to produce Gothic symmetry and lightness has ended in a very gingerbread sort of rostrum, and to the preacher a most uncomfortable, and at first view, insecure pulpit … The Corporation in their robes occupied the seats appropriated to them. I met with great politeness and the collection exceeded my expectations, amounting to nearly £24 [worth just under £2,000 in 2020 terms].[71]

THE CHOIR AND CHANCEL, TEWKESBURY ABBEY-CHURCH.
Presented to the Subscribers to the
CHELTENHAM EXAMINER

Lithographed & Printed   by G. Rowe, Chelt.^m

George Rowe's lithograph of 1830. The elaborate pulpit dates from 1795, and either this pulpit or a new one was later erected against the north-east pillar of the tower in 1849. Note the high altar of 1726 and the floor tiles, which were blue and white and were later moved to the Camera Cantorum and the Chapel of St James, now the Abbey shop

In 1819–20, Thomas Hodges had attempted to restore the quire windows, but with indifferent success. It was to be 1925 before a proper restoration was completed.

Between 1824 and 1830 there was extensive restoration work on the Abbey. The tower exterior was restored, one of the pinnacles being very largely rebuilt and the other three repaired. The turrets on the west front were restored, transept walls and roofs repaired and strengthened and the greater part of the nave paved with Painswick stone. Large parts of the Abbey that had been covered in whitewash were now covered in distemper, as near matching the original stone as possible. The cost came to about £3,000. A subscription list and a parish rate were organised. There was simply no further money available to return to the problem of the quire windows at that point.[72]

In 1828, some restoration work was carried out on the Despenser Monument close by the Founder's Chantry and also the Brien Monument that screens off St Margaret's Chapel.[73] Abbot Richard Cheltenham's tomb and Abbot Wakeman's cadaver also received some attention.[74] In addition, the quire vaulted ceiling was colour-washed.[75]

Royalty briefly touched the lives of the residents of Tewkesbury in 1830. On 26 June, King George IV died, followed by his funeral on 15 July. There was an Abbey service that day, attended by the corporation in their robes. From the time of the King's death until his interment, the great bell in the Abbey tower tolled between 9 am and 10 am every morning, and a muffled peal was rung from 9 pm to midnight on the night of his funeral.[76] In the meantime, King William IV had been proclaimed on 30 June. Somewhat closer to the Abbey, on 19 September, HRH the Duchess of Kent, accompanied by her daughter, the future Queen Victoria, changed horses in Tewkesbury. Sadly, they did not have time to visit the Abbey but would have certainly heard the bells that were rung in their honour.[77]

It was comparatively rare for an ordination to be held outside Gloucester Cathedral, but in 1830 James Gorle of Clare College, Cambridge was ordained deacon in the Abbey by the bishop of Gloucester. It probably occurred because James Gorle had been appointed curate of Walton Cardiff, a small hamlet on the outskirts of Tewkesbury.[78]

The Sir Francis Russell Almshouses were just north of the Abbey. In 1830 they were in such a poor state they required rebuilding. Lindsey Winterbotham donated a strip of land and the two MPs, John Edmund Dowdeswell and John Martin each gave £100 towards the estimated

---

Ministers and vicars of Tewkesbury Abbey from the Restoration to Queen Victoria

Robert Eaton 'The Elder'	1662–68
Cuthbert Browne	1669–(?)1670
Francis Wells	1670–81
Robert Eaton 'The Younger'	1682–87
John Mathews	1688–1728
Henry Jones 'The Elder'	1728–29
Penry Jones	1729–54
Henry Jones 'The Younger'	1754–69
Edward Evanson	1769–77
James Tattersall	1777–91
Robert Knight	1792–1818
Charles White	1818–45

cost of £700 for the accommodation of ten poor widows. The almshouses were rebuilt a little to the east of where they had stood originally. The original site was given to the Abbey to extend the graveyard. The almshouses are still there today.[79]

In 1831, the returns of the vicar of Tewkesbury, Charles White, showed averages over the previous ten years of 125 baptisms, 99 burials and 38 marriages per year.[80] Anthea Jones has noted that only 40% of the women marrying could sign their name, an advance from a third a century earlier. The number of men able to sign their names stayed constant at around two-thirds.[81] In the same year, the bishop took a service at which 'nearly 500 young persons' were confirmed – an astonishingly large number. It was also the year that, for the first time according to a Royal Commission, the vicar was receiving a better income than had been the case earlier. At £376 per annum, his income put him in the top half of the incomes of the roughly 10,500 parish clergy at the time, even though £80 of it had to be given to the assistant curate as his income.[82] On 9 September, King William IV and Queen Adelaide had their coronation. A peal of bells and a special service in the Abbey marked the event.

The following year was difficult for Charles White, the vicar. First, his wife Dorothea died in March. Then, between July and the end of September there was a major outbreak of cholera in the parish. Of 158 who contracted it, 76 died and 82 recovered, and 13 October was declared a day of thanksgiving 'for deliverance from a pestilence so truly afflicting'. Shops were closed, business was suspended. The Abbey and dissenting places of worship were 'remarkably well attended'.[83]

Given that there were increasing numbers of Dissenters, or Nonconformists, in Tewkesbury, it is hardly surprising that resistance to paying the

Sir Francis Russell was Tewkesbury's MP five times between 1673 and 1689. In 1674 he gave ten almshouses and the 'Warkay Gardens' near the Abbey for the benefit of ten poor widows. They were rebuilt in 1830, a little to the east of their original site. They are still in use today

Church Rate increased. Effectively, it was a tax on the whole population, regardless of religious affiliation, to help maintain a Church of England building. In June 1836 the two churchwardens, Henry Brydes and Hugh Martin, gave notice of a Church Rate to help pay for essential repairs to the Abbey. While many of the population agreed, others indicated that they would pay a voluntary contribution but objected to a Church Rate, while still others flatly refused to pay anything. A poll was demanded. In July, the poll result showed that 232 voted for the rate, while 202 opposed it. There were petitions to Parliament, already considering the abolition of the Church Rate. It was the last occasion that such a demand was made in Tewkesbury.[84]

The period from the Restoration to the end of the Regency witnessed the difficulty of keeping the Abbey fabric in barely adequate repair, notwithstanding help from the increasingly unpopular Church Rate.

While the period rejected the more extreme versions of Puritanism, seen in the reinstating of the font, nevertheless worship remained austere, punctuated by music and hymn-singing made possible through the advent of the Milton Organ. The use of the three-decker pulpit and the seemingly haphazard pews and balconies did not help a feeling of ordered beauty. The gradual move from one national Church, represented by the Abbey, that a townsperson was compelled to attend, to a much more diverse Christian community of several denominations was finally accepted in Tewkesbury as elsewhere. The reality of this was underlined by the Repeal of the Test and Corporation Acts in 1828 and the Catholic Emancipation Act of 1829. The Evangelical revival and its emphasis on personal holiness had passed its climax by around 1815. It may have influenced several Abbey incumbents such as Penry Jones, Henry Jones the Younger, James Tattersall and Charles White. Both it and the growing Anglo-Catholic Tractarian movement of the 1830s were to make contributions to the life and worship of the Abbey in years to come.[85] Within the Abbey, the near abandonment of the nave to burials, thus becoming a virtual mausoleum for any who would pay the fee demanded, did little to enhance the Abbey as a place of worship.

The year 1837 was a notable one, for both Tewkesbury and the country. The House of Hanover ended with the death of William IV. William and his two predecessors had been stout, elderly monarchs. They were succeeded by a slim girl who had just reached her majority. Victoria's reign was to prove a period of considerable upheaval for the Abbey.

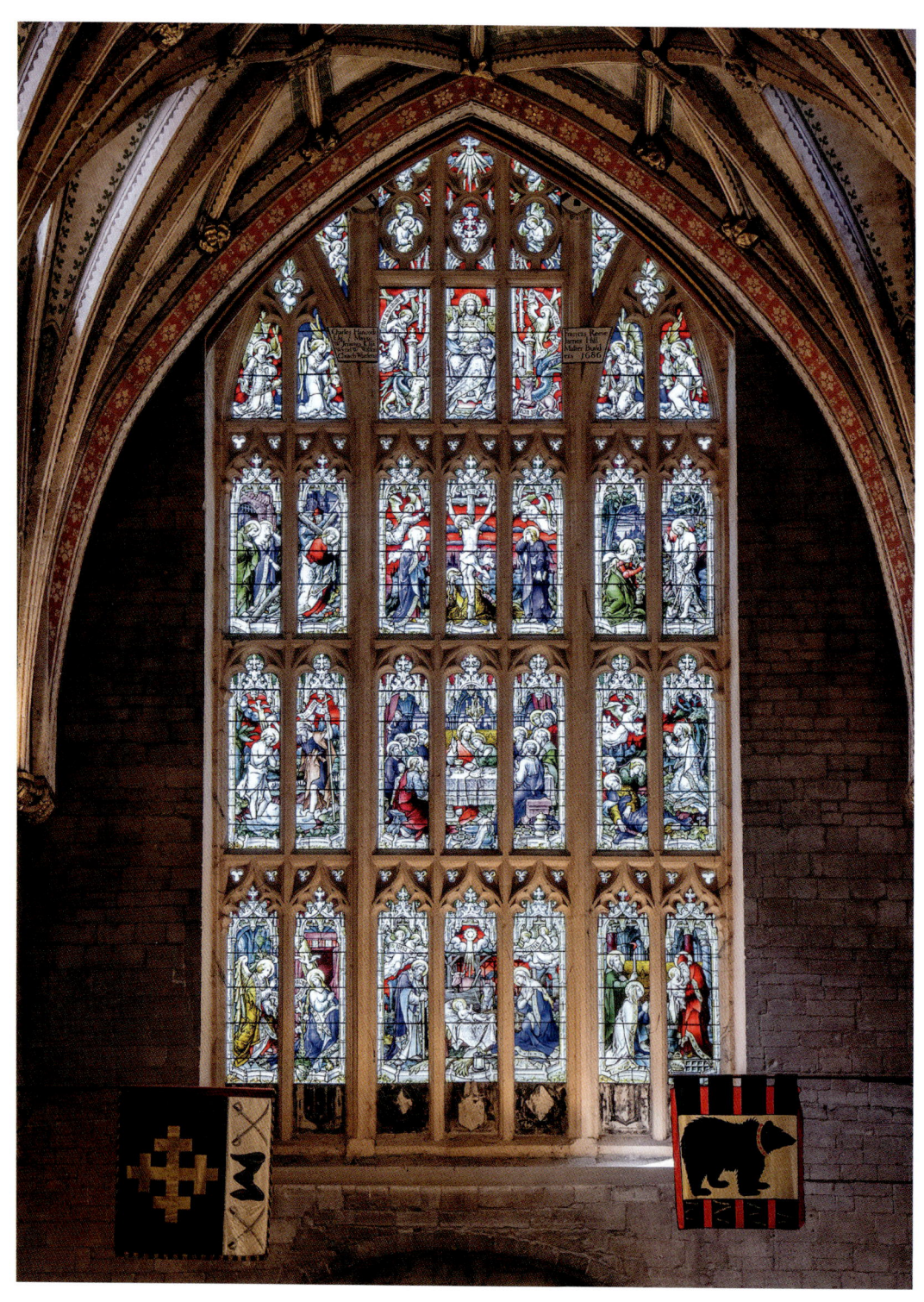

The stained glass in the west window, presented by the Revd Charles Grove in 1886. The glass is by Hardman & Co. and depicts the Life of Christ from infancy through to being seated in Judgement in Heaven

CHAPTER NINE

1837–1920: Victorian Reordering and Restoration to the end of the First World War

Scarcely had Queen Victoria acceded to the throne in June 1837 than Holy Trinity Church in the Oldfield part of Tewkesbury was consecrated and, that August, provided with a licensed clergyman. The new church was built to serve a growing town population nearing 6,000, and provide more free sittings than the Abbey could offer.[1] On Queen Victoria's Coronation Day, 28 June 1838, there was much music-making and bell-ringing. All the shops were closed by midday. There was a morning service in the Abbey and an evening service in Holy Trinity Church.[2]

In 1840, the Abbey held a day-long music festival for the first time in nearly 50 years, which included an orchestra nearly 100-strong. It included both orchestral and choral works, and concluded with 'The Hallelujah Chorus' from *Messiah*.[3] The day may well have encouraged the formation of an Abbey choral society in 1842, the same year that extensive repairs were made to the Milton Organ, and a singing gallery was erected in front of it.[4] It was further renovated and extended in 1848. Henry Willis put in new soundboards and action, added stops and pipes and, for the first time, a pedal-board with two pedal stops.[5] However, the Vestry could be critical of musical standards. In 1858, a Vestry meeting was called to consider how to 'ensure a better performance of the choral part of Divine Service'.[6]

The 1840 Visitation of Clergy in Winchcombe Deanery was held at the Abbey. The guest preacher was the Evangelical Francis Close, incumbent of Cheltenham.[7] He was an enthusiastic, campaigning educationalist, later dean of Carlisle. Dean Close (Memorial) School, Cheltenham, founded in his memory in 1886, was to become closely connected with the Abbey in the twenty-first century.[8]

In 1846, Charles Greenall Davies became vicar, Charles White having left the previous year. White had served from 1818, combining the Abbey living with that of Deerhurst. Davies, aged 41, was also appointed priest-in-charge of Walton Cardiff, rural dean of Winchcombe and a canon of Gloucester Cathedral. During his time, far-reaching decisions were taken. Davies' Church background was Evangelical. He came to Cheltenham to assist Francis Close, and was given the care of St Paul's, a church-plant of Close's, opened in 1831.[9] Paid for by the town and a government grant, it was a 'Free Church', devoid of pew rents, built for the poor at the unfashionable end of Cheltenham.[10] Davies served there from 1836 to 1840. That experience may well have influenced his later actions when vicar of the Abbey.[11]

During Davies' incumbency, several strands in the Abbey's existence came together. The first was that the Abbey itself required major attention, for which the local press and others had agitated for many years. 'The walls were streaming with moisture and there was a damp, musty atmosphere throughout the interior', was one observation.[12] Monuments and other parts of the building were in a very poor state of repair. Externally, in 1849, the dilapidated Abbey gateway had been completely restored. The masonry was renovated by Tewkesbury builder Thomas Collins, while doors of carved oak were added in 1855.[13] The room over the Abbey gateway was later to be used for guilds and classes during the First World War.[14] Already, the Abbey bells had required attention. The major task of rehanging all eight bells was completed by James Cull of Tewkesbury. He erected a new oak frame for them, fixing it on the north-east corner of the central tower instead of the south-west angle where the former frame had stood. Earlier, he had laid down a new bell chamber floor. He also created a new ringing chamber 20 feet higher in the lantern room than before, supported by several new, substantial beams, supported in turn by struts and stone corbels set into the tower. This was a major improvement, the former floor being decayed and dangerous. Thomas Mears of Gloucester recast and tuned the bells. The works cost £443 9s 9d, nearly £35,000 in 2020 money. The bells were 'reopened' on 16 October 1837.[15] The ringing floor lasted until 1886/7 when it was removed and the ringers occupied the old clock room instead.

The present ringing chamber

The second strand was that the interior looked unattractive. The 1820s yellow distempered stonework; the extremely uneven floor of the neglected nave, due to constant burials; the variety of pews and balconies in the transepts and east end had a close but chaotic relationship with each other. True, there had been improvements in the 1790s through replacing many box pews. Edward Edgecumbe of Tewkesbury made them better matched and better ordered, especially in the quire and towards the east end.[16] However, elsewhere it was still somewhat haphazard. The whole was dominated by the organ and its singing gallery on a stone screen separating the nave from the rest of the Abbey. A tall pulpit on the north side of the quire had superseded a more grandiose three-decker pulpit on the south side in 1848.[17] Arguably, it still seemed in danger of eclipsing the importance of the high altar that was now much smaller than that removed at the Dissolution. It is probable that the 1726 altarpiece at the high altar was removed in 1848. The Ten Commandments now in the ambulatory came from it, as does the 'Pelican in her Piety', now on a plinth in St Margaret's Chapel.[18]

The third strand was that, just as church architectural fashion influenced Abbey changes in the fourteenth century with its Decorated style, so did the late nineteenth-century Gothic revival. Largely inspired by Augustus Pugin and the Cambridge Camden Society, this included wide, soaring arches, big windows and the use of space. It was to hugely influence changes to the Abbey interior.

The fourth strand was that the vicar, Charles Davies, was prepared to face the considerable problems involved. Fundraising would be particularly difficult, because of mounting pressure against the traditional, compulsory

This pulpit lasted until the reordering of the whole Abbey later in the nineteenth century. It was the last of the quire pulpits (engraver unknown)

Church Rate, finally repealed in the 1868 Act. A previous Abbey Church Rate in 1836 was implemented with difficulty. Davies and his churchwardens made no such demands. Unfortunately, Gloucester Cathedral was also requiring renovation funds at the time.

However, the Abbey authorities felt that they must act. An initial meeting, called by the churchwardens, Messrs Hanford and Moore, was held in Tewkesbury town hall on 7 May 1864. There were about 20 present. The vicar was chairman, as the invited chairman, Lord Sudeley, was absent. He outlined several proposals: the top of the tower to be restored to its original design, including rebuilding a steeple; the vaulting concealing the interior of the tower to be removed, leaving the interior view open as far as the floor of the ringing room, thereby recreating a 'lantern tower'. Other proposals included removing both organ screen and galleries, and placing the organ 'in a more convenient position' as then unspecified. The pulpit, reading desk and pews were to be replaced. Also proposed was removing plaster covering and whitewash from the walls, roof and columns; the recolouring of the bosses and other carved work in their original condition and the repair of the timber-work and covering of the roof. It was potentially a massive, expensive and possibly controversial undertaking. A committee was formed with Thomas Appelbee acting as honorary secretary.[19]

Charles Greenall Davies, vicar 1846–77

George Gilbert Scott was approached. He admired Pugin, and was arguably the foremost church architect of his day. He was working on Gloucester, Hereford and Worcester Cathedrals and other projects. He spent the morning of 4 August 1864 examining the Abbey before attending an afternoon meeting, chaired by the vicar, which met in the Abbey quire then the vestry to hear Scott's preliminary conclusions. The group consisted of local leading landowners, clergy, two local newspaper editors and key Tewkesbury people such as the churchwardens and several others who had attended the inaugural Town Hall meeting.

Gilbert Scott envisaged a redesigned Abbey interior in which the nave became an integral part of the whole. He suggested that originally the choir – or the monks – were of primary consideration. The congregation were merely of secondary concern. Since the Dissolution of the Monasteries, as Scott put it, in Tewkesbury Abbey's case 'the congregation must be looked to first, and the wants of the choir made subservient to their wants'.[20]

Scott's first proposal was to remove the organ screen and organ, opening out the length of the Abbey for the first time, the nave being for congregational use. He thought the organ might go to the north transept. His second proposal was for an open screen, sited two bays and the width of the central tower nearer the high altar. This meant that the entire Abbey could be admired, but with a clear separation of the congregation from quire and sanctuary. He suggested using moveable chairs for the congregation for the first time. His initial suggestion was to have the quire extending as far as the eastern side of the tower, so that the crossing and transepts were part of the nave. This was later revised.[21] Thirdly, Scott wanted

100   A HISTORY OF TEWKESBURY ABBEY

to remove the interior's yellow distemper. His fourth proposal was to remove all balconies and pews and replace them in the quire with the monastic stalls. These had been sited there until 300 years before but were now either languishing in the transepts or possibly the nave aisles or had been quietly removed by private citizens. There is a tradition that Ripple Church acquired some, although this is open to question. Evidently, some copies would have to be made.

Externally, Scott felt the structure generally was in reasonable repair. However, he proposed work on the south nave aisle fabric. This part of the Abbey, which in medieval days had been protected and supported by monastic buildings, had had to stand unsupported from 1541 and needed strengthening. He also criticised the south aisle roof and all the eastern chapels and aisle roofs that were covered in stone and slate mixed with tiles, and required attention. The damp in the Abbey he attributed to the high ground against the Abbey north wall outside. This arose because of the quantity of graves in the graveyard. In February 1855 an order in council forbade more burials in the Abbey itself and banned churchyard burials from 1 October 1856. However, the latter were later allowed to continue until 1 February 1857. Although the town cemetery opened in the same year, there were still over 50 interments in the Abbey graveyard in certain specified existing vaults and graves.[22] The level of the graveyard must be lowered, insisted Scott.[23] Finally, removing the vaulting under the central tower to re-expose the 'Lantern Tower', and rebuilding the Abbey spire Scott felt were less important. He suggested considering them if funds were available after more urgent matters had been completed.[24]

A restoration committee was formed to organise an appeal. It included many who had attended the Town Hall meeting, prominent landowners such as the Dowdeswells and the Yorkes, local MPs, a local banking philanthropist in Sir Edmund Lechmere, BT, and the mayor, Dr Hitch. Thomas Appelbee continued as secretary. No Church Rate was demanded – a measure of how unpopular and outdated it had become.

Although the restoration committee attracted some funds, it was unwilling to sanction restoration when unable to pay for it. As little was happening, people were reluctant to contribute to the appeal. The impasse was broken by the generosity and drive of Thomas Collins, a local builder and self-made man. Born in 1818 and Tewkesbury-educated, apprenticed as a stonemason, he set up his own business in 1842. By 1881 he was Tewkesbury's biggest employer managing 400 men. Although a life-long, devoted Methodist, he was both baptised and married in the Abbey. He died in 1900.[25]

In two meetings of the vestry on 1 and 6 December 1870, Collins offered to move the old monks' stalls back to just east of their original positions in the quire at his own expense. Canopies of the seats on the south side would have to be reproductions as the originals had disappeared.[26] They would be based on north side originals. The Corporation pew would be removed. The plans were accepted unanimously.[27] In March 1871, the monks' stalls were placed as we see them today. *The Record* reported on 11 March that Mr Collins 'returned the carved oak stalls to their original position, and to these stalls he has added two rows of new seats, carved in the same style as the old ones.' Surplices were provided through private subscription for a choir of men and boys of nearly 30, suggesting that C.G. Davies' views, formerly so Low Church, were changing.[28] Three monks' stalls were later

The choir stalls, removed to the transepts and elsewhere after the Dissolution of the monastery, were partly reinstated and partly reproduced by Thomas Collins and his workforce. He was given permission in December 1870 and carried out the work in 1871

discovered in a Tewkesbury garden in 1908, and were subsequently placed just west of the later Victorian quire screen.[29] Today they are sedilia, or priests' seats, used in 'whole Abbey' worship.

Even after his generosity, little happened. However, Collins was a determined man. In 1872, on his own initiative, he removed wooden galleries in the transepts, taking out pews and restoring pillars damaged when the galleries were installed.[30]

The year 1872 was the last year of recorded pew rentals. They provided only £59 of a total offertory of £218, although many wanted to continue the right to occupy 'their' pew. However, Charles Davies, the vicar, possibly remembering his experience of free seats at St Paul's, Cheltenham, did not object to the disappearance of pews and their replacement by chairs in the nave. At the time of his death late in October 1877, Davies was aware that a Vestry meeting was due, in which it would be proposed that all the seats in the parish church be free. However, compromise triumphed. It was decided unanimously that 'the South Transept and South side of the Church be open for Allotment to those who may apply for sittings but that the North Transept and the North side be absolutely free and un-appropriated'. Regulating seating would clearly be an impossible job for any verger, however efficient, so the same meeting decided to reintroduce sidesmen.[31] In practical terms, the decision meant that 296 out of 600 seats were allocated to named worshippers.[32] The 1879 window in what is now St Dunstan's Chapel is in Charles Davies' memory.[33]

Earlier, Collins' action galvanised the Committee into activity, and during 1874, Scott's approved plans were awarded a Faculty. Then, on 1 October, the Abbey Vestry met and resolved, unanimously, that 'the whole of the interior of the Abbey Church be restored'. This included the stonework being cleaned and re-pointed, the organ gallery and all pews and seats being removed and new seats provided. The glass in the chapels was to be removed; all floors, both wooden and stone, taken up and relaid, and the floor levelled, while monuments or gravestones would be removed where requisite. 'In short', says the official record, 'the Church be generally restored in accordance with the plan and specification of Sir Gilbert Scott'.[34] Temporary hoarding at the head of the nave allowed work at the east end with worship moving to the west of the hoarding.[35] The Vestry resolution led to the area erroneously known as the Old or Lesser Chapter House (in reality the former Chapels of St James and St Nicholas) to be investigated. This had become a Free Grammar School (*see previous chapter*). The archways with the main Abbey had been blocked and the area itself was dilapidated. When unblocked, piles of rubbish up to four feet high were revealed. In the meantime, the grammar school itself had moved. The Freemasons paid for the restoration of the original chapels.[36]

Sir Gilbert Scott noted in 1874 that in the centre of the ceiling in the quire are eight carved oak bosses, 'Tudor Flowers', at the intersection of the ribs, and eight 'stars' in the panel, apparently placed there by King Edward IV after the Battle of Tewkesbury in 1471. On Sir Gilbert Scott's orders, the eight similar stars which now appeared under the tower were copied from those in the quire.[37] No-one quite knows why he chose to do this.

During excavation work in 1875, the floor of the quire and the sanctuary were both carefully examined. 'The soil ... was dug out to depth of 4 feet until the virgin earth was reached, the excavation extending from pier to pier, and for 24 feet from East to West', noted the Revd J.H. Blunt.[38] Earlier, post-Dissolution generations paid scant regard to allowing the bodies of those buried in the chancel to lie in peace.[39] Yet, fortunately, the Abbey verger, W.G. Bannister, was able to observe that, 'the exact position of graves of important persons buried (were) revealed. These were marked by a series of small brasses, adapted to the planning of the tiled floor.' Old medieval tiles were discovered and new Victorian tiles designed from them.[40] Original tiles are still in one of the recesses in the south quire aisle and the Founder's Chantry floor. One identified rediscovered grave, though not marked with a brass, was of Henry Beauchamp, duke of Warwick, King of the Isle of Wight and the Channel Islands, who died in 1446, the area around it 'carelessly' filled with rubble.[41]

Scott found a use for the tiles he removed from the sanctuary and quire, which were replaced with encaustic tiles as seen today. He relaid them in what is now the Camera Cantorum and the Abbey shop.[42]

The colour wash, applied to the whole Abbey, including the vaulting in 1795 and later, was

The black and white tiles in Camera Cantorum, laid here in the 1870s by Sir Gilbert Scott, were previously in the sanctuary in front of the high altar and originally extended to the whole of the quire floor

carefully removed between 1875 and 1879. As Bannister remarks, 'the present treatment, in colour, was carried out under the supervision, and to a great extent by his own hand, by Thomas Gambier Parry … the treatment of the bosses following the original lines'.[43]

The Milton Organ had been played several times by Samuel Sebastian Wesley, Gloucester Cathedral's distinguished composer and organist 1865–76, who had a very high opinion of it, according to Bannister.[44] It was removed from the organ screen and rebuilt in the nave to accompany the congregation while restoration work began on the quire. This was probably the first time the congregation had worshipped in the nave since the Dissolution of the monastery over 300 years before. Later, the organ was re-erected on the floor of the north transept. It was transferred at some point to the south wall of the south transept. It was finally put under the north arch of the crossing, a suggestion made by the distinguished aristocratic composer, organist, scholar and clergyman, the Revd Professor Sir Frederick Gore Ouseley, BT.[45]

The Restoration Committee, meeting in February 1876, asked Scott to enlarge the quire so that the crossing was included. Scott gave way, resulting in the arrangement seen today.[46]

The project was too big for Tewkesbury to raise the necessary money on its own. In March 1877, the year of Charles Davies' death, a meeting, held at Lambeth Palace, reported that £5,000 had already been raised and spent. A National Committee, supported by the Archbishop of Canterbury, A.C. Tait, was formed to assist the Local Committee.[47] In so doing, the Church and the nation acknowledged that Tewkesbury Abbey had national significance. The committee included Lord Sudeley, Earls Beauchamp, Bathurst and Dudley, and local MPs Sir Edmund Lechmere, BT., briefly MP for Tewkesbury, who lived in the Hanleys in Worcestershire; John Yorke, whose family were – and still are – from Forthampton and James Agg-Gardner, then a young Cheltenham MP. Tewkesbury and the Abbey itself were represented by the new vicar, Canon Hemming Robeson, who was vice-chairman, with local auctioneers Charles and Frederick Moore as treasurer and secretary respectively. The committee succeeded in raising over £9,000. However, the whole project reportedly cost more than £18,000 (over £1.5 million in 2020).[48] The cost would have been higher without the drive and generosity of the main contractor, Thomas Collins.

The new vicar, Hemming Robeson was priested in 1858. A curate in Forthampton, he was vicar of Mildenhall, Suffolk, until 1877 when he moved to Tewkesbury Abbey. He had independent means, and proved a generous Abbey benefactor. Robeson appears to have been 'conventional'. He was not associated with the

Evangelical revival or Protestantism on the one hand, nor with the Oxford Movement or being Anglo-Catholic on the other.

Tewkesbury Abbey first attracted national controversy in March 1877 as a result of changes within its walls. William Morris and others felt that people like Sir Gilbert Scott were, by their actions, 'destroying' ancient buildings. The Tewkesbury Abbey project was the latest in a long line of Victorian 'restorations' stretching back 20 years and Morris had had enough. He wrote to the Athenaeum Club, demanding that a society be founded to protect ancient buildings from such 'restoration'. He attracted support, including that of Philip Speakman Webb, the architect. The Society for the Protection of Ancient Buildings (SPAB) was formed with Morris as its secretary. Morris himself never visited the Abbey, although several Tewkesbury citizens may have agreed with his views.

In 1877, change bell-ringing happened for the first time at the Abbey. The Revd C.D.P. Davies, son of the previous vicar, trained a band that rang a peal of Grandsire Triples, recorded on a tablet in the ringing chamber,[49] thereby beginning a tradition that has continued ever since.

It was in the second half of the 1870s that pews and galleries, designed by Edward Edgecombe of Tewkesbury in 1796, were removed.[50] About the same time – in 1878 – the lectern on the south side of the head of the nave was presented to the Abbey by the Revd Charles Grove, a clergyman of independent means who lived at Mythe House, the Twyning side of Tewkesbury. Originally placed centrally, just west of the quire screen, the lectern stood there for almost 20 years. It was moved to its present position ostensibly because visitors, by handling it, were said to be damaging it and turning parts of it black. This was probably a stratagem by the head verger, W.G. Bannister, to obtain Grove's permission to move the lectern. Grove later said that he regretted the move.[51]

The font was also placed in its present position in 1878, although some think 1875. It had been in the present Lady Chapel since 1828.[52] The old font bowl, which dated from at least 1828, was inscribed: 'One Lord, One Faith, One Baptism' from *Ephesians*, chapter 4, verse 5.[53] In its new position, the font bowl and the elaborate font cover were also both new.[54] The font stem is said to be fourteenth-century and may well point to the date of the original font bowl.

Outside the Abbey, in October 1877 a major gale badly damaged the avenue of elm trees leading from the gates to the north porch, requiring them to be cut down. The avenue was replaced by two rows of trees given by churchwarden Benjamin Moore and planted in April 1879.

Sir Gilbert Scott died in 1878, the same year that part of the Abbey churchyard near the north nave aisle was lowered by three feet as part of his plans.[55] He did not see the completion of his scheme for the Abbey. If Augustus Pugin was the main visionary for the English Gothic Revival, Scott was the architectural practitioner who worked to bring it about. Tewkesbury Abbey is an example of its application. Jostling pews, crowded balconies and an indifferent role both for the high altar and the nave gave way to revised, important roles for both altar and nave; soaring arches could be fully seen; the vista of the whole length of the Abbey admired for the first time. In his Will, Sir Gilbert requested that his sons, George Gilbert Scott and John Oldrid Scott continue the work at the Abbey. In April that year, a Vestry meeting agreed.[56] At the same meeting, it was also agreed that Sir Gilbert's plans concerning the altar rails, quire screen and altar should go ahead subject to Faculties. The floor – both wood and stone – should be relaid and cemented and flat gravestones 'be taken up and replaced in the same position or as near thereto as practical' and that the 'remaining portion of the nave and north porch be restored as per plan'.[57]

In April 1879 a second meeting of the national appeal committee agreed to open a further subscription list. The meeting, held in Lambeth Palace library, was chaired by Sir Michael Hicks-Beach BT., MP.[58] Over £9,000 had already been raised and the further subscription list added £6,770 aided by a London Committee. Canon Hemming Robeson and his sister, Mrs Glynn, gave an enormously generous £500 (worth nearly £63,000 in 2020).

In 1607 or 1609 the high altar marble slab had been recovered from its hiding place, probably under the Abbey floor, presumably placed there at the Dissolution of the Abbey monastery in 1541. The slab was part of the high altar during the Archiepiscopal reign of William Laud in the 1630s. Removed from that position again in 1728 or possibly 1730 at the height of Abbey Puritanism, it was cut in two to provide seating in the north porch. It was replaced by a far more modest altar, later put in the Norman chapel in the south transept, eventually becoming the altar in St Margaret's Chapel from 1939.[59]

In 1879 the high altar marble slab was once again returned to its original place of honour and use, although during its transference both halves broke again. All four pieces were put together and placed upon a wooden frame and its installation paid for by Earl Beauchamp.[60]

On 23 September 1879 there was an Abbey rededication service that used elements of what was thought part of the 1121 consecration service, including three bishops.[61] A week of services followed, culminating on 30 September with a festival service of neighbouring choirs, in which nearly 500 choristers took part.[62]

Charles Davies had known that he had to do something about the internal state of the Abbey fabric. In allowing Sir Gilbert Scott, supported by Thomas Collins' commitment, to sweep away Puritan features, notably the high pulpit in the quire and the box pews and galleries concentrated upon it, and bring in a restored high altar, Davies and his churchwardens possibly unwittingly allowed changing forms of liturgy to emerge. Davies' successor as vicar from 1877, the liturgically conformist Hemming Robeson, was simply committed to seeing the project through, as his generous contribution indicates.

The first half of the 1880s was a time of consolidation but also significant developments. The present pulpit, the first built west of the present quire, was designed by J. Oldrid Scott and used for the first time at the Commemoration Festival, 1881. Painswick stone and Purbeck marble were used throughout.[63] Later, during 1914, a reredos, 'A Witness to the Crucifixion', painted by Thomas Gambier Parry, was removed from the chapter house at Gloucester Cathedral. It was installed in the Abbey as the reredos behind the high altar but then transferred to the former St James' Chapel, now the Abbey shop.[64]

In 1883, the Abbey was given the room and area at the west end of the south nave aisle, bought privately at the Dissolution of the monastery. It became a part of the Abbey House estate, owned by the Martin family. It was generously given back to the Abbey by J. Biddulph Martin.[65] The same year, through a special subscription, the Abbey House estate itself was purchased from the Martin family for £10,500. Much of the land was then sold off, leaving Abbey House (whose tenants had been the Healing family) the gatehouse, barn, cottages and land north of the R. Swilgate being transferred to trustees for £6,848 10s.[66] Under a Trust Deed of 1886, the vicar was given the use of Abbey House as a vicarage. In 1965, Abbey House became the official residence of the vicar, rather than Abbey Lodge.[67]

In 1887 the Milton Organ, now on the north side of the quire, was moved to a similar position on the south side by Michell and Thynne, organ builders of Kensington, London.[68] They were already in the Abbey because another of their church organs, originally powered by a water supply and hydraulic apparatus, was being installed on the north side of the quire. It had been displayed at the 1885 Inventions Exhibition in London and in 1886 in Liverpool. The Revd Charles Grove paid about £800 for it (worth some £70,000 in 2020), for which the parish fulsomely thanked him. Originally called the Grand Organ, it became the Grove Organ.[69] The first Abbey recital on it was by George Riseley, organist of Bristol Cathedral.[70] The hydraulic system made the Grove Organ both comparatively noisy and expensive to use. In 1948 an electric motor was substituted.[71]

Also in 1887, the ambulatory's east end wall, which blocked off the demolished former fourteenth-century Lady Chapel, was enhanced with a fine Victorian window depicting the Pharisee and the Publican parable. The publican's face is said to be of the Revd Charles

The Grove Organ, named after its benefactor, the Revd Charles Grove. It was originally shown at the Inventions Exhibition in London in 1885 and the Liverpool Exhibition in 1886. It was powered by water and a hydraulic system, and came to Tewkesbury in 1887. It was powered by electricity from 1948

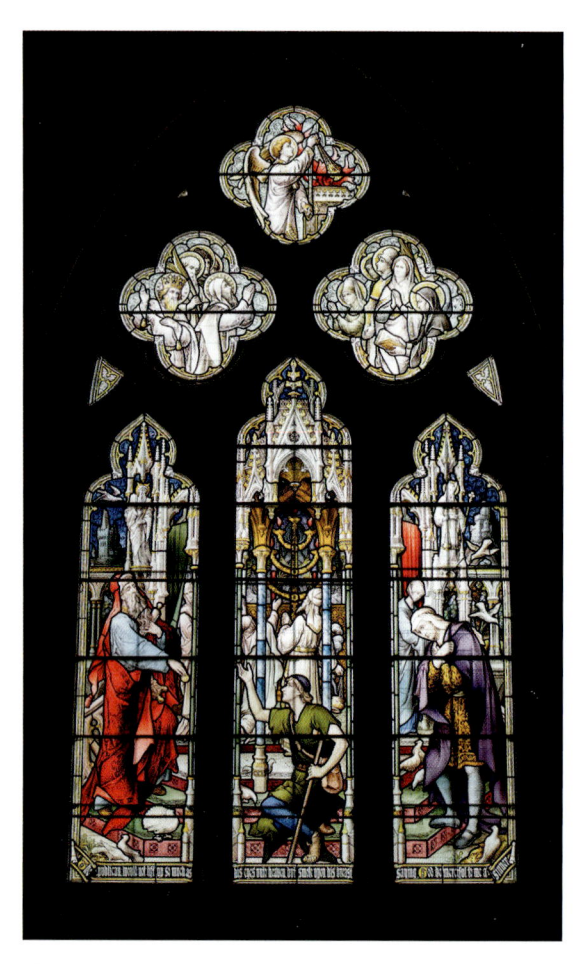

The Pharisee and the Publican parable window by Hardman & Co., of 1887. The publican is a 'faithful portrait' of the donor, the Revd Charles Grove, while his wife is depicted as one of the angelic figures

The Abbey Clock, given by the parishioners in 1887 to mark Queen Victoria's Golden Jubilee, replaced a clock of 1750. The diameter of the clock face is eight feet. The lower image shows the mechanism of the clock

Grove who presented the window, while his wife, Frances Emily, is shown as one of the angels above him. Grove gave both that and a number of stained glass windows to the Abbey, including the west window, in memory of his wife in 1886.[72] He also gave the stained glass windows in the south nave aisle, in 1888, which are by Hardman, as well as five windows in the north nave aisle in December 1891.[73] Charles Grove eventually died in 1896.[74]

The year 1887 was Queen Victoria's Golden Jubilee year. A new clock marking it was installed. There had been an Abbey clock in the sixteenth century, although whether it was precisely in the same position occupied today is unclear. The churchwardens' accounts note it requiring attention or repairs from 1563–64 onwards.[75] The tower clock before the Victorian replacement was by Thomas Steight of Pershore in 1739. The present Abbey Jubilee Tower Clock was started just before 7 am on Tuesday 21 June 1887. The Westminster chimes were used, chiming the 'Cambridge Quarters' as today, first used in Cambridge in 1786. The clock cost £300

The memorial tablet to Dinah Mulock (Mrs Craik) (1826–87) whose best-known book, John Halifax, Gentleman, of 1856, was set in Tewkesbury. The memorial is the work of Hugh H. Armstead

A reconstruction, funded by Thomas Collins, of a bay of fan vaulting in the north-east corner of the original cloister walk. Begun in 1899 and completed in 1900 by his nephew, Francis Godfrey, the work coincided with Thomas Collins' death

(nearly £27,600 in 2020 money), suggested and paid for by the parishioners. The clock face was lowered in 1939.[76]

Another distinguished lady, Mrs Craik, (Dinah Mulock) 1826–87, author of *John Halifax, Gentleman* published in 1856 – a book that was heavily based on Tewkesbury – died the same year. Her memorial tablet can be found on the north-east corner wall of the present Lady Chapel. The author apparently wrote *John Halifax, Gentleman* while staying at a hotel in Tewkesbury. Although born in Staffordshire and buried in Kent, it was decided to have her memorial tablet erected in Tewkesbury Abbey, being the town where her most successful novel was set. A distinguished committee oversaw the tablet's commission in 1890.[77]

Thomas Collins continued working on the Abbey. In February 1893 he unblocked the south doorway and restored it at his own expense, with J. Oldrid Scott having designed the doors.[78] Later, Collins also began to recreate part of the old cloister immediately outside the south door in 1899, so that it acted as a porch.[79]

Late in the summer of 1891, the duke and duchess of Teck visited the Abbey with their daughter, Princess Mary, who later became King George v's Queen. Another royal visitor who came later, in October 1908, was Princess Victoria of Schleswig-Holstein, Queen Victoria's granddaughter, daughter of Princess Helena, herself third daughter of the Queen-Empress.[80]

The end of 1891 and beginning of 1892 included changes of Abbey personnel. The vicar, Hemming Robeson, who oversaw the end of the restoration and reordering of the Abbey, became archdeacon of Bristol. He took with him to Bristol Cathedral Mr Hayward, the Abbey's head verger.[81] Hemming Robeson was also founder of Tewkesbury High School for Girls in 1882, later absorbed into Tewkesbury Comprehensive School in 1972.[82]

The new vicar, the Revd Harry Alsager Sheringham, was also incumbent of Walton Cardiff. Formerly vicar of St Peter's, Great Windmill Street, London, in 1886 he became one of two priests in ordinary to Queen Victoria, in her Chapels Royal. In 1892, when he moved to Tewkesbury, he remained priest in ordinary to the monarch, assisting the sub-dean of the Chapels Royal.[83]

At the outset of Sheringham's Abbey ministry, in 1892 J. Oldrid Scott removed the low wall his father had created separating nave and chancel. He re-erected it at the west end, placing it across the nave just to the east of the font but allowing a large space in the centre for processions. In its place at the entry to the quire he designed the present wooden screen that gives greater emphasis to the division without obscuring the high altar.[84]

Two other significant memorial items date from this time. The first is the eastern circular or rose window occupying space originally at the north-west end of the quire triforium, given in 1892.[85] The second is the triangular window, whose theme is 'Faith, Hope and Charity', occupying a similar space on the south-west side, given in 1893.[86]

Additional colour in the south transept apse chapel was provided in 1893 by the Venetian mosaic in the easternmost lancet. It was executed by Guilio Salviatti, elder son of the famous Commendiatori Salviatti of Venice, who had revived the art of glass mosaic-making. Designed by Clayton and Bell, it was presented anonymously to the Abbey.[87]

In April 1896, Benjamin Moore retired from being a churchwarden after 38 years in post, dying a few weeks later. He and his family had served the Abbey since at least the eighteenth century and had been at the forefront of the restoration and reordering of the building. He had been a generous benefactor. A window by

Hemming Robeson, vicar 1877–92. He left on appointment as archdeacon and canon of Bristol

The wooden screen and Rood were erected in memory of Mrs Harriet Glyn, sister of the then incumbent, the Revd Canon Hemming Robeson, in 1892. It was designed by J. Oldrid Scott. The figures are by R.L. Boulton of Cheltenham. The wrought iron gates were a gift in memory of the Revd Robert Hepworth, a one-time assistant curate at the Abbey from 1823 to 1829

Kempe in St Faith's Chapel is his memorial. Below it is a plaque to two sons, Lieutenants Harold and Lionel Moore, both killed in the First World War. The other window is in memory of Thomas Moore, his other son, churchwarden for 43 years.[88]

Although Harry Sheringham loved his ministry at the Abbey, his personal finances were becoming exhausted. The situation was resolved by exchanging the living for the incumbency of Christ Church, Marylebone. After nearly eight years in Tewkesbury, Sheringham and his family returned to London. He died in 1907. The priest who left Marylebone for Tewkesbury in 1899 was Oswald Wardell-Yerburgh.

Oswald Prior Yerburgh, as he was initially, a Dublin graduate, was a curate at St Peter's, Eaton Square, London between 1881 and 1891. He married banking heiress Edith Wardell Potts in 1889, adding Wardell to his surname by Royal Licence. Rector of Christ Church, St Marylebone in 1891, he came to Tewkesbury and Walton Cardiff eight years later. He was rural dean of Winchcombe 1902–07, then rural dean of Tewkesbury from 1907–13. An honorary canon of Gloucester Cathedral from 1904, for one year, 1908–09, he was proctor in convocation at Canterbury.

The new vicar arrived as Thomas Collins began to build the 'new' cloister bay outside the south door at his own expense, based on the remaining traces of cloister vaulting.

The memorial to Thomas Collins (1818–1900) by R.L. Boulton, with realistically sculpted portrait. A life-long Methodist, Collins was in large part responsible for driving the Abbey restoration and reordering forward, often generously funding the work himself. Note the Decorated-style memorial window above by Powell of Blackfriars, London. Near the base of the window are the heraldic arms of the de Clares, the See of Gloucester, the See of Worcester and the arms of Tewkesbury Abbey

Unfortunately, Collins died in 1900 before it was completed. His nephew and partner, Francis Godfrey, took over.[89] Collins' huge contribution to both Abbey and Tewkesbury was recognised in 1896 when he became an honorary freeman of Tewkesbury Borough, having been elected mayor in 1890.[90]

He worked hard on the restoration and reordering of the Abbey, giving generously to see the project through. In 1906, at the west end of the present Lady Chapel in the south transept, a memorial to him was erected. There is a realistic portrait relief, executed by R.L. Boulton. The window immediately above it, in the Decorated style, is part of his memorial.[91]

The Abbey was bringing visitors, and therefore trade, to Tewkesbury. In 1904 the Town Council claimed 80,000 people a year visited the Abbey.[92] Numbers of worshippers seemed encouraging. In 1908, for example, Christmas and Easter communicants numbered 403 and 570 respectively.[93] People continued to give generously. In 1908, a window was given to St Margaret's Chapel depicting St Margaret of Scotland, with the arms of Dunfermline Abbey, which St Margaret gave lands to support.[94]

In 1912 Archdeacon Robeson died. After Tewkesbury, he had been canon treasurer of Bristol Cathedral and archdeacon of North Wiltshire. His cenotaph, just outside St Faith's Chapel, is said to be the only part of the Abbey that is in Caen stone. It was completed by Percy Bryant Baker, RA, and dedicated in 1914.[95]

In November 1913, Canon Wardell-Yerburgh suddenly and unexpectedly died. He had been in post for 14 years. He and his wife had just given one of two new treble bells to the Abbey to complement the rehanging of bells already there. They had been put in good order in 1912 by Mears and Stainbank. The ring now had ten bells.

Oswald Wardell-Yerburgh, vicar 1899–1913

Ernest Smith, vicar 1914–30

Corbel of the Revd Harry Sheringham,
on the left side of the arch of the west doorway

Corbel of Archdeacon Robeson,
on the right side of the arch of the west doorway

It was decided that the new lobby of the north door, designed by W.D. Caröe, would be a memorial to Oswald Wardell-Yerburgh. The west doors, set in the carefully repaired and restored west front in 1907, with their more recent corbels of Archdeacon Robeson and the Revd Harry Sheringham, were dedicated, with the lobby, by the bishop of Gloucester, Dr Edgar Gibson, in March 1915.[96] During the same year, the quire was fitted with electric light and unsightly gas standards were removed.[97]

The next vicar was the Revd Ernest Frederick Smith. An Oxford graduate, he had held several posts in the American Episcopalian Church before returning to England. In February 1914 he became the new vicar and also rural dean of Winchcombe.[98] It was during his incumbency that choral Eucharist with full Eucharistic vestments was introduced.[99]

In 1914, the Vestry realised that soon they would be replaced by the 'Parochial Church Council', created in 1919 by the convocations of Canterbury and York. The Tewkesbury Abbey Parochial Church Council was to be over 30 members strong. Apart from parochial clergy and two churchwardens, it was to include representatives from 14 different organisations or groups within the parish, from the choir and bell-ringers through to the Young Men's Club, the Girls' Friendly Society and District Visitors, not forgetting four guilds. It was the first time that readers, or lay ministers, were mentioned, suggesting an evolving ministry that had been supported by Canon Wardell-Yerburgh and possibly his predecessor. Reader ministry had been authorised since July 1866.[100] Between 1914 and 1920 there was a church council. The first meeting of the new Parochial Church Council was on 7 April 1920.

In August 1914 hostilities began against Germany. Many men volunteered or were later called up. In his 1915 Easter Vestry address, the vicar remarked upon the 'Roll of Honour which hangs beneath the flag of England at the north-west Entrance and records the names of 550 who have responded to the call of their country's greatest need'. Both Harry Davies, the sub-sacristan, and Percy Baker, the organist,

114   A HISTORY OF TEWKESBURY ABBEY

had volunteered, the latter commissioned into the 'Sportsman's Battalion'.

By 1916, Ernest Smith was reporting that one clergy colleague, Mr Low, a chaplain to the Forces, having been in the front line, was serving in a hospital at Rouen.

The war's end and the huge traumas and sacrifices involved were commemorated by three memorials in Tewkesbury. The memorials inside the Abbey grounds included a 'Calvary' just inside the Gage Gates, initially to commemorate Major James Cartland, killed at the Aisne in May 1918, and other members of his family, relatives of Dame Barbara Cartland, the novelist. It was dedicated in 1919.[101] The Cartland 'Calvary' is today used as the focal point in an Act of Remembrance at the beginning of each Remembrance season.[102]

The second memorial is inside the Abbey itself. It commemorates those lost in the First World War and is found against the south wall at the west end of the south nave aisle. Designed by W.D. Caröe, the lower part is an altar, the base and mensa of which are of Leckhampton stone. The remainder is of pea-grit, chosen to harmonise with the wall. The recess above the altar is of fumed oak divided into four panels bearing 140 names of those from Tewkesbury

This Calvary is found near the Gage Gates and is in memory of James B.F. Cartland, killed in the First World War. He was the father of Dame Barbara Cartland, the romantic novelist. Later, the names of James and Ronald, her two brothers, both killed in the Second World War, were added

Memorial altar by W.D. Caröe. The base and mensa are of Leckhampton stone. The four main panels bear the names of 140 Tewkesburians who made the ultimate sacrifice. The Roll of Honour, commemorating those who volunteered before conscription, can be seen on the left in the photo

and the immediate area who made the ultimate sacrifice. The figures were carved by a Mr Taylorson of London, while the lettering was by F. Coutts, described as one of the oldest choirmen. It was dedicated in 1920.[103]

The memorial outside the Abbey grounds is the town centre Cross, erected where the High Street, Church Street and Barton Road meet. It was unveiled in May 1922, the vicar presiding. It was designed by Abbey architect, W.D. Caröe.[104]

With such sombre thoughts and memories, the Abbey approached the 800th anniversary of its consecration.

The sanctuary and high altar as it might have appeared c.1121. Note the rounded Norman arches, chapels on the ground floor but arches above where there were chapels each side. The pillars were then the same size as in the nave

CHAPTER TEN

1920–2020: From between the Wars to a twenty-first century pandemic

Once arrangements for continuing remembrances of the fallen in the First World War had been completed, the 800th anniversary of the consecration of the Abbey loomed. Some thought that the consecration occurred on 23 October 1123.[1] Subsequent research showed that the presiding Bishop Theulf of Worcester died before 23 October 1123, therefore pointing conclusively to 23 October 1121. However, this revelation came too late for 1921. The celebrations, held in 1923, continued. There were two components. The first was the service on 23 October 1923, the Feast of the Consecration. The Archbishop of Canterbury, Randall Davidson,

The sanctuary and high altar today. The contrast with the situation in Norman times (*opposite*) is great. Note in particular the fourteenth-century windows and the absence of chapels on the first floor

117

preached, followed by a great luncheon at the town hall, and the presentation of the *Compotus Roll* of Henry VIII from the Chapter Library at Winchester to Tewkesbury Abbey.

The second part of the celebrations entailed restoring and renovating the seven fourteenth-century chancel windows. As Sarah Brown has noted, 'This sought to make good, work on the windows in the sixteenth, seventeenth, and eighteenth centuries as well as 1820, 1828 and, externally 1879.' Not all the fragments of the seven windows fitted together, so a 'fragments' window was created in the sacristy. In March 1925 there was a service of thanksgiving and blessing of the seven restored windows. The whole project cost £2,000 (£85,000 in 2020 terms).[2]

Meanwhile, in 1924 a misericord choir stall, apparently used as an armchair in a lady's sitting room, was purchased and presented to the Abbey. It became the vicar's stall, placed just inside the screen on the south side of the quire.[3]

In 1930, Canon Smith was appointed vicar of Yate in Bristol diocese. It is not known whether the addition of Walton Cardiff to the Abbey vicar's responsibilities in 1928 was a factor, although the personal financial cost of the Abbey incumbency certainly was. Under Canon Smith, copes had been recently introduced in services and a choral Eucharist begun at which full Eucharistic vestments were worn. Canon Smith led the parish through the First World War and the 800th anniversary celebrations. He introduced the Parochial Church Council, replacing Vestry meetings. Sadly, he died in March 1933, having just filed for bankruptcy. The coroner's inquest revealed that the Tewkesbury living required an incumbent with private means.[4]

His successor, the Revd Edward Pountney Gough, had been vicar of a variety of benefices. Incense was introduced at the main Eucharist

Edward Pountney Gough, vicar 1930–42

although reservation of the Blessed Sacrament did not happen until 1934. The Abbey was becoming increasingly Prayer Book Catholic in its liturgical tradition.[5]

The Revd C.D.P. Davies died in 1931, son of a former Abbey incumbent and a deeply respected champion of bell-ringing, not least at the Abbey. He had been a founding and prominent member of the Gloucester and Bristol Diocesan Association of Church Bell Ringers. It took nearly two years to recast the existing ten bells and to add two new treble bells to the ring to honour his memory, and on 13 May 1933 they were formally dedicated, the cost borne by the bell-ringers of England. Tewkesbury Abbey now joined an exclusive club of churches with a ring of a dozen bells, as the 52nd member worldwide.⁶ In 1934, St Dunstan's Chapel was refurbished by the bell-ringers of England before dedication. St Dunstan, a late tenth-century Archbishop of Canterbury, is patron saint of bell-ringers; the figure of him was carved by Anton Wagner in 1993. The triptych over the altar is a reproduction of a fifteenth-century Flemish painting. The chapel itself is in the Revd C.D.P. Davies' memory.⁷

St Dunstan's Chapel showing bell and statue of St Dunstan

During 1931 there was a Tewkesbury pageant in which plays were performed in the meadow south of the Abbey.⁸ Canon Gough's interest in drama continued during the 1930s. The west end of the Abbey proved an effective place to hold productions such as T.S. Eliot's *Murder in the Cathedral* and Bernard Shaw's *St Joan*.⁹

Canon Gough founded the Friends of Tewkesbury Abbey in October 1932 at a public meeting. The objectives of the Friends were, and still are, to care for and help preserve the Abbey, together with its goods and ornaments, and safeguard it for future generations. The first contributions they made were to the Warwick Chantry Chapel's restoration and the rebinding of churchwardens' accounts from 1563 to 1703. However, the Friends soon expanded their activities, especially when the Abbey architect, Thomas Overbury (senior), after consulting Sir Charles Peers, Westminster Abbey's surveyor, announced that urgent, expensive work was needed. This included the tower, eastern chapels, nave, crossing and quire parapet. The problems included infestation by deathwatch beetle and would cost £25,000 (nearly £1.8 million in 2020 values). A public appeal was made, the Tewkesbury Festival as well as the Friends made huge efforts and the sum required was raised by July 1939. A service of thanksgiving was held, during which a plaque was unveiled, today found on the south-west pier of the tower.¹⁰ In 1940, Sir Charles and Thomas Overbury collaborated again in conducting an archaeological investigation into the Lady Chapel site at the extreme east end of the Abbey, possibly only the second formal archaeological investigation on the Abbey site. They found 'heraldic tiles, fragments of glass and richly moulded stones.'¹¹ In April 2001 the chapel outline was marked on the ground by stone slabs.¹²

St Faith's Chapel in the south-east corner of the Abbey, was given a stone altar with a wooden reredos in 1936, Peter Murphy's Crucifix being added many years later. The chapel came to have a secondary role. In 1936, Mrs Rees-Mogg presented the Abbey with an ancient cope of Italian workmanship of the late sixteenth or early seventeenth century. The beautiful embroidery was in need of remounting, eventually achieved in 1985. Known as the 'Florentine' Cope, it is worn only by the vicar on special occasions.[13] However, it was not until 2008 that a decision was reached that the Abbey's collection of copes should be kept in a proper quadrant-shaped cope chest. The beautiful, award-winning cope chest at the west end of St Faith's Chapel was made by Tim Jeffree.[14]

An unusual event was an ordination, held in the Abbey in December 1937, by Bishop Arthur Headlam, bishop of Gloucester, when three priests and four deacons were ordained.[15] Equally unusual, in 1938 the Abbey hosted a priests' convention that included the distinguished liturgist Dom Gregory Dix.[16]

In 1939, the high altar had been consecrated for 700 years, and so the Anglican Benedictine abbot of Nashdom, near Burnham, Bucks, presided at Holy Communion on 18 June. The same year, the present Lady Chapel was dedicated by Bishop Headlam, bishop of Gloucester, having been totally refurbished. Its small altar, previously the high altar, was moved to St Margaret's Chapel, while a new stone altar was dedicated for the Lady Chapel.[17] The Cotswold sculptor Alec Miller created the Blessed Virgin Mary and Child statue.[18]

In St Faith's Chapel, a tablet was dedicated in 1943 to the memory of Victoria Woodhull Martin. Born into poverty in America in 1838, she was the first woman to run for the United States presidency, though possibly illegally.

The Lady Chapel. The east window mosaic of 1893 is by Salviati, from a design by Clayton and Bell. The seating round the altar was carved and installed in 2012

Eventually, she married John Biddulph-Martin, a wealthy English banker, moving to the family estate near Tewkesbury. Her daughter, Zula Woodhull, left a large legacy to what became the Abbey Lawn Trust, which allowed Abbey Lawn House and gardens at the Abbey's east end to be purchased in 1940. This was on condition that a tablet to her mother's memory was placed in the Abbey encouraging friendship between Britain and the United States.[19] This bequest led to the Abbey Lawn Trust being created, which today administers grounds and some properties close to the Abbey.[20]

At the beginning of the Second World War, the vicar, appointed an honorary canon of Gloucester in 1939, encouraged people to attend weekly services in the Lady Chapel where there was a particular prayer emphasis on local people serving or about to serve in the forces. The beginning of hostilities also meant that precautions had to be taken. The quire and sanctuary glass was temporarily removed and the windows boarded up.[21]

St Margaret's Chapel, showing the wooden Sacrament House above the altar, designed by Neal Birdsall and made by Dan Windham of Hackford, Norfolk, in 1993

The Victoria Woodhull plaque in St Faith's Chapel, showing her connection to the United States

The cope chest showing the Florentine Cope. The chest is by Tim Jeffree (2008) and the cope is said to belong to the late sixteenth century. It was restored in 1985

With the advent of war, increasing pressures led Canon Gough to seek to retire through ill-health. He was persuaded to stay a further two years and finally retired in June 1942 but died within three years. His memorial was not only the establishment of the Abbey as a centre of well-ordered Catholic liturgy but also the high altar cross, designed by Sir Ninian Comper, the last of the great Gothic Revival architects, and the Gough Room in the Abbey Visitor Centre.[22]

Meanwhile, the Revd Brian Purefoy became vicar. He had farmed near Burford, Oxfordshire before ordination training at Chichester Theological College. He came to Tewkesbury Abbey in 1942, described as, 'A large man both in personality and stature, he was both outspoken and highly popular'.[23]

VE Day, 8 May 1945 – the end of war in Europe – was met with 'relief, thanksgiving and joy' in Tewkesbury. The mayor and corporation led a procession to the Abbey where a service was held, led by the vicar, the vicar of Holy Trinity and the Methodist minister. It is said that 1,500 people crammed themselves into the Abbey. Just over a week later, after another procession from the town hall with many more representatives present, a service of thanksgiving was held in which the Royal British Legion and American Forces flags were received.[24]

Brian Purefoy's incumbency lasted from 1942 to 1963. As soon as the Second World War was over, fabric and related issues surfaced again. First, in 1947 the Milton Organ underwent major restoration, reordering and enlargement to a four manual instrument that included the more modern electrical action, supervised by organist Huskisson Stubington. The console was then on the north side of the quire as there had been the thought – never realised because of lack of funds – that both the Milton and the Grove Organs might be played from the same console. The work on the Milton, begun in 1947, was finished in 1951, and a celebratory recital marking what was in part a new organ was given that July by Francis Jackson, organist of York Minster.[25]

Second, in 1956, an appeal for £50,000 was launched to restore deteriorating stonework, lead roofs and what was described as a 'serious' infestation of deathwatch beetle. In 1959 a statue of the Mother and Child by Darsie Rawlins, the noted ecclesiastical sculptor, replaced a weather-worn medieval version of the same subject above the north porch, though to a fresh design.[26]

Third, there had been concerns over the tonal qualities of the Abbey bells. Between 1960 and 1962, the old late seventeenth- and early eighteenth-century sixth, seventh, eighth and eleventh bells – all originally cast by Rudhall of Gloucester – were preserved as chimes for the Abbey clock. The other bells were recast.[27]

The next year – 1963 – Canon Purefoy was retiring when the vicar of the Abbey was made responsible for Tredington and Stoke Orchard. Sadly, Canon Purefoy retired to Oxfordshire in the September but died in December.[28] His successor was the Revd Cosmo Gabriel Rivers Pouncey. He was ordained in 1934, and Tewkesbury Abbey was his third incumbency.

Sung Eucharist in the Catholic tradition had become a feature of the Abbey's worshipping life since the 1930s. Now Cosmo Pouncey brought in special services for Holy Week in 1964, that included the use of a new Pascal Candlestick. A Humeral Veil was made by the St Mary's Guild as part of the liturgical vestments and, in October 1964, parish Communion – later family Eucharists – was introduced at 9.15 am. An Advent Procession was begun in 1967.[29]

A new tradition began: the start of *Musica Deo Sacra* week in August 1969. A superb

Cosmo Gabriel Rivers Pouncey, Vicar 1963–81

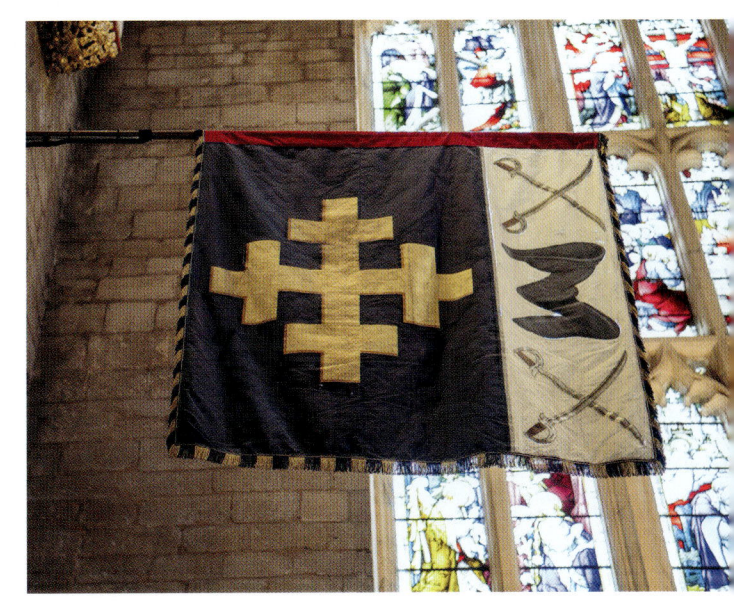

General Ismay was Sir Winston Churchill's top military advisor during the Second World War. For many years he lived in Stanway which belonged to the Abbey before the Dissolution. When the General died, his widow requested that the banner come to the Abbey for safekeeping

choir, recruited from all over the country, was assembled at the Abbey to sing sacred music, perhaps more often performed on the concert platform, back in its rightful liturgical place.[30]

General Lord Ismay, KG, died in 1965. He was Churchill's top personal military advisor during the Second World War and later first Secretary-General of the new North Atlantic Treaty Organisation (NATO). He lived in Stanway for about 20 years. Before the Dissolution of Tewkesbury's monastery in 1540, Stanway had been an Abbey manor and, with Forthampton, one of two private residences of the Abbot. Laura, Lady Ismay, requested that her late husband's Garter Banner, formerly hanging in St George's Chapel, Windsor, came to hang in the Abbey. It is at the west end on the south side.

The year 1971 was the 850th anniversary of the Abbey's consecration, as well as the 500th anniversary of the Battle of Tewkesbury. The 'King Charles' chairs in the Abbey were restored and cushions embroidered for HM Queen Elizabeth II who distributed the Royal Maundy on Thursday 8 April 1971, accompanied by HRH Prince Philip. There were festival services, a *Son et Lumiere*, plays and lectures.[31]

An Abbey Choir School was founded the same year by Miles Amherst (1931–2013), a science teacher, brass player and chorister who had sung in several cathedral choirs. Years earlier, he had visited Tewkesbury Abbey and was captivated by its beauty and superb acoustics but conscious that it had no choir school, which he wished to remedy. Some years later, he returned to explore possibilities. Both the vicar, Cosmo Pouncey, and the Director of Music, Michael Peterson, were enthusiastic. The old Girls' High School building was purchased, close to the Abbey. The Abbey School opened in September 1973 with five pupils and sang its first Evensong on 8 May 1974. Lower parts were supplied by teaching staff and, initially, the Parish Church choir, who still sang the Abbey services on Sundays. The year 1980 was the first year the Abbey School Choir appeared on TV and cut its first record. At one point the Abbey School reached just over 100 pupils and went co-educational in the early 1980s.[32]

The need to keep renovating the Abbey fabric continued. In November 1973, the Bishop of Gloucester launched an appeal to replace the south-west pinnacle of the tower, damaged in a gale. The work was helped by service personnel from RAF Odiham, who lifted four tons of stone by helicopter to the top of the tower where it was carved by master mason John Hopkins to match the other pinnacles. It is said that HM the Queen contributed to a 'treasure' sale that was a part of the appeal, donating a George III oviform cup and cover which sold for £1,300.[33] In 1978, Neil Birdsall, the Abbey architect, undertook what was believed to be the first Quinquennial Abbey inspection. Major work resulted, on the roofs of the chancel and transepts, that took until 1982 to complete.[34]

The year 1973 was also the year in which the Tewkesbury Shield Change Bell-Ringing Competition was launched. Today it is a prestigious, national, ten-bell striking competition that is competed for every May. The Shield is a limited edition Spode plate set in silver. Ten top-class bands, chosen by lot, enter and the competition is fierce. Bands that are successful in gaining a place practise for months in order to do well.

In 1980, St Catherine and St John the Baptist's Chapel was brought back into use, having been used as a museum and store probably since the Victorian restoration.

The year 1980 was also when the Grove Organ was given a complete restoration by J.C. Bishop and Son of London. The lowest five pipes of the 32ft pedal stop had never been included, but now appropriate pipes from what had formerly been part of the Willis Organ in Christ Church Cathedral, Oxford, were installed, completing the stop.[35] The Grove was rededicated by Canon Pouncey in 1981, during his last service before retirement, in memory of the Revd Brian Purefoy. Francis Jackson, organist of York Minster, gave the first recital; who also gave the first recital after the Milton Organ restoration in 1951.[36]

In 1979 there had been an attempt to send the Gambier Parry reredos, which had originally been given to the Abbey in 1914, to the Victoria and Albert Museum in London. However, experts and others insisted that it stay where it was. The reredos came to divide what was St James' Chapel, soon to be the Abbey shop, from the north-east corner chapel of the north transept, which became the Camera Cantorum song school, used by the Abbey and Abbey School Choirs, opened in 1981. New cassock cupboards were set against the screen and in front of the east wall, thereby concealing medieval carvings that had been reset in the east wall in the late 1870s.[37]

Other chapels receiving attention during 1982 included Holy Trinity chantry chapel that has the 'kneeling knight', Lord Edward Despenser, on its roof, facing the high altar. Its conservation was undertaken, roof cleaned and medieval Trinity painting on the east wall cleaned, consolidated, and conserved. The following year, its new altar was consecrated by the bishop of Tewkesbury on the Feast of Corpus Christi (2 June).[38] The Beauchamp and Founder's Chantries had new stone altars consecrated in November 1987, replacing wooden ones. The gate that had been a part of the Beauchamp Chantry became the Founder's Chantry Gate.[39] By St Dunstan's

Chapel in 1983, further conservation work on the Wakeman cenotaph was undertaken in which rusting iron rods were replaced with steel ones.[40] At the extreme south-west point of the nave, the bare room known as Holy Cross Chapel had museum items stored in it from St Catherine's Chapel from January 1980 to 1982, when it reverted back to being a chapel, it having had no real role since 1883 when it was given to the Abbey.[41] St James' Chapel became the Abbey shop in 1983, the year the Abbey tower was floodlit (*see overleaf*).[42]

The new vicar was the Revd Michael Moxon. Trained at Salisbury (Sarum) Theological College, he had been warden of St Paul's Cathedral, College of Canons, London from 1979 until he was appointed to Tewkesbury in 1981.[43]

Visitors or pilgrims entering a church of the Catholic tradition within the Church of England, as well as Roman Catholic churches, often find a holy water stoup near the entrance. This is so that people may sign themselves with the Cross with holy water as an act of self-consecration and spiritual cleansing. This practice was suppressed during the Reformation. Such a stoup, designed by Neil Birdsall, made by Keith Jameson, was set in a recess in the pillar closest to the north door in 1985, paid for anonymously.[44]

As the decade drew to a close, elements of the Abbey community either changed or developed a further step in their stories. The Abbey School joined the Choir Schools Association in 1988. Their choir broadcast their first Radio Three Choral Evensong. Dr Richard Morris became the Abbey's first archaeological consultant in 1990, the same year the Abbey gateway was converted into a holiday apartment by the Landmark Trust. In March 1991, Tewkesbury's Boys' Brigade Company became officially affiliated to the Abbey, a Girls' Company being

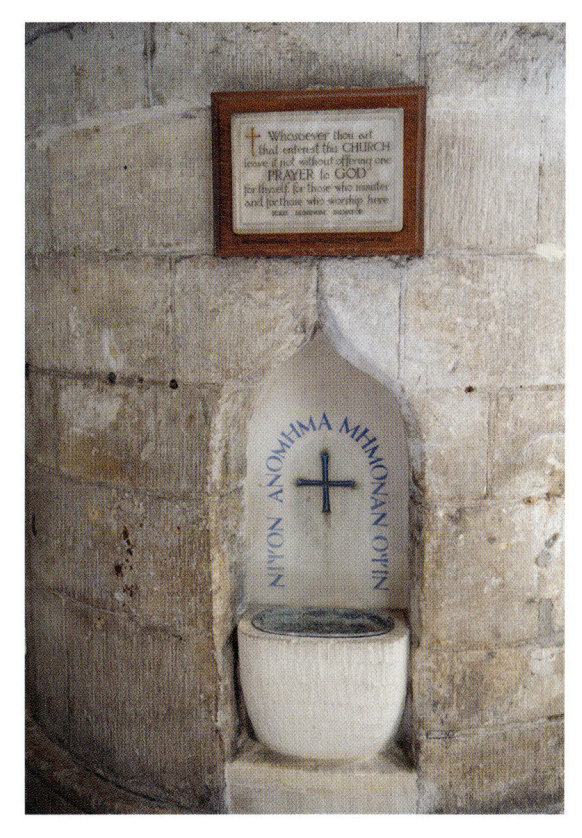

Common before the Reformation, Holy water stoups were subsequently actively discouraged. This one, given anonymously in 1985, was designed by Neil Birdsall and made by Keith Jameson of Winchcombe

founded a little later. Also in 1991 the Greater Churches group was founded, of which the Abbey became a member.[45]

But Michael Moxon had left. He had already been appointed a Queen's Honorary Chaplain in 1986. In 1990, he became Chaplain to the Queen at Windsor, and later a canon there. He was chaplain in Windsor Great Park and was later dean of Truro.[46]

Michael Moxon's successor as vicar was Michael Tavinor. He came to Tewkesbury Abbey in 1990 having been a minor canon, precentor and sacrist at Ely Cathedral from 1985–90 and also vicar of Stuntney, a small village close to Ely.[47]

Michael Edward Tavinor, vicar of Tewkesbury 1990–2002, on appointment as Dean of Hereford

Vicars of Tewkesbury Abbey since Victorian Times

C. Greenall Davies	1846–77
Hemming Robeson	1877–92
Harry Sheringham	1892–99
Oswald Wardell-Yerburgh	1899–1913
Ernest Smith	1914–30
Edward Gough	1930–42
Brian Purefoy	1942–63
Cosmo Pouncey	1963–81
Michael Moxon	1981–90
Michael Tavinor	1990–2002
Paul Rhys Williams	2003–

General Synod, the governing body of the Church of England, finally agreed to the ordination of women in 1992. About 1,000 women were the first to be ordained in this country in 1994. In Tewkesbury Abbey, opinion was divided between those who felt strongly that it was right, those who felt it was wrong and those who were uncertain. Disagreement on this issue was to affect the atmosphere at the Abbey for some years, making life at times difficult for the vicar and for his successor.

The year 1992 was also an important year in the Abbey belfry. The ring of 12 bells was added to by the addition of a 'Flat 6' bell given and installed in order to produce a 'light octave'. The bell, called 'Helen', was given by Eric and Helen Taylor, cast late in 1991 at Loughborough but brought to the Abbey in the New Year.[48]

During 1992–93, considerable activity around the ambulatory and east end of the Abbey occurred. Bruce Induni and a Bournemouth University team conserved and restored the Hugh III Despenser and Elizabeth Montacute tomb on the north side of the high altar as well as the Sir Guy de Brien (Bryan) monument that separates St Margaret's Chapel from the ambulatory.

In St Catherine's Chapel, the 'I am that I am' altar was created by Bryant Feddon in 1992, the same year that St John the Baptist was added to the chapel's dedication. The wooden altar previously there was mounted on wheels and replaced an original wooden nave altar. The following year a bronze gate was added to the aumbry so that holy oils could be kept in that chapel.[49] Dedicated in April 1993 were the 'Our Lady Queen of Peace' statue by Anthony Robinson, seen in the eastern ambulatory, and that of St Dunstan at the entrance to St Dunstan's Chapel, carved by Anthony Wagner.[50]

The Abbey tower was first floodlit in the 1930s

The Upper Room, showing the large painted Crucifix by Peter Murphy, above the altar

A detail of St Faith's Chapel, showing the painted Crucifix by Peter Murphy, above the altar

St Margaret's Chapel, due to its separation from the rest of the east end, owing to the Sir Guy de Brien (Lord Bryan) monument, became the Chapel for the Reservation of the Blessed Sacrament from 1934 in the aumbry in the north wall of the chapel. A sacrament house and hanging pyx was designed by Neil Birdsall. Installed in 1993, it was consecrated on the Feast of Corpus Christi (2 June) 1994.[51]

A £2 million appeal was launched in 1992. HRH Princess Margaret attended the launch service and was to return at the appeal's conclusion in 1997. The appeal embraced a major rebuilding of the Milton Organ; the re-roofing and renovation of the roofs of the eastern chapels and ambulatory and the conversion of the Abbey Halls into the Abbey Visitor Centre.

Further projects included the renovation of the old sacrist's room (which had become an untidy store) into an 'upper room' where quiet,

128 A HISTORY OF TEWKESBURY ABBEY

informal worship was possible. In 1995, work was completed on the roof and walls, including the conservation of some rather faint medieval polychromy (the art of painting or lettering in several colours) by David Perry. The room is dominated by a large Crucifix, fixed into the roof timbers above the altar, painted by Peter Murphy in 1997, and inspired by the Assisi Crucifix, said to have spoken to St Francis.[52] However, much of the cost of restoring and redesigning the room itself was borne by visitors and friends from Tewksbury, Massachusetts, USA. The date of the Our Lady of Tewkesbury sculpture is uncertain. The whole room, together with its furnishings, was dedicated in July 1997.[53]

It had been the hope of several denominations of churches within Tewkesbury to come together as an ecumenical group. This finally happened in 1994. Churches Together in Tewkesbury represented a welcome advance in mutual Christian concern and support to that seen in Tewkesbury three centuries previously.[54] The ecumenical aspect of the Abbey's ministry was further extended in 1996 when it played host to a Methodist Ordination service.[55]

There were further aids to enhance the prayer life of the Abbey. One of these was an ikon of St Benedict, painted by Peter Murphy.[56] It came to be the focus of a small recess in the west wall of the present Lady Chapel that also has a prie-dieu. A second aid was a beam, spanning the arch behind the high altar, designed by Neil Birdsall, from which a two-sided dossal curtain was hung – gold for general use, purple for the penitential seasons – allowing the worshipper to focus on the high altar cross.[57]

A new frontal for St Dunstan's chapel was dedicated in 1995 while in the same year a bracket was presented for the 'Pelican' carving in a new site in St Margaret's Chapel. The pelican

The Ikon of St Benedict, located in a recess in the west wall of the Lady Chapel, was painted by Peter Murphy in 1994

is a mystic emblem of Christ, whose blood was shed for humanity. When she is shown vulning (piercing) herself and nourishing her young while standing on her nest, as in this case, it is referred to as 'the Pelican in her Piety'.[58]

In 1996, Ruth Davis of Bristol and her assistants conserved and cleaned the nave vault paintings from end to end. Coke deposits from the Abbey's Gurney stoves had previously increasingly obscured the nave ceiling's rich colours. A sense of how bad things had become may be gained as a strip of the nave ceiling was deliberately left without being cleaned near the west end of the nave on the north side. Today the remaining Gurney stoves are gas-fired.[59]

One of the major projects of the appeal was the total rebuilding of the Milton Organ by Kenneth Jones and Associates, costing about

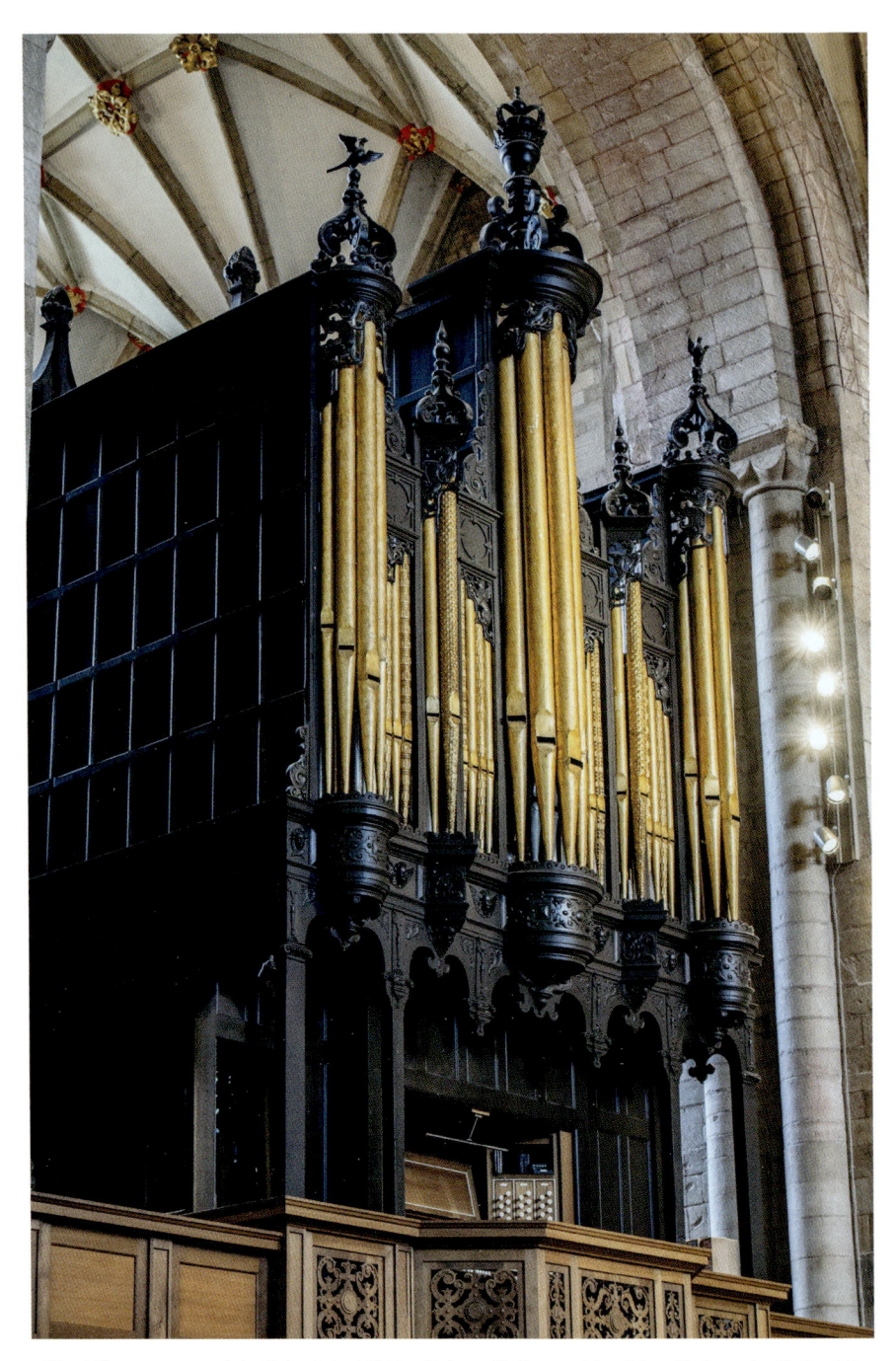

The Milton organ, originally built in 1631 by Robert Dallam at Magdalen College, in Oxford. It consisted of great and chair divisions housed in separate cases. Between 1654 and 1660 it was at Hampton Court (where the poet John Milton knew it). Renatus Harris rebuilt it in Oxford. It was sold to the Abbey in 1737 apart from the chair division which went to Stanford-on-Avon parish church, Northamptonshire. Swell and pedal organs were added in 1796. It has been periodically overhauled, improved and enlarged. It was last overhauled in 2018 and is now a very fine four manual, 68-stop instrument

£500,000. The organ and console, now on the south side of the quire, were raised by about ten feet, allowing the sound to be heard better throughout the Abbey. The new screen/ gallery was designed by David Graebe. As Kenneth Jones observed, 'apart from tiny portable organs, the Milton Organ must be the most moved church organ in existence', 'set up' on at least ten occasions. The 1948 electric action had largely worn out, making the instrument unreliable. Moreover, increasing levels of dust prevented pipes from 'speaking' as they should. The original 1631 front pipes were repaired and restored. The apse organ, built in 1950, was rebuilt but only with the 'echo' organ. It was while space used for the apse organ was being reduced that a medieval twelfth-century painting was rediscovered. It was effectively the foliate 'boss' on the barrel vault of the south transept Norman gallery chapel. Also, there were fragments of painting on the masonry around the doorway.[60] Conservators from the Perry Lithgow partnership stabilised and restored them. The paintings may be found on the ceiling immediately above the floor over the present Lady Chapel sanctuary.[61]

The new Abbey Visitor Centre included offices and parish meeting rooms. In 1996 the tearoom in the centre was opened, initially called the refectory. It extended the Benedictine tradition of hospitality, but also provided a much needed income for Abbey coffers.[62] In September 1999, a sculpture was dedicated outside the Abbey Visitor Centre called 'Touching Souls', a copy of one in Tewksbury, Massachusetts, USA by Mico Kaufman. It showed four children of different ethnicities sitting down together and the soles of their feet touching one another's. The tearoom promptly became the Touching Souls Tearoom.[63]

With roofs and ceilings renewed or restored, the Upper Room completed, the Milton Organ rebuilt and the Abbey Visitor Centre and tearoom already in use, there was a packed Abbey to welcome HRH Princess Margaret to the Thanksgiving Service in April 1997. Just a few months later, however, the mood was very different. Diana, Princess of Wales, died after a car accident in Paris on 31 August 1997. Tewkesbury Abbey opened a Book of Condolence and hundreds queued to sign it. On the day of her funeral, 6 September, over 500 attended a Requiem Eucharist in the Abbey.[64] However, nearly five years later, the Abbey welcomed HRH Charles, Prince of Wales, on 21 July 2002. He was the guest of honour at a 900th anniversary concert of the monks arriving from Cranbourne as well as being the final concert of that year's Cheltenham Festival.

John Belcher retired after 12 years as Abbey Director of Music in 1997. During his time he founded the Abbey Choir Association. The new organist and Director of Music was Carleton Etherington, who came from Leeds Parish Church.[65]

It was announced that from 1 March 1999 the Abbey – and Walton Cardiff – would be joined with Twyning, an ancient parish about three miles from Tewkesbury. Michael Tavinor was inducted as vicar on 18 April 1999. This made little difference to the Abbey community as a whole but clearly had an impact on the workload of the vicar and curate. The joint patrons were now the Lord Chancellor – representing the Crown – and Christ Church, Oxford. Moreover, new estates were being built on the edges of Tewkesbury. The Abbey developed lay ministry, both readers and others who could share some of the pastoral load. From May 1999, authorised members of the laity began to take Holy Communion to the sick at home.[66]

As the nights became darker, many appreciated the new lights recently installed from the north porch to the Gage gates, and of the paving from the north porch round to the west end. Paving was also extended to the cloister walkway in 2002.[67]

As the calendar entered December 1999, two roundels marked the Gospel spot in the nave as the second millennium was reached – and the tower clock-face was refurbished.[68]

All 12 Abbey bells were manned to ring out the old year and ring in the new century and millennium at midnight on 31 December, and also for the special ringing organised at all towers in the country at midday on New Year's Day. Abbey ringers numbered 28 at this time – a record.[69]

Late in 1999 and into the following year, the eighteenth-century Gage Gates were conserved and restored. During the Second World War, the railing on either side had been removed and the metal sent to aid the war effort. Neil Birdsall designed a section of matching railing on either side. The very striking result was erected during March 2000.[70]

In 2000, at the beginning of a new millennium, there had been 43 baptisms, 15 marriages, 3 marriage blessings and 35 funerals at the Abbey. Abbey clergy also conducted 13 funerals at crematoria. On Easter Day, including the Easter Vigil, 844 people attended, of whom 693 received Holy Communion. On Christmas Eve and Christmas Day, 2072 attended services, of whom 1007 received Holy Communion.[71]

In January 2002 Michael Tavinor was appointed Dean of Hereford. He had just completed introducing the parish to Common Worship, then a new form of liturgy.[72] He had also encouraged junior church and youth and vocations to ministry, both ordained and lay. Salaried staff seemed more evident, although the Abbey continued to rely on large numbers of volunteers. Michael Tavinor chose to mark his move from Tewkesbury to Hereford by walking a pilgrimage from one to the other.[73]

Inside the Abbey, the gate behind the high altar was made to mark the 50th anniversary of the accession of Queen Elizabeth II.[74] Tom Denny, the creative designer and glazier, produced two windows for the St John the Baptist and St Catherine Chapel, to mark the coming of the Benedictine monks 900 years before to begin work on building the Abbey in 1102. The theme was *Labore est Orare* – 'To Work is to Pray'. The predominant colours are those of gold and green, and have a considerable impact. The windows were dedicated by the bishop of Gloucester, David Bentley, in October 2002.[75]

On 19 January 2003, the Revd Canon Paul Rhys Williams was instituted as vicar of the Abbey. Having already been an incumbent, he came to the Abbey after being domestic chaplain to Bishop Michael Nazir-Ali of Rochester. In 2001 he had also become an honorary canon of Rochester Cathedral.[76]

A stone altar was installed in St Edmund's Chapel in 2004. Nine years later, it was complemented by a triptych over the altar, created by Silvia Dimitrova, that took four years to plan and two years to execute. It was dedicated by Bishop Martyn Snow, then bishop of Tewkesbury, in November 2013.[77]

The question of women priests presiding at the Eucharist continued to cause difficulties within the Abbey community. While most people now accepted women's ministry, there was a small group of parishioners that did not. Notwithstanding their objections, after much discussion the vicar felt it was time to resolve the matter. In March 2006, the Parochial Church Council overwhelmingly backed his decision

The Chapel of St Catherine and St John the Baptist. The Denny windows were dedicated in 2002, marking the 900th anniversary of when the monks arrived to begin building the Abbey. The altar – 'I am that I am' – is by Bryant Feddon and was dedicated in 1992

St Edmund's Chapel triptych, a modern triptych by Silvia Dimitrova, dedicated in 2013 by Martyn Snow, bishop of Tewkesbury

to invite ordained women to preside at the Eucharist. A little later, two women were among six priests who con-celebrated at the Maundy Thursday Mass in early April, 2006. The die was now cast. Some objectors accepted what had happened; others left the Abbey to worship elsewhere; one or two checked who was presiding at an Abbey celebration before deciding whether to participate or not and one became a Roman Catholic.[78]

The year 2006 was largely focussed on the Abbey School and its choir, which had lost money for years. Miles Amherst had personally subsidised it, but could do no longer. On 24 April, administrators were called in. Neil Gardner, the headmaster, informed several other independent schools. One headmaster, the Revd Tim Hastie-Smith of Dean Close School, Cheltenham, said that he could not save the school, but might be able to save the choir, which had a national reputation. The choir's director, Benjamin Nicholas, immediately contacted him and a campaign began to keep the choir together and transfer it to Dean Close Preparatory School, also in Cheltenham. The trustees and Tim Hastie-Smith knew the Abbey had a wide, broadly Anglo-Catholic approach to Christianity, while the school was decidedly Evangelical in foundation and ethos. It was agreed that both traditions would be honoured. Paul Williams, the vicar and a governor of the Abbey School, was enthusiastically in favour of the plan that would only work if parents, who held the initiative, stuck together. Time was short. Three boys went elsewhere but ten chose Dean Close, enough to make the choir viable. On Thursday 13 July,

The Abbey surrounded by flood water in 2007

the Abbey School Choir sang its last Evensong. The next afternoon the Abbey School held its last speech day. The following term, the choir returned as Tewkesbury Abbey Schola Cantorum of Dean Close Preparatory School, a lengthy title soon shortened to 'Schola' or 'TASC'. Three former Abbey School teachers joined the Dean Close staff.[79]

The ten Abbey School choristers who joined Dean Close Preparatory School were met by three aspiring choristers from the preparatory school itself. They first sang Evensong together on Monday 11 September 2006. It was boys' voices only, with the full four-part choir the next day. A major test for them came a fortnight later on 27 September when they travelled to St Michael's Church, Tenbury Wells, to sing Choral Evensong live on BBC Radio 3, marking the 150th anniversary of St Michael's College. It was a triumph, establishing the reconstituted choir not just in BBC minds but also in those of interested members of the Abbey and the general public.[80] Within two years, the choir represented Great Britain at the closing event of the French Presidency of the EU in Strasbourg.[81]

The year 2007 was dominated by the Tewkesbury flood when 1800 Tewkesbury properties flooded and three people died. It was part of the 'Great Gloucestershire Flood'. Between Friday 20 July and Sunday 22 July nearly six inches of rain fell on an already rain-sodden county, perhaps the greatest flood in the Tewkesbury area since records began in 1766. However, there is a record of one such flood in November 1770. It is suggested that on Sunday 18 November, the flood 'came into the Church and Chancel so that Divine Service could not be performed', although it soon subsided.

In 2007, Tewkesbury quickly flooded, roads were inundated, including the M5 Motorway, where many were stranded. The vicar, Paul Williams, conscious of the continuing heavy rain, met the borough mayor late in the afternoon of 20 July, who requested that the Abbey be opened as a place of refuge. The vicar, assisted by volunteers, opened the Abbey and its visitor centre all night. He later recalled, 'people were sleeping on kneelers – one family was wrapped in an altar cloth'. Over 100 stranded motorists slept in chapels, the nave, in Abbey House or the Abbey visitor centre. For a time, flooding occurred in the Abbey itself, at the west end to a depth of a couple of inches. Some feared flood water might come up through the Clarence vault into the ambulatory but this was prevented. For the most part, services were cancelled, although a wedding was held on 21 July and the vicar held daily evening prayer at the Gage Gates – and several passers-by joined in. The water began to recede significantly after a week. Today, a plaque just above the floor in the north porch of the Abbey shows the depth reached.[82]

The Abbey's external fabric continued to require constant attention. The west end turrets and pinnacles were restored in 2002. A year later, the masonry and glazing of the west window needed work.[83] The tower roof was repaired in 2005 and 2006, and its west face re-pointed, a task completed in 2009. Just over ten years later, in 2019, it was the Camera Cantorum roof that required major repair and restoration. Within the Abbey, it was realised that access for wheelchair users to most of the Abbey had to be made easier. In 2010, a carefully designed stone slope was built from the south quire aisle just opposite the sacristy, which allowed access into the quire itself.

On 16 and 17 December, 1993, the BBC had recorded *Songs of Praise* at the Abbey. Since then, the BBC had broadcast choral evensong both with the Abbey School Choir and later with Tewkesbury Abbey Schola Cantorum on several occasions.[84] BBC local radio had broadcast some carol services as well as inviting the vicar to offer both sacred and secular talks and interviews from time to time. It has been a gently evolving further area of ministry.

Christmas Morning 2010 was memorable as BBC TV broadcast the Abbey service live to the nation, with the vicar presiding, his wife, the Revd Catherine Williams, preaching, the Abbey beautifully decorated and the Abbey Choir in fine voice. In May 2016 the Abbey also welcomed BBC1's *Antiques Roadshow* programme.

One of the ways in which the vicar coped with ever increasing demands on his time and that of his curate was, like his predecessor, by encouraging retired clergy to participate, and also those from the congregations who felt called to non-stipendiary ordained or lay ministry. Apart from some retired clergy and two or three who were already readers, out of this came three local non-stipendiary ministers, and later another Reader.[85] In 2010 they were joined by the Revd Wendy Ruffle, whose brief and calling was to develop a fresh expression of Church, especially in the Priors Park area of the Abbey's parish. Soon, a church community developed called 'Celebrate' that initially met at Queen Margaret's, the local primary school. It grew to about 70 people. A detached house was purchased to act as a base for both worship and other activities while still using the school. Wendy Ruffle was given incumbent status. Much work was still done jointly with the Abbey enabling a unique 'blended' church community, involving as it did the broadly Anglo-Catholic Abbey and the Charismatic Evangelical

The Peregrine falcons

The Peregrine falcons first seem to have come to Tewkesbury Abbey during the winter of 2010–11. The first sighting of the Peregrines was in February 2011.

A nesting tray was put on the upper part of the tower soon after. The situation was kept under observation by David Bagley, a member of the Abbey community, in consultation with the Gloucestershire Raptor Monitoring group. The activity of the falcons is monitored by CCTV and may be seen on the internet.

'CR', a bird identified as having come from Christchurch parish church, Cheltenham, was seen on the tower on 25 September 2014. He was later observed with 'DX', a female known as 'Alice', who came from the Avon Gorge. This female bird had disappeared by March 2015, but within two months a new female bird, 'Bella', had arrived. It was not until May 2018 that three eggs were seen. Although out of three eggs, two hatched, only one chick survived. On 2 July, the surviving chick – a male – was ringed by Tim Bray, using climbing equipment to access the nesting tray, watched by a squawking and distrustful Bella. The chick's identification letters were given as 'PDN' and he is known as 'Paddington'. Increasingly active, the now almost adult Paddington made an attempt to fly, but had to be rescued at the end of July 2018. Since then, he has matured further and flown away, although he did return on one occasion during August of the same year.

A similar situation occurred in 2019, except that two out of three chicks survived. However, attempts to breed in 2020 ended in failure.

The 2021 breeding season resulted in four eggs being laid, of which three hatched and two fledglings survived. One of the two juvenile birds ('P4N') was seen visiting the nesting tray in December 2021.

Male Peregrine falcon, roosting high on the tower photograph copyright © David Bagley

Peregrine falcon chick (P4N) on the tower photograph copyright © David Bagley

'Celebrate'. Through a great deal of goodwill, prayer, thought and discussion the relationship worked, arousing considerable interest both in and beyond the diocese and even internationally. In 2016, the Church at national level paid for a full-time Pioneer Curate, spending 80% of his time with 'Celebrate' and 20% of his time at the Abbey. In the meantime, the Abbey had its own full-time curate.[86]

In 2011–12 the vicar, after consultation, decided to change the seating behind the altar in the Lady Chapel, thereby making Holy Communion in the round possible. There was to be an integral credence table, too. Most of the community thought the idea both excellent and imaginative. However, one or two did not and it took time to resolve the issue. The seating, designed by Neil Birdsall and created by local craftsman Phil Hughes, was dedicated during a Requiem Service held in the Lady Chapel in January 2013. Also dedicated at the same time was a refurbished altar cross and candlesticks.[87]

Between 2014 and 2016, the Abbey community spent £850,000 on a modern, highly flexible lighting system. Virtually instantly, the Abbey could be suitably lit for a service in the quire or a side-chapel, a concert in the nave or a large, whole Abbey act of worship. It followed on from the overhaul of the sound system that had occurred a couple of years earlier.

David Ireson had been director of *Musica Deo Sacra* almost since its inception. He had come across every year from St Albans to direct the Festival, achieving the very highest standards with the *Musica Deo Sacra* choir. In 2017 he retired, handing over the directorship to Carleton Etherington, the Abbey Director of Music.[88] In preparation for the anticipated 2021 celebrations, during 2018 the Milton Organ was given a £100,000 renovation.

The workload for the two churchwardens had increased hugely over the years. At the APCM in 2019 it was decided to add a third. One churchwarden was to look after fabric concerns, a second to deal with all matters regarding employment and the third was to organise what was loosely called 'front of house' issues, such as the sidesmen's rota, who was able to 'meet and greet' for special services and arrangements for numerous occasions. It worked so well that it was tried again the following year.[89]

In 2020, the Abbey community, like the rest of Britain and the world, suffered the pandemic of Coronavirus (Covid-19), following government restrictions and Church of England guidelines. From 24 March for three and a half months, no-one, except the vicar, the head verger and her deputy, was able to enter the Abbey. Other paid staff were put on furlough, while congregations and visitors were in lock-down. Services in the Abbey ceased but by the skilful use of *YouTube*, people could participate in Holy Communion once a week. Initially recorded in the Abbey, they were later offered, through *YouTube* only, from the vicar's private chapel in Abbey House. Each celebration included a homily and a hymn, supplied by members of the Abbey Choir who had to sing their lines individually. Members of the congregation read lessons and led intercessions, recorded separately. Each service was edited and produced by the vicar's son, Harrison Williams, and was watched and appreciated by hundreds of people. A dedicated phone line was also secured, down which the same recorded service was available for those who were without computers. The Abbey community of over 400 people was divided into a dozen groups with whom various Abbey clergy kept in contact. Each week the clergy met in 'Zoom' meetings in order to share what was happening in the Abbey community.

The Abbey opened for private prayer from 14 June but it was not until Wednesday 8 July that any services resumed in the Abbey. In this instance, it was a celebration of Holy Communion. That Sunday, 12 July, a public Holy Communion was held in the Abbey nave, possibly the longest period without a public Abbey service since the Pope's Interdict during the thirteenth century. Nearly 100 people attended, even though there were no hymns or singing, face covering was mandatory and seating and movement were severely restricted. Daily morning prayer in the Lady Chapel resumed. The Abbey was open from 9 am to 1 pm every day. A 'pop-up' shop with light refreshments and card and gift items opened in the tearoom on Fridays, Saturdays and Sundays. The following week 96 adults and five children attended the Abbey service.[90]

Organ music was reintroduced on Sunday 20 September, the Abbey organist, Carleton Etherington, playing before the service, during the distribution and a voluntary at the end.

The following day, the vicar called a meeting of all the lay staff and indicated that the financial future of the Abbey was grim and that changes to staffing patterns would have to be implemented. This difficult exercise was carried out over the following three months, resulting in fewer posts and greater flexibility, even though the Abbey was awarded £185,000 by the government Covid Cultural Recovery Fund, to help it meet some of its expenses.

On Sunday 11 October, the parish choir of 22 voices, duly robed, sang motets during the administration of Holy Communion. They were all 'socially distanced' (that is at least two metres from one another), in the quire, facing the congregation, in chairs just to the east of the choir-stalls. They calculated that it had been 210 days since they had last sung at a service.

The treble bell, 'Sheila', prior to being hoisted into place

The following day, the vicar blessed a new treble bell called Sheila, named after Sheila Taylor, an experienced bell-ringer whose husband, Malcolm, is Tower Captain. It would allow the ring to be more flexible. The bell was hoisted into the ringing chamber and the ring will probably not now be added to or replaced for many years.

In the run-up to Christmas, apart from two carol services with heavily restricted numbers, a carol service was carefully achieved using the parish and Schola Cantorum choirs, directed by Carleton Etherington and Simon Bell respectively, and put on *YouTube*, attracting 6,000 visits. Each part had to be recorded separately in an empty Abbey. There was also a special *YouTube* Christmas celebration on Christmas Eve, in which the parish choir took part, attracting 1,000 visits.[91] The great rise in cases of Covid-19 and the number of deaths meant that scarcely had Christmas been celebrated than a second major lockdown came into force. The Abbey was closed for public services, although open for personal prayer for part of each morning. Hope for 2021 largely centred on promised vaccinations for the population. It seemed that 2021 celebrations might be distinctly muted.

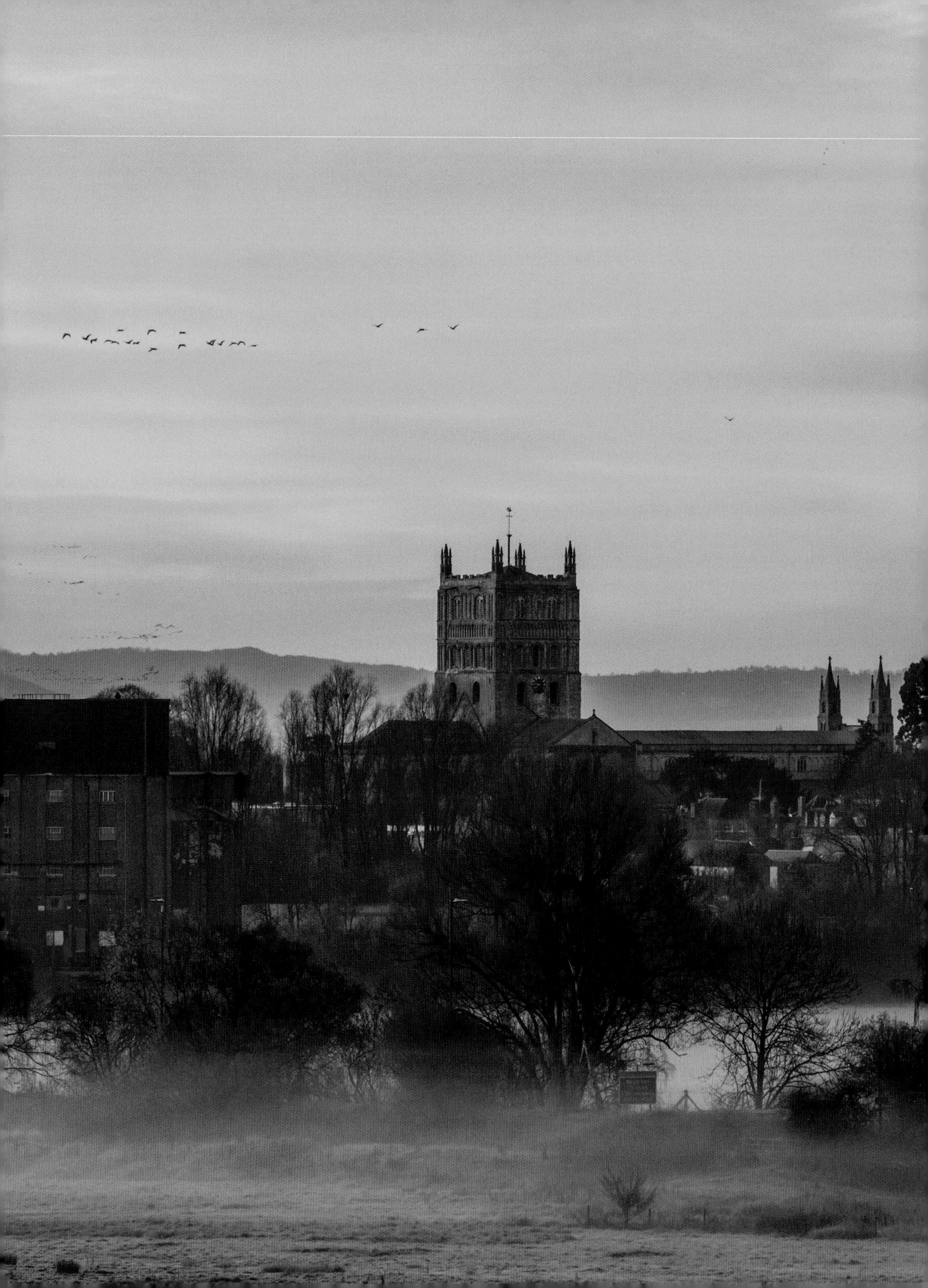

CHAPTER ELEVEN

2021: Celebrating the past, living the present, embracing the future

Although 2021 began in the hope that the Covid-19 situation would improve and celebrations of the 900th anniversary begin, services continued to be banned except for the regular Sunday slots on *YouTube*. A year-long programme of occasions and activities had been planned but almost all became victims of the pandemic and had to be cancelled, to the great disappointment of many people. However, in the early days of 2021, spirits were raised by an Epiphany organ recital on the Milton Organ on *YouTube* by Carleton Etherington, the Abbey organist. Harry Williams, its producer, director and cameraman, was in the organ loft while the pieces were played, so that the organist's hands, and feet, could be seen in action. Simon Bell, director of Tewkesbury Abbey Schola Cantorum, gave a similar – and equally appreciated recital – later that year, in August.

Another Abbey initiative involved a collection of several hundred knitted monks, some undertaking various tasks. Joanne Raywood wrote the script and David Coulton narrated a ten-minute feature, once more on *YouTube*.

At 12 noon on 23 March, the country kept one minute's silence to remember over 126,000 people at that point who were the 'official' victims of Covid-19. The actual loss, in which Covid-19 was a contributory factor, had been put at 145,000.

The Prime Minister, Boris Johnson, thought that it would be appropriate if there was a permanent memorial erected for them. St Paul's Cathedral was thought a suitable place.

The Abbey arranged for an innovative Holy Week and Easter. Palm Sunday was the last Sunday when services would be simply put on *YouTube*. There were services on Maundy Thursday, Good Friday, the Easter Vigil on Holy Saturday and an Easter Day service. For the first time these were live-streamed on *YouTube*, while a limited, ticketed number of the congregation were allowed to come to each service. People were asked not to come to more than one service. The Triduum was not quite the same as usual.[1]

On the morning of Friday 9 April 2021, the Queen's husband, HRH Prince Philip, Duke of Edinburgh died, aged 99, a few weeks short of his 100th birthday. To mark his passing, an Abbey bell tolled and an Abbey flag was flown at half-mast.

However, the sense of sadness was in part dispelled by a special Fitzhamon lecture for the Friends given by Professor John Harper, Emeritus Professor of Bangor University, an expert on medieval church music and liturgy, in April. His lecture, delivered via 'Zoom', was one of the few celebrations that was able to go ahead despite the pandemic. Entitled 'Hallowing God's

House in 1121 – the consecration of the Abbey Church at Tewkesbury', it explored the probable liturgy and music that might have been used on that occasion, 900 years before.

The curate, the Revd Sebastian Hamilton, celebrated Holy Communion for the last time at the Abbey on Sunday 25 April before moving on to a post in Cheltenham. The parish choir, suitably socially distanced and to the east of the screen, returned to lead parts of the worship, this time including the Kyrie, Gloria, Sanctus, Benedictus and Agnus Dei as well as an anthem and a communion hymn. This they continued to do on following Sundays. These services were also live-streamed.

Members of the congregation were also growing used to the tearoom being turned into a 'pop-up shop' for restricted hours on most days, serving thirsty worshippers and visitors with hot and cold drinks, although no meals could be offered. The shop also sold a limited number of gifts for visitors, who had begun to return to the Abbey.

During May, it was announced that as from September 2021 Schola Cantorum would be offering choral scholarships to girls as well as boys. By 2025 it was hoped to have ten boys and ten girls.[2] By the end of June, four girls had been accepted for the following September.

Anomalies arose concerning Covid-19 regulations. Late on Friday 14 May, a government decree resulted in the sudden clamp-down on amateur choirs. The result was that on the following Sunday, only six members of the Abbey Choir were allowed to sing. They managed admirably. However, the new restrictions did not apply to Tewkesbury Abbey Schola Cantorum, as they were perceived as a 'professional' choir. A joke with a certain irony circulated that Covid-19 was a remarkably intelligent virus as it could differentiate between amateur and professional singers!

It was also announced during May that Paul Williams, the vicar, had been appointed a Deputy Lieutenant of Gloucestershire by

Her Majesty Queen Elizabeth II, who distributed the Royal Maundy at Tewkesbury Abbey in 1971. Paul Williams, vicar of the Abbey, was appointed a Deputy Lieutenant of Gloucestershire, a Crown appointment, in 2021

Paul Williams, vicar of Tewkesbury Abbey, in his uniform as a Deputy Lieutenant of Gloucestershire

Edward Gillespie, the Lord Lieutenant. This appointment, to which HM the Queen had 'expressed no objection,' was the first time that an Abbey incumbent had been so honoured.³ It was also at this time that Paul Williams was awarded a Lambeth Doctorate.⁴ He was the first Abbey vicar to achieve such an academic distinction.

It was not until 27 June that Sunday Choral Evensong with the Abbey Choir began again. As in the morning Eucharist, only six singers were permitted. They sat, as in the morning, socially distanced from each other, just to the high altar side of the steps to the east of the choir stalls. The officiant sat on the north side of the nave just west of the screen, but prayed the intercessions from the screen step at the entrance to the quire. The congregation were seated on plastic chairs, socially distanced from each other at the head of the nave.

Sunday 4 July was the Friends' Festival, when the facsimile of the Founders' Book was published as part of the 900th Anniversary celebrations. This was after the Friends' AGM in the nave of the Abbey. Professor Julian Luxford, who had edited the volume, Adrian Ailes, who had contributed a chapter on the heraldry found in the Founders' Book and Professor Susan Powell, who had painstakingly translated the text and added numerous helpful notes were all on hand to speak to the meeting and sign copies. To celebrate the Festival, the bell-ringers rang a quarter peal in 41 minutes of 1320 Cambridge Surprise Minor, the first quarter rung on the new 'light six' and the first tower bell quarter peal since March 2020.

The annual meeting of parishioners and annual parochial church meeting took place in the Abbey on 28 July. A number of the congregation watched the 'streamed' version.

The vicar suggested that the community was passing through 'some of the most challenging times that the Abbey had ever seen,' including wartime. He felt that there were three priorities: first, worship of God; second, the people of God and their pastoral needs; third, the work of God that included the running of the Abbey and parish. He introduced the idea of a new Sunday routine, having only one 'main' service in the morning after the *Book of Common Prayer* Holy Communion at 8 am replacing the pattern of two services at 9 am and 11 am, which had been in place since 1964. The Revd Wendy Ruffle, in her report, echoed what Fr Paul had said, pointing out that in 'Celebrate', now a community of roughly 70, half were children. The level of deprivation was very high. In the week before the end of term in Queen Margaret's School, out of 170 children, 120 were isolating because of Covid-19. Yet adults and children were growing in discipleship.

Elements of normality began to creep back during September 2021. Schools opened. The full Abbey Choir began singing together for the first time in nearly two years, and the congregation were allowed to sing hymns – though still wearing face coverings. From April 2021, Schola Cantorum began to sing mid-week choral evensong again, although the congregation were only allowed into the nave. For the first time, girls sang in that choir – Raffaela Brown, Beth Moody, Alicia O'Connell and Alice Wilson. On Sunday 12 September, Bishop Rachel held a Diocesan Confirmation Service in the Abbey when 20 people were confirmed.

On Wednesday 15 September there was a dinner held in the nave of the Abbey to mark the 900th anniversary of its consecration and dedication. There were over 60 diners, including the town mayor, Mrs Joanne Raywood, her

The parish dinner held in the Abbey to mark the 900th anniversary of its consecration and dedication

HRH Princess Anne, the Princess Royal, who visited Tewkesbury Abbey during 2021

husband and the deputy mayor. It seemed particularly appropriate that during such a year, the mayor was an active member of the Abbey community. The lighting effects were dramatically superb. The following evening the Honourable Company of Gloucestershire entertained HRH Princess Anne, the Princess Royal, in the same place. She, too, was very favourably impressed by the lighting.

On Monday 27 September, the vicar journeyed to Lambeth Palace to receive his doctorate. He was accompanied by Tewkesbury Abbey Schola Cantorum who sang choral evensong in Lambeth Palace Chapel. Choristers compared the beauties of the chapel unfavourably with 'their' Abbey.

The following Sunday there was a Harvest Festival thanksgiving in the morning, together with a baptism, when the Abbey was crowded, not least because the Boys' and Girls' Brigades were present. This was also the first Sunday when the main morning service was not a Eucharist, which was celebrated late in the afternoon instead.

The anniversary of the consecration of the Abbey itself was held on Sunday 24 October, the original date being the 23rd. Instead of the originally planned service, a simple sung Eucharist was held, led by the parish choir. The service included Carleton Etherington's beautiful anthem, 'How Lovely is Thy Dwelling Place', that had been composed for the occasion.[5]

Saturday 30 October was when nations began to assemble in Glasgow for COP 26 to discuss the way forward regarding climate warming of the planet.[6] The Abbey bells rang from 11 am to 12 noon in concert with bell-towers all over the country. They were giving a warning of the impending danger to the planet unless everyone at the conference and beyond made urgent decisions and undertakings that they would keep.

One further celebration that had avoided cancellation was the Festival of Lights held over 2–5 November. Each evening, hundreds of participants flocked to the south door of the Abbey guided by numbers of coloured lights shone against the Abbey at various vantage points. Once inside, each visitor followed a one-way system round the ambulatory accompanied by music, lights and various light shows set up against walls. Finally, the nave was reached where almost all the seating had been removed. A projector, mounted on its own arch near the quire screen, projected a succession of coloured images, dates, occasional pictures and patterns against the west end window and wall, all the Norman pillars and nave vaulting (*see overleaf*). This was accompanied by mainly contemporary, evocative music – although a little plainsong was heard occasionally. From the north door, where visitors came out at the end of the experience, along the path to the Gage Gates, schoolchildren had created a colourful avenue of large, paper-like lanterns tied to stakes. The impact on the public of the whole evening was such that the morning after the first Festival evening the Tewkesbury Roses' Theatre computer, acting as the booking agency, crashed, as all those who now wanted tickets tried to book online. Adjectives such as 'spectacular', 'overwhelming', 'amazing' and 'wonderful' were used. In all, over 5,250 people came on the four nights. The Saturday night, 6 November, was Tewkesbury's Bonfire Night, with an impressive firework display on fields close to the Abbey. Given all the problems and difficulties, it was a memorable week in which to end the immediate celebrations of the 900th anniversary of the Abbey's dedication and consecration.

It has remained an intention that the year be marked further by a modern north door entrance area and a roundel, suitably inscribed, set in the pathway just outside the north door.

While clergy and lay staff had been busy coping with constantly changing regulations from government and the diocese over a two-year period to deal with the pandemic, it had also been a time for reflection. The vicar, looking to the future, came to three conclusions. The first was that, pastorally speaking, the Abbey community had 'come together' even more than before the pandemic and that everyone was looking after everyone else. Out of that had developed an improved system for monitoring those requiring pastoral support.

The second conclusion was that the advent of 'live streaming' of services and the use of *YouTube* had opened up a new congregation that was not just national but worldwide. Links were

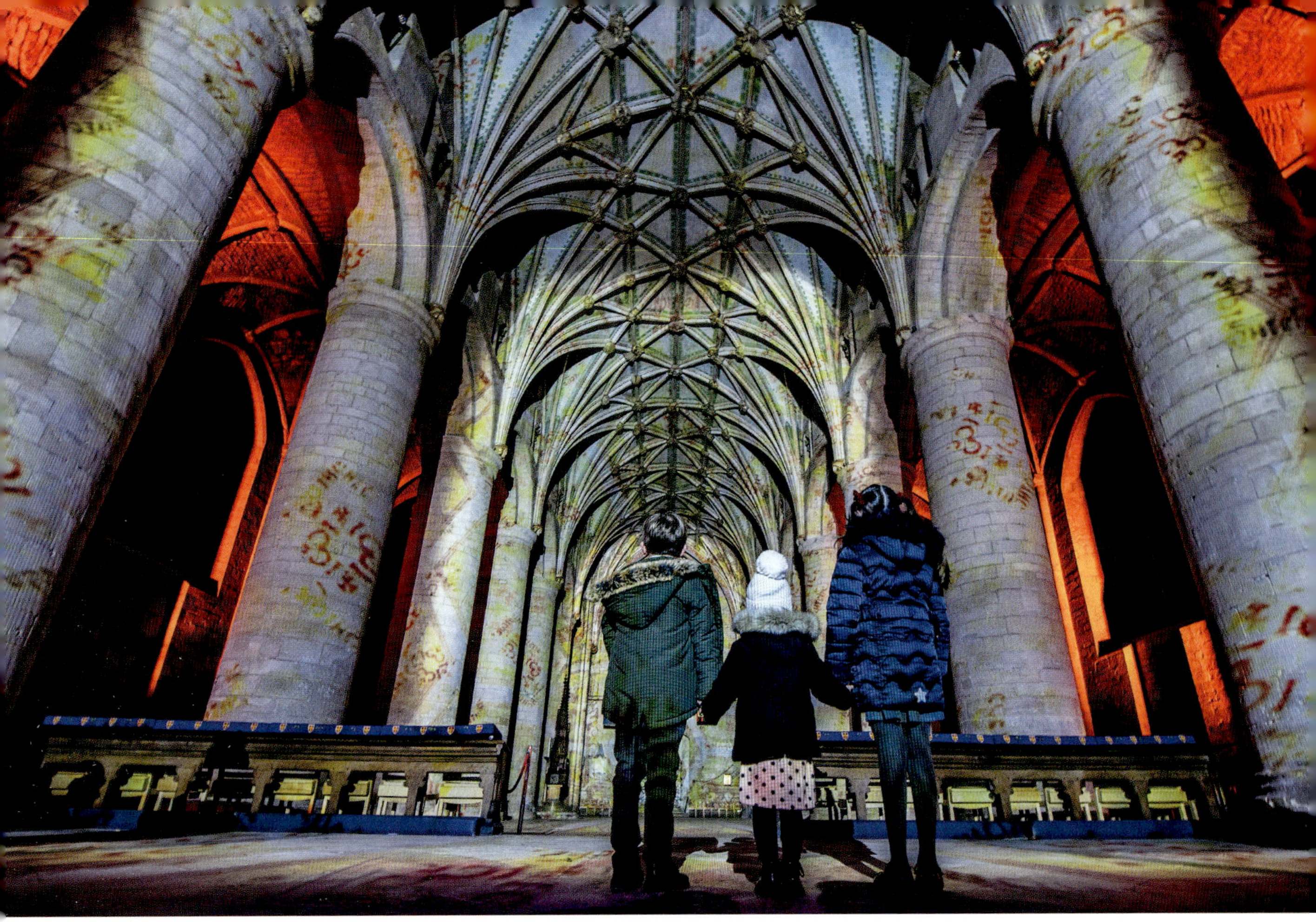

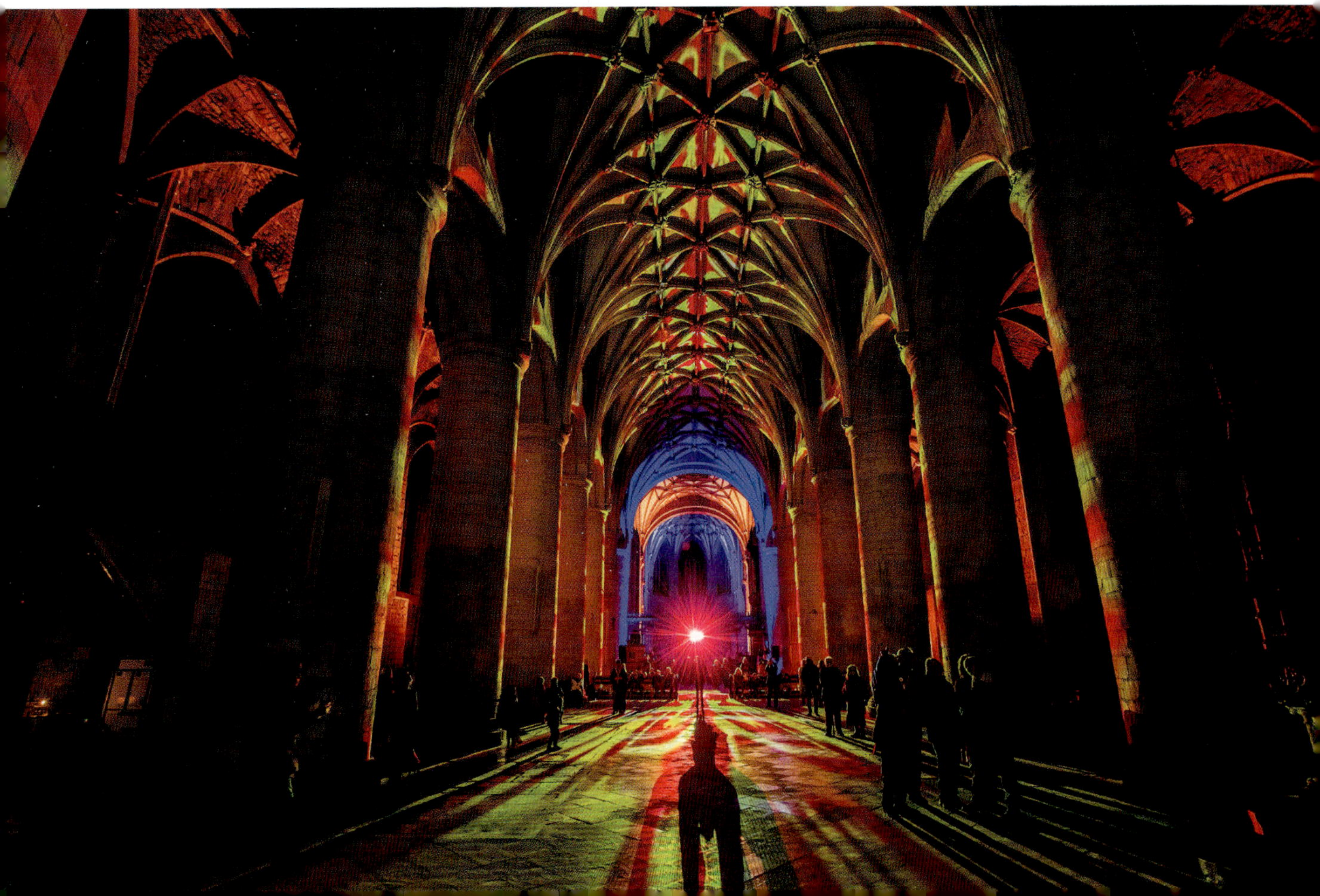

established with the communications department of the Church of England, mainly through the Revd Catherine Williams.[7] This resulted in the Abbey contributing nationally and internationally to services online, both audio as well as visual, especially the morning and evening offices, via the 'Daily Prayer' and 'Time to Pray' apps. Members of the Abbey community welcoming visitors at the north door were beginning to find that some visitors had come because they had seen the services online, echoing the interest evident from the vicar's post bag.

The vicar's third conclusion was that the shape of the church was clearly changing. He felt that this would be seen not only in the liturgy itself but that lay participation would be greater. The nature of ministry itself might change, a situation that 'Celebrate' was already exploring. Moreover, the vicar felt that the Abbey would increasingly be used as a 'resources centre' for surrounding parishes.

However, in the immediate future, and partly as a result of the financial review of 2017, it was agreed to develop and provide a more dynamic and co-ordinated way of raising funds for the Abbey, as well as to centralise existing funds. This scheme was called 'The Abbey Foundation'. At least £1 million a year was required. There were three key aims: firstly, to sustain the Abbey in its role as a place of Christian mission, worship and spiritual sanctuary; secondly to fund and support the Abbey's choirs in the English choral tradition and its music generally; and thirdly to be good stewards of an extraordinarily beautiful and historic church, ensuring excellent maintenance and development where appropriate.[8] There was something symbolic in deciding to formally launch the scheme on Advent Sunday, 28 November – a looking forward to what was to come, although also remaining conscious of the past.

'Locus Iste' is a Latin gradual, based on verses from *Genesis* chapter 28 and *Exodus* chapter 3, used for the anniversary of the consecration of a church.[9] It is sufficiently ancient that a plainsong version of it was almost certainly used at the dedication and consecration at Tewkesbury Abbey in 1121. It has become well known as a beautiful motet by Anton Bruckner.[10]

Locus iste a Deo factus est,
inaestimabile sacramentum,
irreprehensibilis est.

This is the Lord's House,
Which He hath made,
Profoundly sacred,
It is beyond reproach.

As nine centuries of the building of the masterpiece that is the Abbey are celebrated, reflected so aptly in that gradual, so the Abbey is celebrated in a wider sense, too – its community, built on the sure foundation of faith through many generations, that has sustained it through both difficult and uplifting times. The prayer-soaked stones within the Abbey bear abiding witness to both building and community as, under God, the past is celebrated, the present lived and the future embraced.

Opposite: Two images of the Abbey nave during the Festival of Lights in 2021

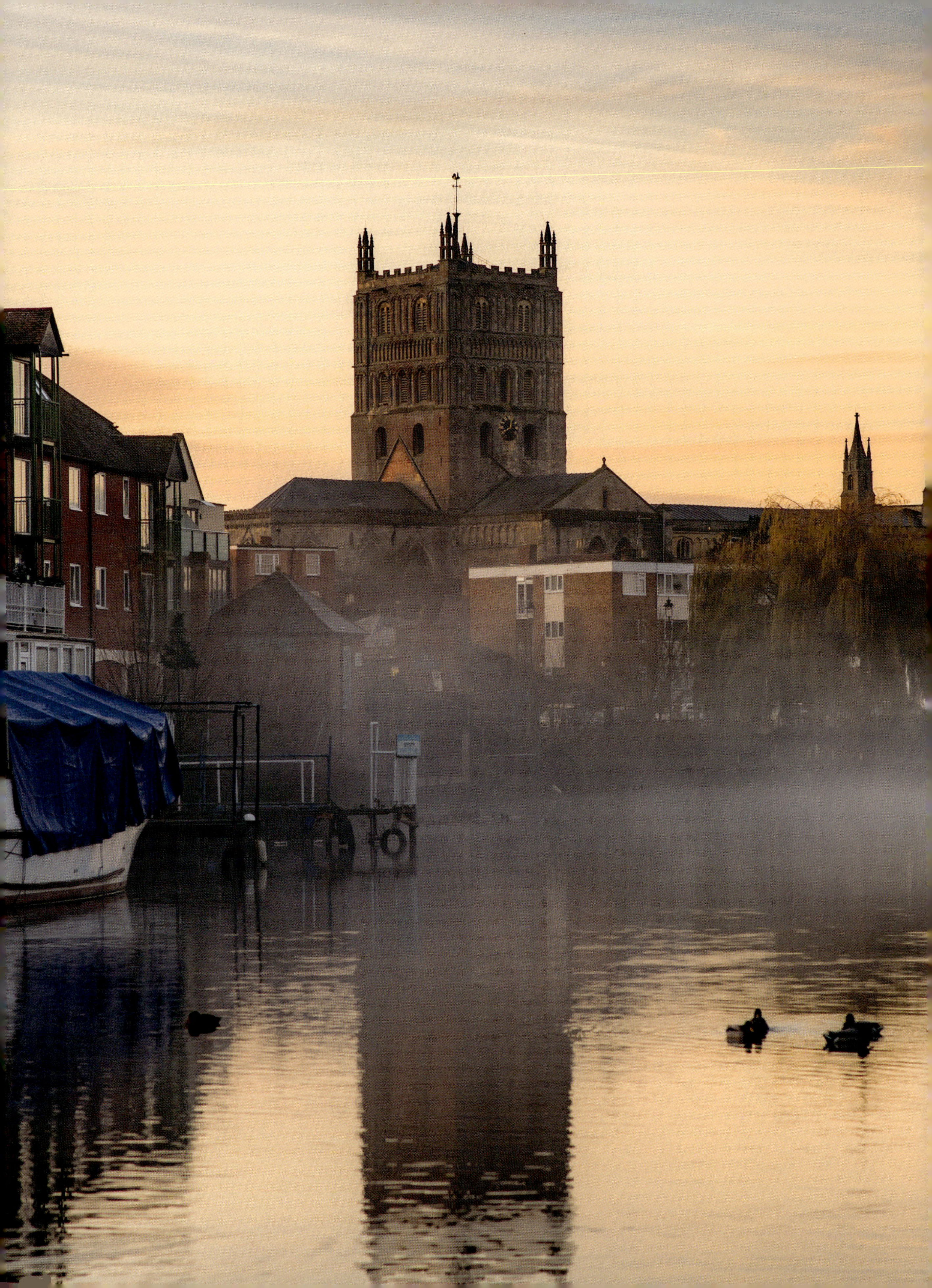

ENDNOTES

Abbreviations

- APCM Annual Parish Church Meeting
- DNB Dictionary of National Biography
- EHS English Historical Society
- FB Atkyns, Sir Robert, *The Founders' Book* (1712 edition, typescript version)
- HAGDRCTA Pat Webley (ed.), Frank Hockaday (et al), *Abstracts from Gloucester Diocesan Records Concerning Clergy at Tewkesbury Abbey 1540–1720*
- TAHAA R.K. Morris & R. Shoesmith (eds.), *Tewkesbury Abbey: History, Art and Architecture* (Logaston Press, 2019)
- THSB Tewkesbury Historical Society Bulletin
- VCH C.R. Elrington (Ed.) *Victoria County History*, Volume 8 (Gloucestershire) (London, 1968)

Chapter One

1. Elrington (ed.), VCH, p. 154.
2. Ingram, *Anglo-Saxon Chronicle* (1993 edition), pp. 232–33, 247; Bolton, Deerhurst Lecture (2006).
3. Beorhtric Tewkesbury burial. See Atkyns (1712) p. 2; Bennett (Cappella edition, 2002) p. 80; Blunt (1898) p. 18. Beorhtric's Wareham burial. See Elrington (ed.), VCH, p. 154 and following; Heighway (TAHAA), p. 6 who, while agreeing that King Beorhtric was buried at Wareham suggests that another Beorhtric, a Tewkesbury lord of the manor, could have been buried in Tewkesbury Church. The possible mix-up may have been deliberate in order to heighten the status and give greater antiquity to Tewkesbury Church.
4. Blair (2005), p. 350.
5. Professor Joyce Hill 'Tewkesbury's Benedictine Heritage', lecture 27 April 2019.
6. Bennett (2002 edition), p. 80.
7. Heighway suggests that there is circumstantial evidence for Tewkesbury Minster being earlier than tenth-century (TAHAA), p. 5. See also Blunt (1898), p. 24; Marples (1992), p. 3.
8. Morris (ed.) and Moore (ed. Vol. 15), Domesday Book Vol. 15 (Gloucestershire) (Folio 163c), pp. 1, 26–33.
9. Prof. Hill, lecture (2019); Atkyns (1712), p.2; Luxford (TAHAA), p. 59.
10. Heighway (TAHAA), p. 5 and endnotes.
11. Prof. Hill, lecture (2019).
12. Bolton; Deerhurst Lecture (2006), p. 11.
13. Blunt, (1898), pp. 21–2 for the legend; Patricia Shakesby has recently (2015–20) researched relevant French material. Her work has not been published.
14. Bennett (2002 edition), p. 56 (although he, too, accepts the Beorhtric legend).
15. Bennett, (2002 edition), p. 57.
16. Blunt (1898), p. 26.
17. See Shakesby's unpublished notes (2008).
18. See Shakesby (2008); M. Hicks (TAHAA), pp. 11–12; Bennett (Capita edition, 2002), p. 81; Gough (1948), p. 3; A. Jones (1987), pp. 22–3; Burial and Founder's Chantry discussed by Morris (TAHAA), pp. 129–30; Lindley (TAHAA), p. 171.
19. Hicks (TAHAA), p. 11.
20. For a discussion of William's claims to the English throne, see M. Ashley, *The Life and Times of William I* (1971), pp. 20–30.
21. R. Allen Brown (1984), pp. 20, 25.
22. ibid.
23. ibid, p. 25.

CHAPTER TWO

1. Atkyns, Translation of *The Founder's Book*, (*Chronica de fundatoribus et de fundatione Eccliae Theokusburiae*) (1712) (typescript p. 3); Luxford, quoting and commenting on *The Founder's Book*. See TAHAA, p. 57.
2. Atkyns (1712) (typescript p. 3); Bennett (Captita edition, 2002), p. 81.
3. Atkyns (1712) (typescript p. 3); Luxford, TAHAA, p. 61.
4. Luxford, TAHAA, p. 58.
5. Luxford, April lecture 2018, pp. 4, 10.
6. Bennett (Capita edition, 2002), Appendix 8 for relevant document; see also Bradley-Birt (1931), p. 45.
7. Luxford lecture (2018), p. 10.
8. Bennett (Capita edition, 2002), p. 95.
9. Bennett (Capita edition, 2002), p. 95; Bettey (TAHAA), pp. 41–2; Bradley-Birt (1931), pp. 44–5.
10. Quoted in Bennett (Capita edition, 2002), endnote 7 on p. 90.
11. Luxford lecture, p. 10, quoting from *The Founder's Book*; Bradley-Birt, p. 153, who notes mason's mark of 'A' can be found on 'many of the lower cornices of the stonework', which may or may not be Alfred's mark.
12. For a more detailed reconstruction of how the Romanesque Tewkesbury Abbey was built, see Prof. Malcolm Thurlby (TAHAA), pp. 89–108.
13. Birdsall & Morris (TAHAA), pp. 272–73.
14. Bryant (2017) article.
15. Cranbourne Monograph, p. 2.
16. Gough, Birdsall & Morris (2010), p. 13.
17. Wimborne Minster Church took 60 years; Christchurch Priory *c.*55 years, whereas it is maintained that both Romsey Abbey and Shrewsbury Abbey took ten years or less to be 'sufficiently complete'. Thirteen English and Welsh cathedrals, whose Romanesque building times are at least roughly (and in some cases precisely) known, took an average of roughly 45 years each to be built.
18. Thurlby (TAHAA), p. 91.
19. Birdsall & Morris (TAHAA), p. 264.
20. Gough, Birdsall & Morris (2010), p. 23.
21. Atkyns (1712 typescript), p. 4; Hicks (TAHAA), pp. 12–13.
22. Bradley-Birt (1931), p. 50; Bennett (Capita edn, 2002), p. 95.
23. Bennett (Capita edn, 2002), p. 95.
24. Blunt (1898), p. 40.
25. Hicks (TAHAA), p. 12.
26. Blunt (1898), pp. 31–33; Hicks (TAHAA), p. 12.
27. Bradley-Birt, p. 56, records that 'the bishops of those same four sees were present 800 years later when the eighth centenary was celebrated'.
28. The *Samson Pontifical* may well have also been worked on by some Canterbury trained scribes. It is generally agreed that it went to Worcester during the eleventh century, where additional material was added. It is evidently the work of several different hands. See Gittos (2013), Appendix, p. 287.
29. Helen Gittos in conversation with the author, March 2019.
30. Pontifical, 'An office-book of the Western Church containing forms for rites to be performed by bishops or those of equivalent status'. See Lee *(*1877), p. 289; Sykes (ed.) (1987), p. 796, col ii. In the case of the *Samson Pontifical*, some rubrics are provided, others not; sometimes at the end of the prayer the comment 'Oratio' meaning a sermon or homily. Often the notes would dodge from one rite to another – in this case between the dedication of a church and a novitiate being accepted into a monastery.
31. Bradley-Birt (1931), pp. 55–8; Blunt (1898), pp. 34–8; John Harper, lecture (2021). Their suggestions, recent research, together with a modern translation of the *Samson Pontifical* reveal a general form of what probably occurred 900 years ago.
32. John Harper, lecture (2021).
33. Galbraith (1967), pp. 86–101.
34. The suggestion concerning the Abbey west end arose from the Romanesque west front of St James Priory, Bristol, whose founder and patron, Robert Fitzroy, was lord of the manor of Tewkesbury and who insisted that St James Priory should be a cell of Tewkesbury Abbey. It seemed likely that the west fronts of the two churches might be similar. There was a study of a variety of Romanesque west fronts around England and Wales as well as discussions with Professor Malcolm Thurlby and also Neil Birdsall, FSA, Tewkesbury Abbey architect and surveyor for 30 years.
35. Harper, Fitzhamon lecture (2021).
36. Blunt (1897), pp. 34–8 suggests that 'the common people' would have been present inside the Abbey. Helen Gittos has said, in conversation with the author (July 2019), that there is no evidence for that at all and that it would have been most unlikely. John Harper in his 2021 Fitzhamon lecture suggests that no laity would have been allowed in at this point other than possibly the lord of the manor.
37. Bradley-Birt (1931), p. 57; Gittos (2013), p. 233. Blunt (1897), p. 36 suggests that 'time had been' when three alphabets were used. Greek, Latin and Hebrew, 'as the title on the Cross was written in those three tongues', but Hebrew was 'early discontinued'.
38. Gittos (2013), p. 234.

39 Chrism Oil is olive oil mixed with balsam. It is consecrated by a bishop. Anointing with it represents the gift of the Holy Spirit.
40 www.catholic hierarchy org/bishop/btheulf.html.; Bradley-Birt (1931), p. 55 and Blunt (1897), p. 34 say little – the dedication date is quoted from the *Annals of Tewkesbury,* which is accepted as inaccurate; A. Jones corrects this (1987), p. 23.
41 Gittos (2013), pp. 237–40. See also Harper, Fitzhamon lecture (2021).
42 Harper, Fitzhamon lecture (2021).
43 ibid.
44 Gittos (2013) pp. 237–40; Harper, Fitzhamon lecture 2021.
45 Harper Fitzhamon lecture (2021).
46 See the *Book of Revelation*, Chapter 21, v 14. 'And the wall of the city has twelve foundations, and on them are the twelve names of the twelve apostles of the Lamb' (NRSV, 1998 edition).

Chapter Three

1 Bettey (TAHAA), pp. 41–2.
2 ibid, p. 44. See also Bennett (2002 edition), p. 95.
3 Originally married to Henry V, Holy Roman Emperor, Matilda later married Geoffrey, Count of Anjou, after her first husband's death in 1125.
4 See John of Worcester (ed. Weaver), *Anecdota Oxoniensa,* pp. 56–7, quoted in Poole (1955), pp. 139–40.
5 For Worcester version, see Florence of Worcester, *Chronicle* (EHS) Vol. ii, pp. 119–20, in Page and Willis-Bard (eds.), *VCH, Worcestershire* Vol. 4 (1924), pp. 376–90 online. For Tewkesbury version, see John of Worcester (ed. Weaver), p.603. Also Elrington (ed.) *VCH, Gloucestershire* Vol. 8 (1968), Borough of Tewkesbury entry, pp. 110–18, online. See also Bennett, (2002 edition), p. 15, endnote (to chapter 2) no. 19.
6 St James' Priory, Bristol, *Visitors' Booklet* but also Bettey (TAHAA), p. 41.
7 Gough (1948), p. 9; Blunt, though for 'steeple' read 'tower' (1898), p. 108.
8 Bennett (2002 edition), p. 95; Bettey (TAHAA), p. 44.
9 Marples (1992 edition), p. 15; Masse (1900), p. 8; Blunt (1898), p. 40–2; Bradley-Birt (1931 edition), p. 64. He adds a description of the tomb.
10 For the terms of the Charter see Bennett (2002 edition) appendix one, pp. 287–88.
11 See Poole (1955), p. 330 footnote.
12 Ibid, p. 348, footnote 4 (quoting Pipe Roll 30 Hen II, Introduction, p. xxix). For a labourer, see p. 414; usual wage a silver penny a day. There were 240 pence per £. Another 60 pence would represent five shillings or 25 pence today – a total of 300 pence altogether. No work on Sundays nor major Holy Days, thus taking up the additional 65 days of the year. But the worker worked for free on his lord's land as part of his vassalage. Thus £1 25p per year income is probably too high an estimate.
13 Bennett (2002 edition), p. 82.
14 Bradley-Birt (1931), p. 157.
15 Bennett (2002 edition), p. 82.
16 A. Jones (1987), p. 57.
17 M. Harris (1989 edition), pp. 1–2.
18 Elrington (ed.), Vol. 8, pp. 167–69.
19 Hicks (TAHAA), pp.13–14; Bennett (2002 edition), p. 9; Blunt (1898), p. 44; Bradley-Birt (1931), pp. 66–7. Evidence from *The Annals of Worcester, The Annals of Winchester* – which almost certainly give a distorted account – and *The Annals of Tewkesbury.* Bennett (2002 edition), quoting Dugdale's *Monasticon,* mentions two charters given to the Abbey, p. 82.
20 Masse, pp. 8–9; Blunt (1898), pp. 45–6; Bradley-Birt (1931), pp. 69–70.
21 For life of Abbot Alan, see especially Harris, pp. 1–4; Bennett (2002 edition), pp. 95–6; Bettey (TAHAA), pp. 44–5; A. Jones (1987), p. 57. His tomb lies close to the door to the Sacristy.
22 Poole (1955), pp. 297–8.
23 ibid, pp. 444–46, 456–58.
24 Blunt (1898), p. 46.
25 Poole (1955), p. 448.
26 ibid pp. 456–57.
27 Bennett (2002 edition), p. 96.
28 ibid.
29 Gough (1948), pp. 4, 22; Masse (1900), p. 9.
30 Bennett (2002 edition), p. 87, quoting Hale's book *History and Analysis of the Common Law* (1713) in which Hale (1609–76) states that seven pairs of these charters were sent to some of the greater monasteries; and that he had seen the one at Tewkesbury, under the seal of that King (John), which differed in a trifling degree from the Great Charter.

31 For details of barons present at Runneymede, go to https.//www.magnacharta.com/bomc/profile-of-magna-charta-sureties-and-other-supporters. Two who held the 'Honour of Gloucester' and who were alive at this time (but were not present) were Countess Isabel of Gloucester, who held the Honour from 1217–18 when she died. She was succeeded by her nephew, Almeric Montfort, son of Countess Isabel's sister, Mabel, who also was not present at Runneymede. He died without an heir in 1221. At that point Gilbert de Clare (I), son of Richard (died 1217) both of whom had been at Runneymede, became earl of a combined earldom of Hertford and Gloucester.

Chapter Four

1. See https.//www.geni.com/people/Amaury-V-de-Montfort-comte-d-Evreux for further genealogical information. Also Hicks (TAHAA) p.13 and family tree.
2. ibid.
3. Bennett (2002 edition), p. 58; for Glamorgan reference, see Poole (1954 edition) pp. 297–98.
4. Hicks (TAHAA), p. 13 (family tree) and p. 16; see also Blunt (1898 edition), p. 46.
5. Blunt (1898 edition), p. 46.
6. R.B. Patterson, Isabella, Suo Jure Countess of Gloucester; DNB (2004) (online edition 2006); also Hicks (TAHAA), p.16; Blunt, (1898 edition), p. 46.
7. Masse (1900), p.9; Blunt (1898 edition), pp. 47, 49–50; also de Clare family tree, Hicks (TAHAA), p. 13.
8. Bettey (TAHAA), p. 45; Bennett (2002 edition), p. 96.
9. Masse (1900), p. 12.
10. H.R.Luard (ed.) *Annales Monastici Vol. I.*, Rolls Series, Vol. 36 (London 1862), 'Annales de Theokesberia AD 1066–1263', pp. 84–6, quoted in Bettey (TAHAA), p. 45.
11. Davis (2013) pp. 136–37; Blunt (1898 edition) pp. 50–1.
12. Morris and Thurlby (TAHAA) (2003), p. 109–10.
13. ibid.
14. Morris & Thurlby [TAHAA] p.112; Elrington, VCH (1968), pp. 154–65; Bennett (2002 edition), p. 83.
15. Neil Birdsall has argued for the probability of an external door here, noting the symmetry between the transept entry to the chapel and the passageway entry, also the perceived need for townsfolk to have external access, which they would not otherwise have had.
16. Morris & Thurlby (TAHAA), p. 111.
17. ibid, p. 112. There is a possibility that one of the chapels was dedicated to St Eustace but this does not appear to have happened. See Morris & Thurlby (TAHAA), p. 116.
18. Bennett (2002 edition), p. 83.
19. Bradley-Birt (1931), p. 162.
20. Davis (2013), p. 139.
21. Page; VCH Vol. 2 (1907), pp. 61–6.
22. Bettey (TAHAA), p. 45.
23. Masse (1900), p. 12; Bennett (2002 edition), p. 83; Morris (TAHAA), p. 145.
24. There is some date discrepancy here. Blunt (1898), p. 55; Bradley-Birt (1931), p.78. For the later visitation, see Blunt p. 55 and A. Jones (1987), p. 33; also Elrington (1968), pp. 110–118.
25. Blunt (1898), pp. 52–4.
26. ibid; See also F.B. Bradley-Birt, p. 162; also Page (Worcs) VCH Vol. 2, pp. 61–6.
27. Bettey (TAHAA), p. 45; Page (Worcs) VCH Vol. 2, p. 62.
28. ibid. also Bradley-Birt (1931), p. 162; Blunt (1898), pp. 52–3.
29. ibid (all three).
30. Bennett (2002 edition), p. 82; Elrington (ed.) (1968), p.110–18; A. Jones (1987), p. 30.
31. Blunt (1898), p. 55; Bradley-Birt (1931), pp. 20, 78; A. Jones (1987), p. 33.
32. Gough (1948), pp. 4–5; A. Jones (1987), p. 33.
33. Elrington VCH Glos Vol. 8, pp. 110–18.
34. Hicks (TAHAA), pp. 25–7; Goodchild (2005), pp. 39–62.
35. Bradley-Birt (1931), pp. 24, 177–79.
36. Morris & Grueninger (2015 edition), pp. 191–93.
37. Bennett (2002 edition), pp. 278–79.
38. Parish Magazine, October 1891.
39. Tavinor (TAHAA), pp. 285–86.
40. There is a discrepancy here. Davis, quoting Michael Altschul, *A Baronial Family in Medieval England. The Clares* (John Hopkins Press, 1965), pp. 61–2, maintains that the bride-price was 5,000 marks (p. 143); Bradley-Birt (1931) says 7,000 marks (p. 78), also Blunt (1898) (p. 55). In the event, Earl Hugh died in 1240, apparently still owing money to the King on the deal.
41. Blunt (1898), pp. 52–3.
42. Masse (1900), pp. 13, 74; also Gough (1948), p. 23; Webley (2020), p. 1.
43. Morris & Thurlby (TAHAA), p. 114.
44. Webley (2020), p. 1
45. Atkyns (1712), p. 3, quoted by Morris & Thurlby (TAHAA), pp. 114, 116.
46. Atkyns (1712), p. 6.
47. ibid; also Gough (1948), p. 4; Masse (1900), pp. 9, 80.
48. Bettey (TAHAA), p. 17.
49. Bennett (2002 edition), pp. 87–8.
50. ibid.
51. ibid, p. 96.
52. A. Jones (1987), p. 33; Elrington, VCH (1968), pp. 110–18.

53 Bennett (2002 edition), p. 96; Bettey (TAHAA), pp. 46–7.
54 Bettey, p. 47.
55 ibid; also Bennett (2002 edition), p. 96.
56 Atkyns (1712), p. 6; Masse (1900), p. 80; Blunt (1898), p. 62.
57 Bennett (2002 edition), p. 82. Copy of the Charter, p. 306.
58 Davis (2013), p. 270.
59 ibid, pp. 271, 275; Atkyns (1712), p. 6.
60 ibid, pp. 282–86; Gough (1948), p. 5; Blunt (1898), pp. 64–5.

CHAPTER FIVE
1 Gough (1948), p. 5; See also Atkyns (1712), p. 6.
2 Masse (1900), p. 10.
3 Gough (1948), p. 5; Atkyns (1712), p. 6.
4 Gough (1948), p. 10; Masse (1900), pp. 10, 79; Blunt (1898), pp. 63–4.
5 Bettey (TAHAA) (2003), p. 46.
6 VCH Page (ed.); Gloucestershire (1907), Vol. 2, pp. 61–66.
7 Simon Jenkins (1999), p. 228; see also A. Jones (1987), p. 37.
8 Birdsall & Morris, (TAHAA) (2003), p. 21; detailed discussion, Brown (TAHAA), pp. 183–96.
9 Elrington VCH, Gloucestershire, (1968), Vol. 8, pp. 154–65; Cox (1914), p. 206; A. Jones (1987), pp. 37–8.
10 The *Arma Christi* might include a range of objects, for example, chalice, torch, lantern, sword, flagellum, Veronica's veil, reed sceptre, pitcher of gall and vinegar, hammer, spear.
11 Brown (TAHAA), p. 193.
12 The figure might also be Elizabeth Montacute, Eleanor's daughter-in-law, bur unlikely. See Brown (TAHAA), p. 188.
13 The shields include those of Tewkesbury Abbey, Despeer, England, as adopted by Edward III, although only the top right quarter survives, and it is probable that it was not a part of the original window and was inserted later; Munchensi (through Joan Munchensi, Countess of Pembroke, there is a link to the de Clares) and finally d'Amory (Elizabeth de Clare had made Lord (Roger) d'Amory her third husband in 1317).
14 Morris (TAHAA), pp. 138–42.
15 Blunt (1898), p. 66–7 and fn. The tomb of Eleanor and her husband was transferred to what had been the abbot's personal manor house at Forthampton Court, Forthampton where it can still be seen.
16 For detailed discussion on vaulting, see Morris (TAHAA) (2003), pp. 131–38; see also Bradley-Birt (1931), pp. 216–18.
17 Birdsall & Morris (TAHAA) (2003), p. 262.
18 Bettey (TAHAA), p. 48.
19 Blunt (1898), p. 69; Gough (1948), p. 16. See also Lindley (TAHAA) (2003), pp. 168–69; also Luxford (TAHAA) (2003), p. 59.
20 Information from Louise Soothill-Ward of Slapton Parish Council, November 2020.
21 Atkins (1712), p. 3; confirmed by Bennett (2002 edition), p. 97; Morris (TAHAA), pp. 124–30 discusses the Perpendicular style involved while Lindley (TAHAA), p. 171 discusses its place in the Abbey's history. See also Vince in (TAHAA) (2003), pp. 197–204.
22 Hayman (2010), pp. 5–13, 26. One also appears on the street side of the Gage Gates, a 1959 replacement of the one on the original gate of 1712.
23 Morris (TAHAA), pp. 129–30, 136.
24 Morris (TAHAA) (2003), pp. 129–30; Blunt (1898), p. 76.
25 Blunt (1898), p. 76; Luxford's lecture, p. 21; Lindley (TAHAA) (2003), pp. 172–76; Included in the dedication were Saints Mary Magdalene, Barbara and Leonard. Floor discussed by Vince (TAHAA) (2003), p. 198.
26 On fifth earl's death, see Masse (1900), p. 11; On Lady Isobel's death and burial, see Atkyns (1712), pp. 10–11. See also Bennett (2002 edition), p. 137 and her requests p. 85. Atkyns says burial on her father's right-hand side; Bennett that she was buried in the Warwick Chantry.
27 Atkyns (1712), pp. 3–4; Bennett (2002 edition), p. 85, except that the latter suggests that the Priory was given by Henry Beauchamp, duke of Warwick. For Abbot Parker's death, see Bennett (2002 edition), p. 97.
28 Atkyns (1712), pp. 9, 12; Bradley-Birt (1931), pp. 118–19; also Bannister (1925), p. 83.
29 See Masse (1900), pp. 12, 79; also Bradley-Birt (1931), pp. 118–19, 120–25; also discovery of possible Duke Henry tomb, Bannister (1925), p. 83.
30 Bettey (TAHAA) (2003), pp. 50–1; Atkyns (1712), p. 11; Masse (1900), p. 12 and Bennett (2002 edn), p. 86.

CHAPTER SIX
1 Masse (1900), p.12; Gough (1948), p.6.
2 Jacob (1985 edition), p.547.
3 Details in Goodchild's 160-page study of the battle. *Tewkesbury. Eclipse of the House of Lancaster – 1471* (2005), plus local booklets. See also Smurthwaite, *The Ordnance Survey Battlefields of Britain* (1984), pp.114–16; A. Jones (1987), pp.42–4; Bradley-Birt (1931), pp.135–44; Bennett (2002 edition), pp.295–300.
4 The Sun in Splendour badge was King Edward IV's personal favourite. When he was earl of March, he had won the Battle of Mortimer's Cross, Herefordshire, in February 1461, against the Lancastrians, when he and his comrades had seen what appeared to be three suns in the sky. See Morris (TAHAA), p.130.

5 McN. Rushforth, *Transactions of BGAS, Vol. XLVII*, pp. 131–49; see also Blunt (1898), pp. 91–2; Goodchild (2005), pp. 131–35.
6 Masse (1900), p. 14.
7 See Rushforth for detailed discussion, '*The Burials of Lancastrian Notables in Tewkesbury Abbey After the Battle, 1471*' (Bristol and Gloucestershire Arch. Soc., Vol. XLVII); see also Goodchild (2005), pp. 60, 65, 89, 110 and 113.
8 Atkyns (1712), p. 13; Bannister (1925), p. 46; Blunt (1898), p.84; Bradley-Birt (1931), pp. 125–7; Hick (TAHAA) (2003), p. 30.
9 Masse (1900), p. 12; Blunt (1898), p. 85.
10 Masse (1900), p. 12; Gough (1948), p. 8; Bradley-Birt (1931), pp. 129–31.
11 Bradley-Birt (1931), pp. 127–9.
12 Luxford Lecture (2018).
13 Bennett (2002 edition), p. 97.
14 Bennett (2002 edition), pp. 97–8; Luxford, lecture (2018), p. 3; Bettey (TAHAA) (2003), pp. 67–8.
15 Bennett (2002 edition), pp. 38–9; dendrochronological evidence for the re-roofing by Dr Andy Moir in his Friends' lecture, 13 March 2021.
16 Bettey (TAHAA) (2003), p. 65.
17 Bradley-Birt (1931), pp. 24, 177–79.
18 Bettey (TAHAA) (2003), p. 67.
19 ibid.
20 See Wilkinson article, THSB (2013), pp. 8–14.
21 Litzenberger (1998), p. 80.
22 Bettey (TAHAA) (2003), p. 68.
23 Ibid. Bettey's evidence is based on letters and papers of King Henry VIII. Other authorities (e.g. VCH Vol. II, Bradley-Birt, Bennett,) base their evidence on Sir William Dugdale, (*Monasticon Anglicanum. A History of the Abbies and other Monasteries in England and Wales*, Vol. II, 1819 edition). He suggests that there was a brief rule by an Abbot John Walker in 1531, about whom nothing is known. Examination shows that Dugdale inserted this information on hearsay evidence only. Bettey's evidence appears considerably stronger. In his endnotes to his chapter (Note 18) he specifically states that 'the list and dates of the last three abbots given in VCH Glos Vol. II, p. 65, is incorrect.'
24 ibid. The Act of Supremacy 1534 made Henry VIII 'Supreme Head' of the Church of England. This Act was repealed by Queen Mary. Queen Elizabeth I and her successors were given the title 'Supreme Governor' of the Church of England by the Act of Supremacy, 1558. Thus, there was no clash with the Bible, where Jesus Christ is explicitly named as Head of the Church.
25 Morris and Grueninger (2015), p. 176; see also Lacey (1972 edition), p. 147.
26 See discussion in Morris and Grueninger (2015 edition), pp. 193–94.
27 Bank of England figure, based on £1 in 1534 equivalent to £922.79p, in 2017. For Tewkesbury's comparative wealth, see Julian Luxford Lecture of April 2018, p. 3.
28 Bennett (2002 edition), p. 108, note 3.
29 Bettey (TAHAA) (2003), p. 69.
30 Starkey (2004), pp. 527–30.
31 Letter to Cromwell, 24 October 1535 quoted by Morris and Greninger (2015 edition), pp. 191, 193).
32 see Joanna Denny; *Anne Boleyn. A New Life of England's Tragic Queen*; London; Piatkus Books (2007 edition).
33 Litzenberger (1998), p. 80.
34 Luxford (TAHAA) (2003), p. 53.
35 Bennett (2002 edn), pp. 102–5; Bettey (TAHAA), pp. 70–2.
36 Bennett (2002 edn), Appendix 15, pp. 322–24 for details.
37 Wilkinson THSB No. 22 (2013), p. 13; see also A. Jones (1987), pp. 53–4; Bennett (2002 edition), pp. 102–109; also appendix 15, pp. 322–24.
38 Litzenberger (1994), Introduction, pp. x–xii.

Chapter Seven

1 A. Jones (TAHAA) (2003), p. 75.
2 Bennett (2002 edition), pp. 104–5.
3 Warmington (1997), p. 19.
4 Bettey (TAHAA) (2003), p. 72; Bannister (1925), p. 44.
5 A. Jones (TAHAA), p. 81.
6 See Webley (HAGDRCTA), Hockaday PRO (Chantry Cert. 22, No. 61, 23; No. 52).
7 Webley (ed.) (HAGDRCTA), where Sherwood is named as 'Priest and Curate'; also a witness to Alexander Pyrry's Will For Davis, see TA list; also Bennett, p. 158. For Greene, who witnessed a number of Wills including that of Edward Tyndale, see Webley, Hockaday Abstracts. Referred to as 'Curate'.
8 A point made by the Abbey archivist, Pat Webley.
9 Bradley-Birt (1931), pp. 129–31; Gough (1948), p. 8.
10 Bettey (TAHAA), pp. 72–3.
11 Philip Lindley dated the cadavar carving. He and Neil Birdsall, the Abbey's former Surveyor, agree about the effigy's deficiencies. (Lindley TAHAA, pp. 180–82).
12 Briggs (1983 edition), pp. 121, 128.
13 Elrington, VCH, pp. 167–69.
14 Litzenberger (1994), Introduction, p. x.
15 Briggs (1983 edition), p. 121; Litzenberger (1994) p. xii; Beaver (1998), p. 148.

16 Blunt (1898), p. 108.
17 Litzenberger (1994), p. 4.
18 Elrington (VCH), pp. 154–65.
19 Litzenberger (1994), p. 6.
20 A. Jones (TAHAA), p. 78.
21 Litzenberger (1994), p. 126; Aldred (TAHAA), p. 210.
22 A. Jones (1987), p. 25.
23 Masse (1900), p. 56.
24 Bennett (2002 edition), p. 274; Aldred (TAHAA), p. 210.
25 Litzenberger (1998), p. 93.
26 Beaver (1998), p. 149.
27 ibid, p. 126.
28 Litzenberger (1994), Introduction, p. xiii endnote 30; Masse (1900), p. 16; Bennett (2002 edition), p. 119; Aldred (TAHAA), p. 209.
29 Masse (1900), p. 16; Bennett (2002 edition), p. 119.
30 Aldred (TAHAA), p. 209.
31 A. Jones (TAHAA), p. 79.
32 Litzenberger (1994), p. xii; Masse (1900), p. 16; Elrington (VCR), pp. 122–31.
33 The term 'Puritan' was coined during the 1560s, see Briggs (1983 edition), p. 120.
34 See Masse (1900), p. 16; Beaver (1998), pp. 78, 79; A. Jones (1987), p. 68.
35 Aldred (TAHAA), pp. 209–10.
36 Litzenberger (1994), p. 88.
37 Masse (1900), p. 17; Litzenberger (1994), p. 96; Blunt (1898), pp. 112, 113.
38 See Patterson & Bishop, Chartered Architects, 'An Outline History of the Abbey House, Tewkesbury and its Adjoining Buildings' (1964).
39 Beaver (1998), pp. 144–45.
40 ibid, pp. 158, 180–89.
41 Warmington (1997), p. 15.
42 Gough (1948), p. 11; Masse (1900), p. 17; Bennett (2002 edition), p. 119; Aldred (TAHAA), p. 209.
43 According to Bannister (1925), p. 72; see also Bennett (2002 edition), pp. 275–6; Webley (2020), p. 1.
44 Beaver (1998), p. 133.
45 Litzenberger (1994), p. 116.
46 Gough (1948), p. 8.
47 Aldred (TAHAA), p. 206. Also Litzenberger (1994), p. 103.
48 Beaver (1998), p. 81.
49 Litzenberger (1994), pp. 129–32 for some applicants.
50 Aldred (TAHAA), p. 207.
51 Litzenberger (1994), pp. 112–13, 123, 126–27, 138 ref. meals for Archdeacon's visitations.
52 ibid, p. 126; Aldred, p. 210.

53 Elrington, VCH, pp. 154–65.
54 Beaver (1998), pp. 158, 182–83.
55 Masse (1900), p. 55; Blunt (1898), p. 109 footnote.
56 Beaver (1998), pp. 140, 185, 186.
57 ibid.
58 Litzenberger (1994), p. 116; Aldred (TAHAA), p. 210.
59 Beaver (1998), pp. 186–87.
60 ibid, pp. 184, 188.
61 Briggs (1983), p. 140.
62 A. Jones (1987), p. 67.
63 Beaver (1998), pp. 77, 187–88.
64 A. Jones (1987), p. 68.
65 Davies (1959 edition), pp. 190–4.
66 Warmington (1997), p. 113.
67 Bennett (2002 edn), p. 159; Beaver (1998), pp. 225–28, 231–32.
68 Churchwardens' Accounts for 1645, p. 317.
69 Beaver (1998), p. 230.
70 ibid p. 225.
71 A. Jones (1987), p. 76.
72 Bennett footnote 3, p. 144.
73 GRO. D2688, f.93v., quoted in Beaver (1998), p. 216.
74 Bennett, (2002 edn), fn. 15, p. 165; Beaver (1998), pp. 218–19.
75 Aldred (TAHAA), p. 206; A. Jones (TAHAA), p. 82.
76 A. Jones (1987), p. 75; Beaver (1998), p. 230; Eisel (TAHAA), p. 238.
77 Beaver (1998), pp. 230–31.
78 ibid, pp. 231–32.
79 ibid, pp. 254–55.
80 Davies (1959 edition), p. 197.
81 ibid, p. 198.
82 Aldred (TAHAA), p. 209.
83 K. Jones (TAHAA), p. 243.
84 Beaver (1998), p. 229.
85 Churchwardens' Accounts, 1661, p. 359.
86 Beaver (1998), pp. 249–50.
87 Elrington, pp. 154–65; Loosley (article, 2017), p. 22.

Chapter Eight
1 Clark, p. 10.
2 Briggs, p. 154.
3 Bennett, p. 159.
4 Churchwardens' Accounts, pp. 367, 372, 380–81, 386–87.
5 Churchwardens' Accounts, pp. 365–66.
6 Beaver, p. 229.
7 GRO. TBR A ½, p. 43; also Beaver, p. 229.
8 Churchwardens' Accounts, p. 359.
9 Churchwardens' Accounts, pp. 380–81.
10 Masse, p.20; Rushforth, p. 147.

11 Aldred (TAHAA), p. 209.
12 Churchwardens' Accounts 1685, pp. 171–74.
13 Gough, pp. 10, 46; Masse p. 17; Blunt p. 104; detailed comment by Birdsall & Morris (TAHAA), p. 263; also Churchwardens' Accounts, pp. 471–74.
14 Aldred (TAHAA), p. 210.
15 Bennett, p. 159.
16 TA Archives.
17 University College, London; *Records of Four Tewkesbury Vicars,* vol. 9; Sermons on Public Events and Occasions 1691–1708; Vol. 15; Pious Maxims, Meditations and Occasional Observations, relevant passages both found in Beaver, pp. 317–18.
18 Briggs pp. 154–55.
19 Churchwardens' Accounts, 1690, pp. 485–86.
20 George Clark, p. 166.
21 Churchwardens' Accounts, pp. 498–500.
22 A. Jones (TAHAA), p. 83.
23 Churchwardens' Accounts, 1663–1680.
24 Churchwardens' Accounts, p. 462.
25 ibid, p. 553.
26 Churchwardens' Accounts (Vestry), p. 527.
27 Bradley-Birt, pp. 225–26; Masse, p. 62.
28 Bennett (2002 edition), p. 119; Dendrochronological analysis given by Dr Andy Moir in a Friends' lecture, 13 March 2021.
29 Masse, p. 30; Banister, p. 23.
30 Aldred (TAHAA), p. 210.
31 Aldred, (TAHAA), p. 209.
32 Bennett (2002 edition), p. 277; Aldred, p. 208.
33 Aldred, (TAHAA), pp. 207–8; Elrington, pp. 154–65, Masse, p. 18; Gough, supported by Webley, maintains the marble was not cut until 1730. See p. 23; Webley (2020), p. 1.
34 Webley (2020), p. 1.
35 J. Birdsall (TAHAA), p. 227; Elrington, pp. 154–65; Bennett, Appendix 17, p. 328.
36 Churchwardens' Accounts, p. 20.
37 Bennett, p. 159.
38 TA Archives.
39 Webley transcription, Churchwardens' Accounts, p. 23.
40 ibid.
41 Vestry Minutes 1736, p. 24.
42 Elrington, pp. 154–65.
43 Williamson, p. 99.
44 ibid.
45 ibid.
46 Gough p.21; Masse, pp. 18, 98.
47 Aldred (TAHAA), p. 205.

48 K. Jones (TAHAA), p. 243; Williamson, p. 99.
49 Williamson, pp. 99–100.
50 Vestry minutes 1737, p. 25.
51 North, p. 51.
52 J. Birdsall, (TAHAA), p. 232.
53 Masse, p. 30; Dixon, Cockburn, Webley, pp. 38–9; A. Jones, p. 130; Aldred (TAHAA), p. 216.
54 A. Jones (1987), p. 130.
55 Aldred (TAHAA), p. 216.
56 Webley, p. 40.
57 ibid, p. 41.
58 Bennett (2002 edition), p. 167; Appendix 23, p. 345.
59 Aldred (TAHAA), p. 206.
60 Bennett (2002 edition), p. 162.
61 Elder (2016), p. 77; Bennett (2002 edition), pp. 278–79; Bradley-Birt, p. 25; C.R. Elrington, pp. 154–65.
62 Bennett (2002 edition), p. 162, also fn. 27 p. 168.
63 Bannister, p. 65; Bennett (2002 edition), p. 162.
64 Bannister, p. 65.
65 Bennett (2002 edn) fn. 3 p. 144; Aldred (TAHAA), p. 211.
66 Camp & Round, p. 11.
67 Vestry Minutes, 1794.
68 Masse, p.98; Williamson, p.100; K. Jones (TAHAA), p.243; Bannister (1923), p. 40.
69 1827 Vestry Minutes transcription, Webley p. 160.
70 Verey (ed.), pp. 12–13.
71 Verey, (ed.), p. 33.
72 Masse, pp. 18–19, 32; Bennett, (2002 edition), pp. 123–25; Brown (TAHAA), p. 184; Aldred, (TAHAA), pp. 211–13.
73 Blunt p. 123; Bennett (2002 edition), pp. 135–36.
74 Blunt, p. 124; Bennett (2002 edition), p. 140.
75 Masse, p. 73.
76 Bennett (2002 edition), p. 10.
77 ibid, p. 13.
78 ibid, p. 1.
79 1830 Vestry transcription, pp. 169–70.
80 Bennett (2002 edition), p. 59.
81 A. Jones, 1987, p. 133.
82 A. Jones (TAHAA), p. 84.
83 Bennett, (2002 edition), pp. 83, 106–8, 109.
84 Bennett (2002 edition), p. 273.
85 Woodward, *The Age of Reform 1815–1870*; Clarendon (2nd edition, 1962), pp. 502–21

CHAPTER NINE

1. Bennett (ed.), p. 313; A. Jones pp. 134–35. The Revd Edward Foley was the new clergyman.
2. Bennett (ed.), p. 372.
3. Bennett (ed., Vol. ii), pp. 12–3; Erlingham (ed.), pp. 122–31.
4. Erlingham (ed.), pp. 122–31; fn. Tewkesbury Yearly Register Vol. II, p. 87; Williamson, p. 100; Webley (transcript) p. 186.
5. K. Jones (TAHAA), p. 243; Masse, p. 98; Williamson, p. 100.
6. Vestry Meeting 14 January 1858 (transcription. P. Webley). Jabez Jones was the offending Organist.
7. Bennett (ed., Vol ii) p. 10.
8. Whitney, pp. 10, 306–12.
9. A. Deuchar, *Unpublished Notes on the work of Brian Torode and Others*, Tewkesbury Abbey Archives.
10. Pakenham, p. 105.
11. Deuchar, Webley, *Unpublished Notes*.
12. See Aldred (TAHAA), p. 214 quoting *Tewkesbury Abbey. A Record of its Restoration and Re-opening in 1879 GRO P329/1 CW4/10 n.p.*
13. Masse, p.24; Elrington (ed.), pp. 122–31.
14. Webley transcription, Vestry minutes 1915, pp. 261–63.
15. Beeson p. 6; Masse p. 55; Bennett p. 400, Eisel (TAHAA), p. 241; Bannister, p. 38; David Bagley lecture; Webley, *Vestry Meeting Minutes 1704–1928* (VMM) Folio 79, p. 185.
16. C. Elrington, (ed.), pp. 154–65.
17. Aldred (TAHAA), p. 207; A. Jones (2012), pp. 4–9.
18. Bennett, 1848 Register; Webley (2020) p. 1; Aldred (TAHAA), pp. 207–8; Tim Jeffreys constructed the plinth.
19. *The Tewkesbury Weekly Record*, 14 May 1864.
20. *Gloucestershire Chronicle*, 6 August 1864.
21. Aldred (TAHAA), p. 214–15; Webley, *Unpublished Notes*.
22. J. Birdsall (TAHAA), p. 232; Webley, *Unpublished Notes*.
23. *Gloucestershire Chronicle*, 6 August 1864.
24. ibid.
25. A. Jones (2012), pp. 27–8.
26. A. Jones (2012), p. 3.
27. Vestry Minutes, transcribed Webley, p. 218.
28. *Tewkesbury Weekly Record*, 11 March 1871.
29. A. Jones (2012), p.3; Aldred, p. 215.
30. Aldred (TAHAA), p. 215, A. Jones (2012), p. 3.
31. Aldred (TAHAA), p. 216; Webley; Vestry Minutes 1877 Transcript. Litzenberger's transcripts, Churchwardens' Accounts, refers to Tudor and Stuart sidesmen (see pp. 30, 44, 45, 46 etc.) Also, a Vestry meeting on 26 April 1698 appointed two.
32. GRO 329/1 CW 2/4; P329/1 CW 3/6 quoted in Aldred p. 217.
33. Masse, pp. 60–1.
34. Vestry Minutes, 1874, p. 218. Scott was knighted in 1872.
35. A. Jones (2012), p. 3.
36. ibid, p.9; Aldred (TAHAA), p. 216.
37. Bannister, p. 36.
38. GRO P329 CW 4/30, quoted by Aldred (TAHAA), p. 215.
39. ibid, p. 215.
40. Brasses designed by J.T.D. Niblett. See Bannister, p. 79; Masse, p. 76. Medieval tiles copies produced by Godwin of Lugwardine. See Aldred (TAHAA), p. 215.
41. Bradley-Birt pp. 118–19.
42. Webley, *Unpublished Notes to CEW*.
43. Bannister (1925), p. 31.
44. Bannister (1925), p. 85.
45. K. Jones (TAHAA), pp. 243–45; Webley, *Unpublished Notes to CEW*.
46. *Tewkesbury Register*, Saturday 4 March 1876; Aldred (TAHAA), p. 214–15; Webley, *Unpublished Notes*.
47. Bannister, p. 17.
48. Aldred (TAHAA) Notes, No. 75, p. 308.
49. Eisel (TAHAA), p. 241.
50. Elrington (ed.), pp. 154–65.
51. Lectern inscription reads. '*Hoc Donum dedit Carolus Gulielmus Grove Easter 1878. Ad Gloriam Dei et conservandam memoriam Uxoris Carissima*' – that is, 'Charles William Grove presented this gift, Easter 1878, to the glory of God and to perpetuate the memory of his dearly loved wife.' Frances, his wife, died in 1886. Masse, p. 44.
52. Rushworth claims that it was 1875. Masse, p. 20; Bennett p. 121; Rushforth, p. 147. This discrepancy explained by Masse, who suggests that from 1875 to 1878 the font was 'in one of the two North East Chapels', i.e. St Edmund's Chapel, before returning to the nave. John Coney's 1820 print shows the font in the nave, but two bays further east than the present font.
53. Bennett, p. 121.
54. Presented by Benjamin and Mary Thomas, he a long-serving churchwarden.
55. Morris, Webley and Kendrick p.11; J. Birdsall (TAHAA), p. 233.
56. Methven, p. 28.
57. Webley (transcription) Vestry Meetings, 1878.
58. later Chancellor of the Exchequer, MP for East Gloucestershire, including Tewkesbury.
59. Gough, p. 23; Bradley-Birt, pp. 222–23; Webley (2020), p. 1.
60. Aldred p. 216; Webley (2020), p. 1.
61. Masse p. 20; confirmed by Methven, p. 28; Bradley-Birt, p. 230; Jones (2012), p. 20; Bannister, p. 18.
62. Methven, p. 28; Bannister, p. 18.

63 Pulpit presented by Mrs Glynn, Archdeacon Robeson's sister, given in memory of her husband, Edward. Bannister, 1923 handbook, p. 23 and history, c.1925, p. 83.
64 Gough, p. 15; Gough, Birdsall, Morris, p. 16; Aldred (TAHAA), p. 216; Webley (Transcription) Vestry 1914, p. 259.
65 Bradley-Birt, pp. 218–19; Aldred (TAHAA), p. 217; Bannister, p. 31.
66 Gough p. 10; Masse pp. 23–4; A. Jones (TAHAA) p.86 and also (2012), p. 171; Birdsall (TAHAA), p. 234. Helen Healing, daughter of Samuel, Abbey House tenant, died in 1915, and was the last person interred in the churchyard, by special dispensation.
67 Elrington (ed.), pp. 154–65; A. Jones, 1987, p. 171.
68 Williamson, p. 101; K. Jones (TAHAA), p. 245.
69 Webley, Vestry transcription, 4 August 1887, p. 233; change of name, Peterson (TAHAA), p. 251.
70 Masse, p. 98; Gough, p. 15; Gough, Birdsall and Morris, p. 15; Bradley-Birt, p. 231; Roy Williamson, pp. 105–6; Peterson (TAHAA), p. 251.
71 Peterson (TAHAA), p. 252.
72 Bannister, 1923, p. 54. In 1887 it replaced a stained glass window of the crucifixion given in memory of a Mr Sproule. That window was moved to the present Lady Chapel and again in 1945. Currently stored in the roof space. For other windows, see Masse, p. 46; Bannister, p. 32.
73 Webley, Parish Mags 1888 and 1891. The Holy Cross Chapel window was in memory of H.P. Moore by his brother, C.W. Moore.
74 Peterson (TAHAA), p. 256. Grove is buried in a Tewkesbury cemetery mausoleum.
75 D. Bagley lecture; Litzenberger (ed.), pp. 41, 51, 71, 78, 90.
76 Bannister noted (pp. 38–9) that, 'The exterior of the clock-face is 8ft in diameter, the minute hand is 2ft 11 ins long; the pendulum bob weighs 2 cwt and the striking hammer is about 60 lbs.' Webley, transcription from June 1887 Parish Magazine; Bannister (1923), p. 54; Beeson, p. 7; Masse, p. 53; Aldred (TAHAA), p. 216; Bannister (1925), pp. 38–9, D. Bagley lecture.
77 The committee included Lord Tennyson, Robert Browning, Matthew Arnold, Professor Huxley, Sir John Millais and Holman Hunt among others, including unnamed ladies. Memorial executed by Hugh Armstead, RA. See Gough, p. 19; Masse, p. 67; Birdsall (TAHAA), p. 226; Bannister (1925), p. 54.
78 Masse, p. 50; Aldred (TAHAA), p. 217; A. Jones (2012), p. 28; *Parish Magazine* February 1893.
79 A. Jones (2012), p. 28.
80 North, p. 16. Married in 1893, George became King in 1910. For 1908 visitors, see Tavinor (TAHAA), p. 276.
81 Webley. Parish Magazine for 1892.
82 Further details, see endnote 95.
83 Bannister (1925), p. 65; Webley, *Unpublished Notes on Harry Alsager Sheringham*.
84 Aldred (TAHAA), p. 216, Webley photographic evidence. Screen given by Archdeacon Robeson and nephew E.F. Glynn in memory of the Archdeacon's sister, Mrs Harriet Glynn who had earlier given the pulpit in her husband's memory. Masse, pp. 45–6; Bannister (1923), pp. 34–5; Bannister (1925), p. 83; Bradley-Birt, p. 231.
85 Glazed in memory of Mary Moore, wife of Benjamin Moore, a long-serving churchwarden. Masse, p. 53; Bannister (1925), p. 39.
86 Given by the Revd W.H.F. Hepworth in memory of his mother; Masse p. 69; Bannister (1925), p. 56.
87 Bannister (1923), pp. 44–5; Bannister (1925), p. 56.
88 Webley, Vestry transcription, 1896; Masse, p. 64.
89 A. Jones, pp. 170–71; Bannister (1923), p. 18.
90 Elrington (ed.), pp. 110–18; A. Jones (2012), p. 28.
91 The window was designed and executed by a Mr Powell of Blackfriars, London. See Birdsall (TAHAA), p. 226; Bannister (1925) p. 54–6. Near the window's base are the de Clare arms, the see of Worcester and those of Tewkesbury Abbey. At the top are the Masons arms, the Corporation of Bricklayers, the Plasters' Company and the Carpenters.
92 A. Jones (1987), p. 183.
93 Tavinor (TAHAA), p. 275.
94 Tavinor (TAHAA), p. 276; Bannister (1925), p. 42. The window is a memorial to Alan Rokeby Law, given by Miss Plumer Price and Miss Butler. The window also has the arms of Scotland, St Andrew and Edmund Ironside, St Margaret's grandfather.
95 Webley, transcription of January 1914 Vestry minutes, p. 255; J. Birdsall (TAHAA), pp. 230–31. From the 1920s until the Girls' Grammar School he founded was absorbed into Tewkesbury Comprehensive School in 1972, girls and Old Girls of the School visited the Abbey on Commemoration Day for a service, including the School Hymn. '*For All the Saints*' – traditionally, each girl or Old Girl visited the Archdeacon's memorial and gently patted his head!
96 Bannister (1925), p. 22; Parish Magazine, February 1908 – Sheringham and Robeson are seen either side of the outside of the west doors; Crockford, p. 999; Aldred (TAHAA), p. 217; Tavinor (TAHAA), p. 276.

97 Webley transcription, Vestry minutes 1915, pp. 261–63.
98 Bannister (1925), p. 65; Tavinor (TAHAA), p. 277.
99 Tavinor (TAHAA), p. 277.
100 Webley (transcription), Parish Magazine 1914, p. 257; Crockfords (2014–15), p. 999.
101 Birdsall (TAHAA), p. 234; Webley (transcription), p. 273.
102 The other Calvary, at the south-east corner of the Abbey grounds, is a memorial and gravestone to the Revd Ernest Smith's mother, Mrs Elizabeth Smith, who died in 1916. Birdsall (TAHAA), p. 234; Webley *Unpublished Notes to CEW*.
103 Bannister (1925), pp. 35–6; Webley (transcription) 1919 Vestry, p. 273
104 Dixon et al, p. 6.

CHAPTER TEN

1 e.g. Lionel Gough, J.B. Bradley-Birt, J.H. Blunt and J. Charles Cox.
2 Brown (TAHAA), pp. 183, 187–88; Methven, p. 29; Aldred (TAHAA), p. 218; Bannister pp. 51-2; Sarah Brown was sometime head of research for places of worship at English Heritage; Gordon McNeil Rushforth, a medieval stained glass scholar, advised. Fragments window supervised by Walter Tower of Kempe & Co.
3 Morris (TAHAA), p. 139; Bannister, p. 74.
4 Tavinor (TAHAA), pp. 277–78; Bannister (1925), pp. 35–6; Elrington (ed.), pp. 154–65.
5 Tavinor (TAHAA), p. 279; Blessed Sacrament information by Pat Webley.
6 Eisel (TAHAA), p. 241; Beeson, p. 6; Malcolm Taylor, Tower Captain, Tewkesbury Abbey. Today there are currently 145 rings worldwide of 12 bells.
7 Gough, p. 16; Webley (2020), p. 2.
8 Tavinor (TAHAA), pp. 281–82.
9 ibid p. 282.
10 Aldred (TAHAA), p. 218; Tavinor (TAHAA), p. 282; Methven, p. 29; A. Jones (1987), p. 171; Friends of Tewkesbury Abbey website.
11 Birdsall & Morris (TAHAA), p. 257. The first was an archaeological excavation of the land alongside the south wall of the south aisle, following the purchase of the Abbey House estate in 1885. See Friends' Annual Report, 1940 and Parochial Magazine, May 1940.
12 Gough, Birdsall and Morris, p. 13; Parish Magazine, May 2001, p. 1.
13 See Friends' Annual Report, 1936; also July 1954 Parish Magazine.
14 Webley (2020), p. 2; the altar and reredos in memory of a Miss Holmes; the award winning wooden cope chest was by Tim Jeffree.
15 Tavinor (TAHAA), p. 281; Crockford, p. 999.
16 Tavinor (TAHAA), p. 280.
17 Webley (2020), pp. 1–2.
18 Gough, p.19; see also Gough, Birdsall, Morris, p. 19.
19 The plaque is said to be of polished Hopton Wood sandstone from Derbyshire, carved by G. Kruger Gray, CBE, RA, painter, sculptor and medallist.
20 Tavinor (TAHAA), p. 282; Gough, p. 12; J. Birdsall (TAHAA), pp. 230–31, 234; Aldred (TAHAA), p. 218.
21 S. Brown (TAHAA), p. 186; Tavinor (TAHAA), p. 282.
22 Gough, Birdsall and Morris, p. 11; Tavinor (TAHAA), pp. 280, 283. Canon Gough is buried externally between the Lady Chapel apse and the sacristy.
23 Tavinor (TAHAA), p. 283–84.
24 *Tewkesbury Register*, Saturday 12 May and Saturday 19 May 1945 editions.
25 Williamson p. 102; K. Jones (TAHAA), p. 245; Methven p. 29. The work was done by J.W. Walker and Son. Contributions to the cost were made by the Pilgrim Trust and the Friends of Tewkesbury Abbey among others.
26 A. Jones (TAHAA), p. 171; Methven, p. 29; Gough, Birdsall & Morris, p. 13, Tavinor (TAHAA), p. 284.
27 Eislen (TAHAA), pp. 241–42; Methven, p. 20 Bells recast by John Taylor & Co Ltd of Loughborough, the tenor now weighing over 27 cwt. and having a diameter of 53 inches.
28 Tavinor (TAHAA), p. 285; Elrington (ed.), pp. 154–65.
29 Tavinor (TAHAA), p. 286.
30 Parish Magazine, May 1969.
31 Tavinor (TAHAA), p. 286.
32 Massey, *Church Times*, 24 May 2013; Whitney, p. 303–5.
33 Methven, p. 30.
34 Birdsall & Morris (TAHAA), p. 267.
35 Williamson, p.107; Peterson (TAHAA), p. 253.
36 Peterson (TAHAA), p. 253; Williamson, p. 108.
37 Birdsall & Morris (TAHAA), pp. 267–68.
38 Birdsall & Morris (TAHAA), pp. 265–66; June 1983 Parish Magazine, p. 18.
39 Parish Magazine, November 1987, p. 1; Webley (2020), p. 2.
40 Tavinor (TAHAA), p. 287; Parish Magazine, Oct. 1983, p. 1.
41 Parish Magazine, April 1982, p. 3.
42 Floodlighting. Pat Webley in correspondence, March 2021.
43 Crockford's (2014 edition), p. 618.
44 Birdsall & Morris (TAHAA), p. 270; Parish Magazine, December 1986, p. 17.

45 Whitney, p. 305; Parish Magazine, March 1991, p. 9; Tavinor (TAHAA), p. 287.
46 Crockford's (2014 edition), p. 618. When he left Windsor he was appointed a Lieutenant of the Victorian Order (LVO) by HM the Queen.
47 ibid, p. 854. He was a graduate of Durham and Oxford Universities, held a Master of Music degree from King's, London and was an ARCO.
48 Beeson, p. 6; Eislen (TAHAA), pp. 241–42.
49 Webley (2020), pp. 2, 3. New Chapel altar given by the Friends of Tewkesbury Abbey. The Guild of St Raphael gave the Holy Oils aumbry.
50 Given in memory of George Taylor, a long-serving Abbey server (died 1991). 'Our Lady Queen of Peace' was given by the Friends; Webley, *Unpublished Notes to CEW*.
51 Birdsall & Morris (TAHAA), pp. 266, 268–69; Parish Magazine, March 1992, p. 11; also January 1993, p. 8, also April 1993, p. 2; Gough, Birdsall, Morris, pp. 16–18; Parish Magazine June 1994. Sacrament house and hanging pyx executed by Dan Windham of Hackford, Norfolk; pyx and its metal cage were made by Keith Jameson of Winchcombe in memory of the Revd Gerald Edmunds.
52 Given in memory of Ted Francis Potter.
53 Our Lady of Tewkesbury sculpture in memory of Bill Moore. Birdsall & Morris (TAHAA), p. 268; Parish Magazine, November 1996, p. 4; Also Parish Magazine, July 1997 pp. 1–3.
54 APCM reports 1994, p. 6; 1995, p. 10.
55 APCM report 1996, p. 11.
56 Peter Murphy, who created the ikon, painted the Crucifix in St Faith's Chapel and the hanging Crucifix in the Upper Room. The ikon given in memory of Mrs Honor Patrick by her husband, George.
57 Beam for dossal in place 1995 (Parish Magazine, February 1996, p. 5). Dossal in place in 1996 (Parish Magazine, April 1996, p. 11).
58 Parish Magazine, May 1995, p. 15 and July, p. 13; APCM Report 1995, p. 15. Bracket by Tim Jeffree.
59 Birdsall &Morris (TAHAA), p. 281; Parish Magazine, August 1996, p. 11–12. Paid for by Stella Norton's generous bequest.
60 K. Jones (TAHAA), p. 245; Gough, Birdsall & Morris, p. 22; Methven pp. 30–1. Kenneth Jones and Associates of Bray, County Wicklow, Ireland.
61 Birdsall & Morris (TAHAA), p. 262; Methven, p. 31.
62 Tavinor (TAHAA), pp. 287–88; Methven p. 30.
63 Parish Magazine, November 1999, p. 1. Original outside the United Methodist Church, Tewksbury, Mass.
64 APCM report 1998, p. 11.
65 APCM report 1997, p. 28.
66 Parish Magazine, April 1999, p.1; APCM report 1999, p. 11; APCM report, 2000, p. 6.
67 APCM reports 2000 p. 26; 2002, p. 28.
68 Parish Magazine, December 1999, p. 1; Gough, Birdsall & Morris, p. 14.
69 APCM report 2000, p. 36.
70 Parish Magazine, March 2000; Birdsall & Morris (TAHAA), p. 270. The blacksmith was Peter Crownshaw of Tenbury Wells (Worcs).
71 APCM report 2002, p. 9.
72 ibid, p. 12.
73 Tavinor (TAHAA), pp. 287–88; junior church activities developed. However, POPITS for mothers and toddlers began later, in 2007.
74 Once more, the ironwork was created by craftsman blacksmith Peter Crownshaw. See Gough, Birdsall & Morris, p. 17; Birdsall & Morris (TAHAA), p. 270.
75 Gough, Birdsall & Morris, p. 18; APCM report 2002, p. 27.
76 Parish Magazine, December 2002, p. 7; Crockford's (2014 edn), p. 956. Paul Williams was a master of theology from St Andrew's University; trained at Westcott House, Cambridge.
77 Given by the Friends of Tewkesbury Abbey.
78 APCM report, 2006, p. 17.
79 Whitney, p. 306. Dean Close School and the Abbey began a sporting relationship in 1896 when, for three years, they played football matches, at one point each raising two teams. The Abbey pitch was on the Ham. (See *Decanian*, 1896–98.) Since the 1950s, Dean Close Chapel Choir have always sung at least one Choral Evensong a year in the Abbey.
80 ibid, p. 309.
81 The EU ceremony was broadcast live to 39 countries. The Choir has also produced two BBC Radio 2 Choristers of the Year. Laurence Kilsby (2009) directed by Benjamin Nicholas and Cassian Pichler-Roca (2018) directed by Simon Bell.
82 Bennett's Annual Register 1833, pp. 140–42; Bradley-Birt, p. 207; Gloucestershire Media *The Great Gloucestershire Flood, 2007*; 2007; pp. 7–8, 39, 127; Borough of Tewkesbury Overview and Scrutiny Committee *Review of the Council's Response to Flooding*, July 2007, especially pp. 6–8; APCM report 2009, pp. 9–10.
83 Birdsall & Morris (TAHAA), pp. 262–63.
84 APCM reports 1993, pp. 24, 29; 1995, p. 30.
85 The Revds David Coulton, Carolyn Methven and Charles Whitney, and later a Reader, Katie Etherington.

86 The Pioneer Curate was the Revd Ed Sauven, who, with others, has since set up a Fresh Expression of Church in Stroud. The Abbey Curate was the Revd Sebastian Hamilton who moved on to St Stephen's Church, Tivoli, Cheltenham.
87 The disagreement was eventually resolved by the Consistory Court. For dedication, see Order of Service, 27 January 2013. The Cross and candlesticks were re-silvered in memory of Joan Webley; the seating and credence table was given in memory of the parents of the Revd Charles and Mrs Anne Whitney.
88 Carleton Etherington was also appointed a Fellow of the Guild of Church Musicians about this time, marking his 20 years at the Abbey, in recognition of his outstanding work, notably the high standards of musicianship that he had encouraged and maintained.
89 APCM, that is the Annual Parochial Church Meeting. There had been four churchwardens 1721–9 and again in 1736. In 2019 Peter Smail and Nikki Hawley were joined by John Parkes. In 2020, Nikki Hawley and John Parkes were joined by Nancy Oakes
90 Abbey Parish Bulletins 12 & 19 July 2020.
91 Abbey Parish Bulletins 20 & 24 December 2020; Vicar's report to Council of the Friends of Tewkesbury Abbey, 6 February 2021.

CHAPTER ELEVEN

1 Triduum means a religious observance lasting three days. In the Abbey's case, the Triduum refers to the fairly well-known Liturgical Paschal Triduum that lasts from the evening of Maundy Thursday to Easter Sunday, beginning with the Holy Communion that usually includes feet-washing on the Thursday evening and the taking of the consecrated wafers to an altar of repose where a watch is kept. On Good Friday a cross is solemnly unveiled and placed on the high altar. Holy Communion is given from the wafers consecrated the previous evening. At the Easter Vigil, late on Holy Saturday, the Pascal candle is solemnly blessed and lighted at the beginning of the first Eucharist of Easter.
2 Girl choristers for Schola Cantorum had been under discussion since at least 2019. Simon Bell, Director of Schola Cantorum, presented a paper examining options and proposals in March 2021. In April, after the Trustees of Tewkesbury Abbey Foundation had approved the idea, there were discussions between Tewkesbury Abbey, Tewkesbury Abbey Foundation and Dean Close Foundation which resulted in the announcement that girls would be allowed to become choristers from September 2021.
3 While the Lord Lieutenant of a county has the right to appoint the Deputy Lieutenants, the Monarch has the right of veto.
4 The thesis title for the vicar's doctorate was. *'Chasing the Lady. The Virgin Mary in Early Modern English Liturgical Texts 1534–1562.*
5 The Abbey Choir sang Haydn's *Missa Brevis Sancti Joannis de Deo* (the Little Organ Mass). Carleton Etherington had become the Abbey organist and minister for music in a staff reorganisation brought about by Covid-19 and the financial pressures that had resulted.
6 COP 26 stands for the 26th United Nations Climate Conference of the Parties organised by the United Kingdom and Italy, 31 October to 12 November 2021.
7 The Revd Catherine Williams is a Christian writer, retreat leader and spiritual director based at Tewkesbury Abbey where her husband, Paul, is vicar.
8 See *Laying Foundations for the Abbey's Future*, a leaflet explaining Tewkesbury Abbey Foundation, published November 2021. Tewkesbury Abbey Foundation was formally registered on 12 December 2019 but it took two years before it could be formally launched. Its chairman was John Jeffreys, a former Abbey churchwarden.
9 A responsorial chant or short anthem. *Locus Iste* is based on the Old Testament stories of Jacob's ladder and his quote. 'Surely the Lord was in this place and I knew it not' (Genesis 28 v. 16) and the burning bush where Moses was told 'put off thy shoes from off thy feet for the place wherein thou standest is holy ground' (Exodus 3, v.5).
10 The Austrian Anton Bruckner's motet was composed in 1869.

BIBLIOGRAPHY

PRIMARY SOURCES

Atkyns, Sir Robert, *The Founders' Book* (dated 1712) (typed copy given by TAA in Founders' Book File)

Bennett, James, *The History of Tewkesbury*, appendices, notably appendices 4–7, 9, 11–15, 17

Bennett, James (ed.), *Tewkesbury Yearly Register and Magazine vol.I* (1830–39) & *vol. II* (1840–49) (Tewkesbury, James Bennett 1840 & 1850)

Churchwardens, *The Churchwardens' Accounts 1563–1624* (Transcribed by hand)

Fendley, John (Ed.), *Bishop Benson's Survey of the Diocese of Gloucester 1735–1750* (The Bristol and Gloucestershire Archaeological Society; 2000)

Fish, Simon, *Supplication for the Beggars*; (?)Antwerp; Johannes Grapheus; 1529 as found in Carroll, Gerald L. & Murray, Joseph E., *The Yale Edition of the Complete Works of St Thomas More* vol. 7; (New Haven; Yale University Press; 1990)

Ingram, Revd J., *Anglo Saxon Chronicle*, reprint of 1823 edition by Longman, Hurst, Rees, Orme and Brown

Litzenberger, C. J. (ed.), *Tewkesbury Churchwardens' Accounts, 1563–1624* (Stroud): Alan Sutton for Bristol and Gloucestershire Archaeological Society, 1994)

Luxford, Julian (ed.), *The Founders' Book: A Medieval History of Tewkesbury Abbey* (Donington: S. Tyas, 2021)

Morris, John (gen. ed.), *Domesday Book: Volume 15, Gloucestershire* (London & Chichester; Phillimore [Vol. ed.: John S. Moore] & Co Ltd, 1982) [Folio 162 to 171]

Munden, Alan (ed.), *The Religious Census of Bristol and Gloucestershire 1851* (Bristol and Gloucestershire Archaeological Society; 2015)

Savage, Anne, *The Anglo Saxon Chronicles* (London: William Heinemann Ltd, 1982)

Webley, Pat (compiled & edited), *Items from Frank S. Hockaday (et al) Abstracts from Gloucester Diocesan Records Concerning Clergy at Tewkesbury Abbey 1540–1720* (unpublished)

— (transcr.), *Parish Magazines 1879–2004 (with gaps)*

— (compiled & transcr.), *Tewkesbury Abbey Clergy 1540–1840* (unpublished)

— (transcr.), *Vestry and Parish Meeting Minutes 1660–1703*

— (transcr.), *Vestry Meeting Minutes 1704–1928*

ALSO:

University College, London University: Special Collection – *Vicars' Papers (of Four Successive Vicars of Tewkesbury)* – 40 volumes c.1680–c.1770 (repository 0 1 0 3).

UNPUBLISHED PAPERS

Morris, Richard K., *West Front Works 2002–2004: Archaeological Report* (2005)

Shakesby, Patricia, *Robert Fitzhamon* (2008)

Various, *Tewkesbury Abbey: A Record of its Restoration and Reopening in 1879*, GRO P329/1 CW4/10 n.p.

Webley, Pat, *Harry Alsager Sheringham 1852–1907* (2019)

—, *Tewkesbury Abbey Altars* (2020)

ARTICLES

Bannister, W.G., 'Harry Alsager Sheringham, Vicar of Tewkesbury 1892–1899' (*Tewkesbury Abbey Parochial Magazine, May 1907*)

Benson, Derek, 'Ripples from The French Revolution in Tewkesbury' *(THS Bulletin No. 23, 2014)* pp. 6–13

Bryant, Richard, 'A Carved Romanesque Springer with Voussoirs in Church House Gloucester Cathedral' (*Journal of the British Archaeological Assn*, 170, 2017) pp. 180–95

Camp, Bill & Round, D., '91 Church Street and J.M.W. Turner' (THS *Bulletin No. 8*, 1999; Woodard Award Winner*)* pp. 5–11

Dixon, John, with Cockburn, Jack & Webley, Pat, 'Gage of the Gates' (*THS Bulletin No. 19*, 2010) pp. 38–9

Devereux, Janet, 'The Poet, The Ploughman, The Kitchener and the Lady' (*THS Bulletin No. 8*, 1999) pp. 21–6

Galbraith, V. H., 'Notes on the Career of Samson, Bishop of Worcester (1096–1112)' *English Historical Review* vol 82 No.322 (Jan 1967) (OUP) pp. 86–101

Gittos, Helen, 'Sources for the Liturgy of Canterbury Cathedral in the Central Middle Ages', *Transactions of the British Archaeological Association* Vol. xxxv (2013), pp. 41–8

Hare, Michael, 'The Anglo-Saxon Church of St Mary, Deerhurst: A Reassessment of the Early Structural History', *Transactions of the Bristol and Gloucestershire Archaeological Society* (2018) pp. 197–235

Hope, William St John, 'Quire Screens in English Churches, with Special Reference to the Twelfth Century Quire Screen Formerly in the Cathedral Church of Ely', (*Archaeologia, 68* 1917) pp. 43–110

Kitabayashi, Hikaru, 'The Burley Family Ancestry of Thomas Mallory', (1425–1469), *(KG 1377, Number (63) online in 2007 for Genealogy Forum (generation 8)*

Litzenberger, C. J., 'The Coming of Protestantism to Elizabethan Tewkesbury', in Collinson, Patrick and Craig, John (eds), *The Reformation in English Towns 1500–1640* (Basingstoke; Macmillan; 1998), pp. 79–93

Loosley, John, 'Royal Arms in Bristol and Gloucestershire Churches' in *Transactions of Bristol and Gloucestershire Archaeological Society.*, Vol. 135, 2017

Methven, C.F., 'Tewkesbury Abbey: Restorations Past and Present' (*THS Bulletin No. 8*, 1999) pp. 27–31

Morris, Richard K., Webley, Pat and Kendrick, David, 'The Easthope Monument Tewkesbury Abbey', (*THS Bulletin No. 17*, 2008) pp. 11–19

Rushforth, G. McN., 'The Burials of Lancastrian Notables in Tewkesbury Abbey after the Battle, 1471' (*Transactions of the Bristol and Gloucestershire Archaeological Society* Vol. XLVII)

Wherrett, Rosemary, 'They Left a Lasting Impression: Some of Tewkesbury's Early Photographers' (*THS Bulletin No. 24*, 2015), pp. 35–42

Wilkinson, Tom, 'Did The Purchase of Tewkesbury Abbey Reflect the Continuation of Traditional Catholic Belief?' (*THS Bulletin No. 22*, 2013) pp. 8–14

LECTURES

Bagley, David, *Tewkesbury Abbey's Bells and Clocks* (unpublished)

Bassett, Steve, *The Origins of the Parishes of the Deerhurst Area* (Deerhurst Lecture 1997, published 1998)

Bolton, Timothy, *Conquest and Controversy: The Early Career of Odda of Deerhurst* (Deerhurst Lecture 2006, published 2007)

Harper, John, *Hallowing God's House in 1121: the Consecration of the Abbey Church at Tewkesbury* (unpublished Fitzhamon Lecture, given to the Friends of Tewkesbury Abbey, via 'Zoom', 24 April 2021)

Hill, Joyce, *Tewkesbury's Benedictine Heritage* (unpublished Annual Fitzhamon Lecture given to the Friends of Tewkesbury Abbey, Saturday 27 April 2019, in the Parish Hall)

Luxford, Julian, *The Founders' Book: Art, Heraldry and History in Late Medieval Tewkesbury* (unpublished Fitzhamon Lecture given to The Friends of Tewkesbury Abbey, Saturday 28 April 2018, in the Parish Hall)

Moir, Andy, *A New Timeline for Tewkesbury* (unpublished dendrochronological lecture to the Friends of Tewkesbury Abbey given via 'Zoom', 13 March 2021)

Mortimer, Richard, *Deerhurst, Pershore and Westminster: Do We Know What We Think We Know?* (the Deerhurst Lecture 2018, published 2019)

Parsons, David, *Liturgy and Architecture in the Middle Ages*, (the Third Deerhurst Lecture 1986, published 1989)

GUIDES AND MONOGRAPHS

Anon, *Cranbourne With Boveridge* (revised Cranbourne: Cranbourne Church edn, 1997)

Anon, *St James Priory – The Story* (HLF, c.2015)

Bannister, W.G. [2], *Handbook and Guide to Tewkesbury Abbey*, Eighth and Octo-Centenary Edition [i.e. 1923], Tewkesbury: P&P by R.A. Newman (late W. North)

Beeson A.W., *Tewkesbury Abbey Tower* (Tewkesbury, BloxSoft, Monograph 1993)

Forsyth, Marie, *The Great FitzHamon: The Story of Robert FitzHamon, The Norman Founder of Tewkesbury Abbey* (Private Pub.; printed in Gloucester by Severn; 2019)

Gough, Lionel, *A Short Guide to the Abbey Church of St. Mary the Virgin at Tewkesbury* (Tewkesbury: Friends of Tewkesbury Abbey, 1948)

Gough, Lionel, Birdsall, Neil and Morris, Richard K., *A Concise Guide to the Abbey Church of St Mary the Virgin* (7th revised edition, Friends of Tewkesbury Abbey, 2010)

Harris, Margaret, *Alan, Abbot of Tewkesbury* (Tewkesbury; Friends of Tewkesbury Abbey; 1989 edn)

Hayman, Richard, *Church Misericords and Bench Ends* (Oxford; Shire Publications, 2009)

—, *The Green Man* (Oxford; Shire Publications, 2010)

Hebron, Stephen, *Life in a Monastery* (London; Pitkin Publishing, 2018)

Knight, Robert (Revd), *A Cursory Disquisition on The Conventual Church of Tewkesbury and its Antiquities* (Reprint: India, Pranava Books; originally 1818)

Marples, Mary J., *The Founders of Tewkesbury Abbey* (Tewkesbury; The Friends of Tewkesbury Abbey; edition 1982 – this ed. 1992)

Masse, H.J.L.J., *The Abbey Church of Tewkesbury with Some Account of the Priory Church of Deerhurst, Gloucestershire* (London: George Bell & Son, 1900)

Petit, J.L., *The Abbey Church of Tewkesbury* (Cheltenham; Henry Davis; 1848)

Robeson, Hemming, *A Short Paper on Tewkesbury Abbey* (Tewkesbury: W. North, 1882)

Strawford, G.F., *A Walk Around and About Tewkesbury Abbey* (Tewkesbury; Tewkesbury Abbey & Tewkesbury Civic Society, 1992, reprinted 2011)

BOOKS

Ashley, Maurice, *The Life and Times of William I* (London; George Weidenfeld & Nicholson Ltd in association with Book Club Associates [BCA]; 1973)

Bannister, W.G., *Tewkesbury Abbey: As It Was and As It Is* (Worcester; Phillips & Probert Ltd., c.1925)

Beaver, Daniel C., *Parish Communities and Religious Conflict in the Vale of Gloucester 1590–1690* (Cambridge, Massachusetts, USA; Harvard University Press, 1998)

Bennett, James, *The History of Tewkesbury* (Tewkesbury: James Bennett, 1st edn, 1830. This ed. by Cappella, 2002)

Blair, (William) John, *The Church in Anglo-Saxon Society* (Oxford; Oxford University Press; 2005)

Blunt, Revd J. H., *Tewkesbury Abbey and Its Associations* (London; Simkin, Marshall, Hamilton, Kent & Co. Ltd. 1st edn 1875, 2nd edn 1898)

Bradley-Birt, F.B., *Tewkesbury: The Story of Abbey, Town and Neighbourhood* (Worcs; Phillips & Probert, 1931 ed.)

Briggs, Asa, *A Social History of England* (Book Club Associates with Weidenfeld and Nicolson; 1983 ed.)

Brown, R. Allen, *The Normans* (London; Guild Publishing edition; 1984)

Clarke, W.K. Lowther, *Liturgy and Worship* (London; SPCK; first published 1932; this reprint 1947)

Cox, J. Charles, *Gloucestershire* (London; Methuen, originally 1914)

Cressy, David, *Bonfires and Bells: National Memory and the Protestant Calendar in Elizabethan and Stuart England* (originally London; Weidenfeld & Nicholson Ltd., 1989. This edn, Alan Sutton Publishing Ltd., 2004)

Davies, Godfrey, *The Early Stuarts, 1603–1660* (Oxford at the Clarendon Press, 1959 edn)

Davis, Paul R., *Three Chevrons Red: The Clares: A Marcher Dynasty in Wales, England and Ireland* (Almeley; Logaston Press, 2013)

Dyde, W., *The History and Antiquities of Tewkesbury* (London; G. Wilkes; second and enlarged edition, 1798)

Elder, David, *Literary Tewkesbury* (Tewkesbury; Tewkesbury Historical Society, 2016)

Elrington, C.R. (ed.), *Victoria County History, Volume 8.* (London; 1968, digitized & on Internet)

Foot, Sarah, *Monastic Life in Anglo-Saxon England c.600–900* (Cambridge; CUP; 2009 edn)

Friar, Stephen, *A Companion to the English Parish Church* (Stroud; Alan Sutton Publishing; 1996)

Gittos, Helen, *Liturgy, Architecture, and Sacred Places in Anglo-Saxon England* (Oxford; OUP; 2015 edn)

Gloucestershire Media, *The Great Gloucestershire Flood 2007* (2007)

Goodchild, Steven, *Tewkesbury: Eclipse of the House of Lancaster – 1471* (Barnsley; Pen & Sword Military, 2005)

Hogan, Rose, *Mrs Craik, Author of 'John Halifax, Gentleman'* (London; Athena Press, 2009)

Jenkins, Simon, *England's Thousand Best Churches* (London; Penguin, 1999)

Jones, Anthea, *Tewkesbury* (Chichester; Phillimore & Co Ltd., 1987)

Lacey, Robert, *The Life and Times of Henry VIII*; (London; Weidenfeld & Nicholson & Book Club Associates; 1972 edn)

Lee, Frederick George, *A Glossary of Liturgical and Ecclesiastical Terms* (London; Bernard Quaritch, 1877)

Mackie, J.D., *The Earlier Tudors, 1485–1558* (Oxford; OUP, 1952)

Morris, Richard K., & Shoesmith, Ron (eds), *Tewkesbury Abbey: History, Art & Architecture* (Almeley; Logaston Press, 2003)

Morris, Sarah & Grueninger, Natalie, *In the Footsteps of Anne Boleyn* (Stroud; Amberley Publishing, 2015 edn)

Page, William (ed.), *VCH (Worcestershire) Vol. 2* (London; 1907, digitized & on internet)

Page, William, & Willis-Bard, J. W. (eds), *Victoria County History (Worcestershire), vol. 4* (London; 1924, digitized and on internet)

Pakenham, Simona, *Cheltenham: A Biography* (London; Macmillan, 1971)

Petit, J.L., *The Abbey Church of Tewkesbury (*Cheltenham; Henry Davies, 1848)

Platt, Colin, *The Architecture of Medieval Britain: A Social History (*New Haven; Yale University, 1990)

Poole, A.L., *Domesday Book to Magna Carta 1087–1216* (Oxford; Clarendon Press, second edn, 1955)

Starkey, David, *Six Wives: The Queens of Henry VIII* (London; Vintage Edition, 2004)

Verey, David (ed.), *The Diary of a Cotswold Parson: the Reverend F. E. Witts 1783–1854* (Gloucester; Alan Sutton, 1986)

Warmington, A.R., *Civil War, Interregnum and Restoration in Gloucestershire* (Woodbridge; The Boydell Press; 1997)

Warner, Kathryn, *Hugh Despenser The Younger and Edward II; Downfall of a King's Favourite* (Barnsley; Pen & Sword History, 2018)

Whitney, C.E., *At Close Quarters: Dean Close School 1884–2009* (Almeley; Logaston Press, 2009)

Williamson, Roy, *The Organs of Gloucester, Tewkesbury and Cirencester from the XVth century* (Cheltenham; Roy Williamson, 1991)

INDEX

Abbey House 51, *57*, 71
Abbeys local to Tewkesbury 2
Abbots of Tewkesbury Abbey 15
   Alan (1186–1202) 8, 27–29, *28*
   Benedict (1124–37) 8, 23, 25
   Fromund (1162–78) 8, 25, 27
   Gerald (Giraldus) (1102–9) 8–10, 14, 23
   Henry (Beoly or Beeley) (1509–34) 8, 56–58
   Hugh (1214–15) 8, 29
   John Abington (or de Salys or Salis) (1443–?1467) 8, 51
   John Cotes (1328–47) 8, 44
   John de Strensham or Streynsham (1468–81) 8, 53, 55
   John Wakeman (or Wick or Wicke or Wyth) (1534–40) 8, 57–60, *67*
   (*see also bishops of Gloucester*)
   Peter (1215–31) 8, 29, 31–32, 34
   Richard Cheltenham (1481–1509) 8, 56–57, 62
   Richard de Norton (1276–82) 8, 37
   Robert (1110–24) 8, 14, 23
   Robert (1182–83) 8, 27
   Robert of Forthampton or Forthington (1232–54) 8, 34–35, 37
   Roger (1137–61) 8, 24–25
   Thomas Chesterton 8
   Thomas de Kemsey (1282–1328) 8, 37, 39, 41
   Thomas de Stoke (1255–75) 8, 37, 41
   Thomas Legh (1347–61) 8
   Thomas Parker (1390–1420) 8, 46, 51
   Walter (1203–14) 8, 29
   William de Bristol (or Bristow) (1421–42) 8
Abingdon Abbey 58
Aelfgar 5
Aelfric 1
Ailes, Adrian 143
Alley, Edward 72

Alfred, monk of Tewkesbury 10
Anne, HRH Princess Royal 144, *144*
Anselm, Archbishop of Canterbury 34
Arthur, Prince of Wales, death and funeral 56
   Masses for 62
Ashchurch parish and chapel/ church 65
Athelweard Meow, lord of Tewkesbury Manor 3
Athelwold, Bishop of Winchester 2
Anglo-Catholic Tractarian movement 95
Anglo Saxon Chronicle 1
Anglo-Saxon Church 2
ap Gurgant, Nicholas 27
Arches, Court of 39
Audley, Sir Humphrey 55
Avon, River 27

Bach, John, bailiff 81
Bagley, David 137
Baker, Percy 114–115
Baldwin, Archbishop of Canterbury 27
Baptists 74
   Collett, Henry 83
Baron, Master Henry 55
barons 1
Barnet, Battle of 53
Bathurst, Earl 104
Bayard, Thomas, commissioner 58
Beard, Stephen 66
Beauchamp, Earl 104
   restoration of Abbey high altar 106
Beauchamp, Lady Anne 51
Beauchamp, Lady Anne, the younger 51
Beauchamp, Henry, duke of Warwick 51
   grave site discovered 103
Beauchamp, Isabella, countess 51
Beauchamp, Richard, fourth earl of Warwick 51
Beauchamp, Richard, fifth earl of Warwick 51

Beauchamp, arms of 51
Beaufort, Edmund, duke of Somerset 53, 55
Beaufort, John, marquis of Somerset 55
Beaulieu Abbey 36
Becket, St Thomas, Archbishop of Canterbury 27
Belcher, John 131
Bell, Simon 139, 141
Benedictine reforms 2, 4
Benedictine Rule 2
Beotric (Brictric, Berthric, Brihtric, Beorhtric) lord of Tewkesbury Manor 4–5
Beotric, possibly from Kent 5
Bible, Authorized King James 72
Birdsall, Neil, Abbey surveyor 124, 125, 128, 132, 138
bishops, Anglican (Church of England)
   reinstated to the House of Lords 79
   removed from the House of Lords 74
   their temporary abolition 74
Black Death 46
Blessed Virgin Mary 4
   dedication of Abbey to 16–22, 36
   increasing veneration of 32
   possible first Abbey Lady Chapel 32
Boleyn, Queen Anne 58, 59
Book of Common Prayer 63, 76, 77
   new version published 79
Boulter, Thomas 83
Boulton, R.L. 111, 113
Boyne, battle of the 83
Bredon Hill quarry 11
Briohtric, King of Wessex 2
Bristol 9, 23, 31
   Cathedral 12, 13, 32
   people kill Hugh 1 Despenser 4
   Priory of St James at 15, 24–25, 80
   monks at Black Death 46
   Prior Robert 57

Bristol Priory cont.
   priory sold 65
   priory surrendered 60
  surrendered to Henry II 26
Bromley, Mrs 89
Brown, Raffaela 143
Brown, Sarah 118
Bruckner, Anton 147
Bryan, Lord (*see de Brien*)
Brydes, Henry 94
Burghersh, Elizabeth 51
Burnett (Somerset) 57
Burney, Fanny (Madame d'Arblay) 89
Bushley (Worcs) 57
  Bredon School 87
  Dowdeswell, William, MP 87
  parish & chapel/ church 65
  Payne's Place 54
  Pull Court 57, 87

Caen stone 11
Calendar
  Gregorian 88
  Julian 87–88
Calvary
  relics said to be from 34
Cambridge Camden Society 99
Camden, Lord Chancellor 89
Canterbury, Archbishops of 2
  Anselm, St 34
  Baldwin 27
  Becket, St Thomas 27
  Cranmer, Thomas 65, 66, 73
  Davidson, Randall 117
  Dunstan, St 2, 119, *119*
    chapel in Abbey 118, *119*
  Langton, Simon 29
  Laud, William 72, 85
  Tait, Archibald Campbell (A.C.) 104
  Warham, William 58
  Wichelsey, Robert 39
Cardiff and castle 9
Caröe, W.D. 114, 115–116
Cartland, Dame Barbara 115
Cartland, James 115
Cartland, Ronald 115
cathedral chapters and deans
  abolished 74
Catholic Emancipation Act 95
Catholicism, Roman 75
  Holy Days & Sundays 76
Charles, HRH Prince of Wales 35, 131

Cheltenham
  Agg-Gardner, James, MP 104
  Dean Close (Memorial) School 97
  Festival, final concert 131
  St Paul's Church 97, 102
  Visitations to 84
Chichester Theological College 122
Christ Church, Oxford University 131
Church of England
  communications department 147
  General Synod 126
Church Street shops, Tewkesbury 51
Civil War 1 75
Clarence, George, duke of 53–56
Clayton & Bell 110
Clergy of Tewkesbury Abbey
  (*see Tewkesbury Abbey, General*)
Close, Francis 97
Collins, Thomas 98, 101, *102*, 106, 109, *109*, 111–113, *112*
Comper, Sir Ninian 122
Congregationalists (*see United Reformed Church*)
Cooke, Richard, Abbey churchwarden, 77, 80, 81
Copner, John 85
Cornwall, Richard, earl of 36
Coulton, David 141
Council of Winchester 2
Coutts, F. 115, 116
Craik, Mrs, memorial 109
Cranbourne, Dorset 5
  Abbey/ monastery/ priory in 3, 7, 9
  priory surrendered 60
  numbers at Black Death 46
  Abbot of 9
  anniversary (900th) of monks leaving for Tewkesbury 131
  church porch 11
  statue of Christ 12
Cranmer, Archbishop Thomas 65, 66
  reforms of 73
Crécy, Battle of 46
Cromwell, Oliver
  becomes Lord Protector 76
  death of 78
  hears Milton Organ 77
  improves ministers' pay 75
Cromwell, Richard 78
Cromwell, Thomas 58, 59
Cross of Christ relics 34

Dallam, Robert, organ builder 87
Dallam, Thomas, organ builder 87
Davidson, Randall, Archbishop of Canterbury 117
Davies, C.D.P. 105, 118–119
Davies, Harry 114–115
Davis, Ruth 129
Dawlish, Devon 5
Dean Close (Memorial) School 97, 134
  Headmaster of 134
  Preparatory School 134
de Brien, Sir Guy (Lord Bryan), KG 46
de Burgh, Hubert, Lord Warden of the Cinque Ports 31, 34, 35
de Burgh, Maud, wife of Gilbert III de Clare 39
de Capella, Richard, bishop of Hereford 16
de Clare, Eleanor 41–45, *42–43*, *45*
de Clare, Gilbert I, earl of Gloucester 29–30
de Clare, Gilbert II, (Red Earl) earl of Gloucester 37, 39
de Clare, Glbert III, earl of Gloucester 37, 39
de Clare, Margaret, marries Piers Gaveston 37
de Clare, Richard I, earl of Gloucester 29–30, 31
de Clare, Richard II, earl of Gloucester, 34, 35
de Clare – arms of 51
de Lacy, Maud, daughter of the earl of Lincoln 35–36
de la Zouch, Lord (William de Mortimer) 43, 44
de Mandeville, Geoffrey, earl of Gloucester (and Essex) 29–30, 31
de Montfort, Amaury (Amauri) v 31
Deerhurst 2
  deer park 27
  parish & chapel/ church of 65, 90
  priory 51, 60, 65, 84
Denny, Tom 132, *133*
Despenser family 40
Despenser, Lord Edward, KG
  'kneeling knight' 45–46, *49*, 51, 124
Despenser Elizabeth, (née Montacute) wife of Henry III Despenser 46
Despenser, Hugh I 41
Despenser, Hugh II (marries Eleanor de Clare) 41, 42–3

168   A HISTORY OF TEWKESBURY ABBEY

Despenser, Hugh III 45–46, 48
Despenser, Isabella 51
Despenser heraldry 46, 82
Devizes Castle 35
Diana, Princess of Wales 131
Dimitrova, Silvia 132, *133*
Dix, Dom Gregory 120
Dissolution of the Monasteries 1, 27, 57, 59, 60, 63
Doddo 1
Domesday Book/ survey 1, 2, 3, 7
Dowdeswell, Richard 72
Down and Connor, Bishop of 55
Drake, Richard 66
Dublin, Bishop (later Archbishop) Grene 16
Dudley, earl of 104
Dunstan, Archbishop of Canterbury 2
Dureford, Abbot of 32
Dyde, William 90

Eastleach (Glos) 62
Edgar the Peaceful, King 2
Edgecombe, Edward 91, 99, 105
Edmund, duke of Somerset, masses for 62
Edmund, earl of Richmond, masses for 62
Edward, Lancastrian Prince of Wales 53, 54, 55
  Masses for 62
Eldon, Lord Chancellor 89
Elfric (*see Aelfric*)
Elizabeth I, Queen 63, 66, 68
Elizabeth II, Queen 1, 35, 123, 124, 132, *142*, 143
Elizabethan Settlement 66
Ely Cathedral 125
Erle, Walter 65
Etherington, Carleton 131, 138, 139, 141
Evangelical revival 95
Evesham Abbey 2

Fairford Parish Church 32, 41
Falcons, Peregrine 137, *137*
Feddon, Bryant 126, *133*
Ferrers, William 68
Fish, Simon 59–60
Fitzhamon, Robert 6, 7, 9, 14
  buried in Chapter House 6, 14
  reburial in Abbey 14, 37
Fitzhamon, Sybil (wife of Robert) 7, 9
Fitzhamon lecture 141

Fitzroy, Robert, first earl of Gloucester 14, *14*, 15, 17, 24–25
  supports Empress Matilda (Queen Maud) 23
Fitzroy (Fitzcount), William, second earl of Gloucester 25, 31
  marries Hawise 26
  three daughters, Mabel, Isabel (Isabella), Amice buried at Keynsham Abbey 26
Fitzroy, Robert (son of William) 26
Flaxley, abbot of 32
Foliot, Gilbert, bishop of London 27
Forthampton
  parish & chapel/ church 65
  Court 58, 104, 123
Founder's Almsmen 27, 66
Founders' Book, The 9
Fox, George 76–77
Franklin, Thomas 65

Gambier Parry, Thomas, reredos 106, 124
Gerald (Giraldus) of Avranches, Abbot of Cranbourne 7, 9
Gillespie, Edward, Lord Lieutenant of Gloucestershire 143
Glamorgan 26, 27
Glastonbury 1
Gloucester
  garrison at 24
  Miles, constable of 24
Gloucester Abbey (*see St Peter's Abbey, Gloucester*)
Gloucester and Bristol Diocesan Assn of Church Bell Ringers 118–119
Gloucester, bishops of
  Bentley, David 132
  Frampton, Robert 84
  Gibson, Dr Edgar 114
  Goodman, Godfrey 72, 73
  Headlam, Arthur 120
  Treweek, Rachel 143
  Wakeman, John 65, 66
  Warburton, William 88
Gloucester Cathedral 10, 99
  painting/ reredos of 106
  Wesley, S.S., organist of 104
Gloucester College (*see Worcester College, Oxford University*)
Gloucester, countesses of
  Amice (weds Richard I de Clare) 31
  Eleanor 41–45, *45*
  Isabel (Isabelle) 27, 31, 34

Isabel Marshall 31, 34–36
Joan of Acre 37
Isobel of Luisgnan 37
Mabel 14, 15, 17
Maud (daughter of earl of Ulster, marries Gilbert III de Clare) 39–40
Gloucester, diocese of, established 60
Gloucester, earls of and lords of the Manor of Tewkesbury
  de Clare, Gilbert I (sixth) 29–30, 31, 36, 42
    first patron buried before high altar 32
  de Clare, Gilbert II (Red Earl) (eighth) 37
  de Clare, Gilbert III (ninth) 37, 39–42
  de Clare, Richard I (fifth) 29–30, 31
  de Clare, Richard II (seventh) 34, 35, 37
  de Mandeville, Geoffrey (fourth) 27, 29–30, 31
  Fitzroy, Robert (first) 14, *14*, 15, 17, 23, 24–25
  Fitzroy (Fitzcount) William (second) 14, 15, 23, 25–27, 68
  John, Prince (third) (given up when marriage annulled) 26–30
Gloucestershire
  estates in 5
  monastic lands in 65
Glynn, Mrs Harriet 106, 111
Godfrey, Francis 113
Goldcliff Priory 51
Gorle, James 93
Great (Gloucestershire) Flood, 2007 1
Great Malvern Priory 2
Grene, Bishop of Dublin 16
Grove, Charles 81, 96, 105, 107, *108*
Grove, Frances Emily 81, *108*
Gunpowder Plot 76
Gupshill Manor 53

Haines, William 73
Hawling, Samuel, burial of 84
Hale, Sir Matthew 29
Hampden, Sir Edmund 55
Hampden Court, London 77
  Milton Organ there 87
Hanford, Mr 99
Harper, Professor John 141
Harris, Renatus, organ builder 87
Hastie-Smith, Timothy 134
Hawise de Beaumont marriage 26
Hayward, Mr Bailiff 85

INDEX 169

Haylward Snow, lord of Tewkesbury
    Manor 3
Healing family 107
Hepworth, Robert 111
Hereford
    Capella, Bishop Richard de 16
    people in, kill Hugh II Despenser 41
Hill, William, Tewkesbury Town Clerk 72
Hill, William, bailiff 81
Hodges, Thomas 93
Hopkins, John, master mason 124
Hugh, lord of Tewkesbury Manor 2
Hughes, Phil 138

Independents (*see United Reformed Church*)
Induni, Bruce 126
Interdict of Pope Innocent III 29
Ireson, David 138
Isabel (Isabelle), daughter of Earl
    William 27, 31
Isabella of Angoulême 31
Ismay, General Lord (Lionel) 'Pug', KG
    123, *123*
Ismay, Laura, Lady 123

Jackson, Francis, organist 122, 124
Jameson, Keith 125
Jeemes, John 83
Jeffree, Tim, master craftsman 121
Jesus (Christ) of Nazareth 1
John, lord of Somerset, masses for 62
John, Prince, (lackland) earl of Cornwall
    (*see King John*)
Johnson, Boris, Prime Minister 141
Jones, Dr Anthia 94
Joseph of Arimathea 1

Kaufman, Mico, sculptor 131
Kemble, Mr, bailiff 85
Kempe, Charles E. 111
Kent, HRH Duchess of 93
Keynsham, Abbot of 32
King's Court of Augmentation 63
Kings of England
    Charles I 75
    Charles II 78, 79
    Edgar the Peaceful 2
    Edward I 35, 37, 39
    Edward II 37, 41
    Edward III 37, 46
    Edward IV 35, 53, 55, 103
    Edward VI 63, 66, 68

George I 84
George III 35, 89
George IV 93
Henry I 10, 14
Henry II 25–26, 27, 31
Henry III 32, 34, 35
Henry VI 51, 53
Henry VII 56, 62
Henry VIII 35, 37, 56, 57, 61, 118
    supreme head of Church of England 58
James I 75
James II 83
John 26–30, 29, 35, 36
Richard II 35, 37
Richard III 35
William I 5
William II, (William Rufus) 5–7
William III 83
William IV 93, 95
King of Scotland
    Alexander I 37
Kingston, Sir William 58

Lambeth Palace 104
Lancastrian army 53–55, 56
Langton, Simon, Archbishop of
    Canterbury 29
Laud, William, Archbishop of
    Canterbury 72–73, 85
Layton, Richard, Dean of York 59
Lechmere, Sir Edmund, BT. 101
Leckhampton stone 115
Leicester, earl of, daughter marries
    William Fitzroy (Fitzcount) 26
Leight, Mrs 71
Leland, John, antiquary 60
Lewknor, Sir John 55
Little Malvern Priory 54
Litzenberger 66–67
Llandaff, Bishop Urban of 16
London, Bishop Bonner of 65
Lord Chancellor 66, 75, 131
Lord Warden of the Cinque Ports and
    Constable of Dover Castle 31
Luxford, Professor Julian 143

Magdalen College, Oxford University
    77, 87
Magdalen Pontifical 16
Magna Carta 1, 29
Major-Generals appointed 77
Malmesbury Abbey, Wiltshire 2

Mandeville, Geoffrey (*see de Mandeville*)
Mansfield, Lord, Lord Chancellor 84
Margam Abbey 15
Margaret, HRH Princess, Countess of
    Snowdon 128, 131
Margaret (Meggota) 35–36
Margaret of Anjou, Henry VI's Queen
    53–54
Margaret, second wife of Hubert de
    Burgh 35
Marriages secularized 76
Martin family 106–107
Martin, Hugh 94
Martin, J. Biddulph 106, 120
Martin, Victoria Woodhull 120–121
Mears, Thomas, of Gloucester 98
Mears & Stainbank 114
Mearson, Nicholas 73
Mildenhall, Suffolk, vicar of 104
Miller, Alec 120
monasteries
    Cranbourne, Dorset 3
    improvements in discipline etc. 2
monks 1, 31
    Opus Dei 4, 23
monarch as appointer of Abbey
    incumbents 66
monasteries 1
    Dissolution of 45
Monk, General 78
Monmouth, duke of, rebellion 83
Montacute, Elizabeth 46, *48*
Moody, Beth 143
Moore, Benjamin 110–111
Moore, Charles, Treasurer, national
    committee 104
Moore, Frederick, Secretary, national
    committee 104
Morris, William 105
Mulock, Dinah, memorial 109
Murphy, Peter 119, 128, 129
Mythe, the 3

Nashdom, Anglican Benedictine Abbot
    of 120
Nazir-Ali, Bishop Michael of
    Rochester 132
Neath Abbey 15
Neville, Anne 51, 53
Neville, Isabelle 51, 53
Neville, Richard, sixth earl of Warwick,
    51, 53

Despenser, Hugh III 45–46, 48
Despenser, Isabella 51
Despenser heraldry 46, 82
Devizes Castle 35
Diana, Princess of Wales 131
Dimitrova, Silvia 132, *133*
Dix, Dom Gregory 120
Dissolution of the Monasteries 1, 27, 57, 59, 60, 63
Doddo 1
Domesday Book/ survey 1, 2, 3, 7
Dowdeswell, Richard 72
Down and Connor, Bishop of 55
Drake, Richard 66
Dublin, Bishop (later Archbishop) Grene 16
Dudley, earl of 104
Dunstan, Archbishop of Canterbury 2
Dureford, Abbot of 32
Dyde, William 90

Eastleach (Glos) 62
Edgar the Peaceful, King 2
Edgecombe, Edward 91, 99, 105
Edmund, duke of Somerset, masses for 62
Edmund, earl of Richmond, masses for 62
Edward, Lancastrian Prince of Wales 53, 54, 55
  Masses for 62
Eldon, Lord Chancellor 89
Elfric (*see Aelfric*)
Elizabeth I, Queen 63, 66, 68
Elizabeth II, Queen 1, 35, 123, 124, 132, *142*, 143
Elizabethan Settlement 66
Ely Cathedral 125
Erle, Walter 65
Etherington, Carleton 131, 138, 139, 141
Evangelical revival 95
Evesham Abbey 2

Fairford Parish Church 32, 41
Falcons, Peregrine 137, *137*
Feddon, Bryant 126, *133*
Ferrers, William 68
Fish, Simon 59–60
Fitzhamon, Robert 6, 7, 9, 14
  buried in Chapter House 6, 14
  reburial in Abbey 14, 37
Fitzhamon, Sybil (wife of Robert) 7, 9
Fitzhamon lecture 141

Fitzroy, Robert, first earl of Gloucester 14, *14*, 15, 17, 24–25
  supports Empress Matilda (Queen Maud) 23
Fitzroy (Fitzcount), William, second earl of Gloucester 25, 31
  marries Hawise 26
  three daughters, Mabel, Isabel (Isabella), Amice buried at Keynsham Abbey 26
Fitzroy, Robert (son of William) 26
Flaxley, abbot of 32
Foliot, Gilbert, bishop of London 27
Forthampton
  parish & chapel/ church 65
  Court 58, 104, 123
Founder's Almsmen 27, 66
Founders' Book, The 9
Fox, George 76–77
Franklin, Thomas 65

Gambier Parry, Thomas, reredos 106, 124
Gerald (Giraldus) of Avranches, Abbot of Cranbourne 7, 9
Gillespie, Edward, Lord Lieutenant of Gloucestershire 143
Glamorgan 26, 27
Glastonbury 1
Gloucester
  garrison at 24
  Miles, constable of 24
Gloucester Abbey (*see St Peter's Abbey, Gloucester*)
Gloucester and Bristol Diocesan Assn of Church Bell Ringers 118–119
Gloucester, bishops of
  Bentley, David 132
  Frampton, Robert 84
  Gibson, Dr Edgar 114
  Goodman, Godfrey 72, 73
  Headlam, Arthur 120
  Treweek, Rachel 143
  Wakeman, John 65, 66
  Warburton, William 88
Gloucester Cathedral 10, 99
  painting/ reredos of 106
  Wesley, S.S., organist of 104
Gloucester College (*see Worcester College, Oxford University*)
Gloucester, countesses of
  Amice (weds Richard I de Clare) 31
  Eleanor 41–45, *45*
  Isabel (Isabelle) 27, 31, 34

Isabel Marshall 31, 34–36
Joan of Acre 37
Isobel of Luisgnan 37
Mabel 14, 15, 17
Maud (daughter of earl of Ulster, marries Gilbert III de Clare) 39–40
Gloucester, diocese of, established 60
Gloucester, earls of and lords of the Manor of Tewkesbury
  de Clare, Gilbert I (sixth) 29–30, 31, 36, 42
    first patron buried before high altar 32
  de Clare, Gilbert II (Red Earl) (eighth) 37
  de Clare, Gilbert III (ninth) 37, 39–42
  de Clare, Richard I (fifth) 29–30, 31
  de Clare, Richard II (seventh) 34, 35, 37
  de Mandeville, Geoffrey (fourth) 27, 29–30, 31
  Fitzroy, Robert (first) 14, *14*, 15, 17, 23, 24–25
  Fitzroy (Fitzcount) William (second) 14, 15, 23, 25–27, 68
  John, Prince (third) (given up when marriage annulled) 26–30
Gloucestershire
  estates in 5
  monastic lands in 65
Glynn, Mrs Harriet 106, 111
Godfrey, Francis 113
Goldcliff Priory 51
Gorle, James 93
Great (Gloucestershire) Flood, 2007 1
Great Malvern Priory 2
Grene, Bishop of Dublin 16
Grove, Charles 81, 96, 105, 107, *108*
Grove, Frances Emily 81, *108*
Gunpowder Plot 76
Gupshill Manor 53

Haines, William 73
Hawling, Samuel, burial of 84
Hale, Sir Matthew 29
Hampden, Sir Edmund 55
Hampden Court, London 77
  Milton Organ there 87
Hanford, Mr 99
Harper, Professor John 141
Harris, Renatus, organ builder 87
Hastie-Smith, Timothy 134
Hawise de Beaumont marriage 26
Hayward, Mr Bailiff 85

Haylward Snow, lord of Tewkesbury Manor 3
Healing family 107
Hepworth, Robert 111
Hereford
   Capella, Bishop Richard de 16
   people in, kill Hugh II Despenser 41
Hill, William, Tewkesbury Town Clerk 72
Hill, William, bailiff 81
Hodges, Thomas 93
Hopkins, John, master mason 124
Hugh, lord of Tewkesbury Manor 2
Hughes, Phil 138

Independents (*see United Reformed Church*)
Induni, Bruce 126
Interdict of Pope Innocent III 29
Ireson, David 138
Isabel (Isabelle), daughter of Earl William 27, 31
Isabella of Angoulême 31
Ismay, General Lord (Lionel) 'Pug', KG 123, *123*
Ismay, Laura, Lady 123

Jackson, Francis, organist 122, 124
Jameson, Keith 125
Jeemes, John 83
Jeffree, Tim, master craftsman 121
Jesus (Christ) of Nazareth 1
John, lord of Somerset, masses for 62
John, Prince, (lackland) earl of Cornwall (*see King John*)
Johnson, Boris, Prime Minister 141
Jones, Dr Anthia 94
Joseph of Arimathea 1

Kaufman, Mico, sculptor 131
Kemble, Mr, bailiff 85
Kempe, Charles E. 111
Kent, HRH Duchess of 93
Keynsham, Abbot of 32
King's Court of Augmentation 63
Kings of England
   Charles I 75
   Charles II 78, 79
   Edgar the Peaceful 2
   Edward I 35, 37, 39
   Edward II 37, 41
   Edward III 37, 46
   Edward IV 35, 53, 55, 103
   Edward VI 63, 66, 68
   George I 84
   George III 35, 89
   George IV 93
   Henry I 10, 14
   Henry II 25–26, 27, 31
   Henry III 32, 34, 35
   Henry VI 51, 53
   Henry VII 56, 62
   Henry VIII 35, 37, 56, 57, 61, 118
     supreme head of Church of England 58
   James I 75
   James II 83
   John 26–30, 29, 35, 36
   Richard II 35, 37
   Richard III 35
   William I 5
   William II, (William Rufus) 5–7
   William III 83
   William IV 93, 95
King of Scotland
   Alexander I 37
Kingston, Sir William 58

Lambeth Palace 104
Lancastrian army 53–55, 56
Langton, Simon, Archbishop of Canterbury 29
Laud, William, Archbishop of Canterbury 72–73, 85
Layton, Richard, Dean of York 59
Lechmere, Sir Edmund, BT. 101
Leckhampton stone 115
Leicester, earl of, daughter marries William Fitzroy (Fitzcount) 26
Leight, Mrs 71
Leland, John, antiquary 60
Lewknor, Sir John 55
Little Malvern Priory 54
Litzenberger 66–67
Llandaff, Bishop Urban of 16
London, Bishop Bonner of 65
Lord Chancellor 66, 75, 131
Lord Warden of the Cinque Ports and Constable of Dover Castle 31
Luxford, Professor Julian 143

Magdalen College, Oxford University 77, 87
Magdalen Pontifical 16
Magna Carta 1, 29
Major-Generals appointed 77
Malmesbury Abbey, Wiltshire 2

Mandeville, Geoffrey (*see de Mandeville*)
Mansfield, Lord, Lord Chancellor 84
Margam Abbey 15
Margaret, HRH Princess, Countess of Snowdon 128, 131
Margaret (Meggota) 35–36
Margaret of Anjou, Henry VI's Queen 53–54
Margaret, second wife of Hubert de Burgh 35
Marriages secularized 76
Martin family 106–107
Martin, Hugh 94
Martin, J. Biddulph 106, 120
Martin, Victoria Woodhull 120–121
Mears, Thomas, of Gloucester 98
Mears & Stainbank 114
Mearson, Nicholas 73
Mildenhall, Suffolk, vicar of 104
Miller, Alec 120
monasteries
   Cranbourne, Dorset 3
   improvements in discipline etc. 2
monks 1, 31
Opus Dei 4, 23
monarch as appointer of Abbey incumbents 66
monasteries 1
   Dissolution of 45
Monk, General 78
Monmouth, duke of, rebellion 83
Montacute, Elizabeth 46, *48*
Moody, Beth 143
Moore, Benjamin 110–111
Moore, Charles, Treasurer, national committee 104
Moore, Frederick, Secretary, national committee 104
Morris, William 105
Mulock, Dinah, memorial 109
Murphy, Peter 119, 128, 129
Mythe, the 3

Nashdom, Anglican Benedictine Abbot of 120
Nazir-Ali, Bishop Michael of Rochester 132
Neath Abbey 15
Neville, Anne 51, 53
Neville, Isabelle 51, 53
Neville, Richard, sixth earl of Warwick, 51, 53

Newburgh, Sir William 55
Nicholas, Benjamin 134
Nonconformity
  clergy 72
  possible leader of 72
  'Godly' individuals 76
  worship 71, 72
Norman invasion & conquest 1066 2, 5
NATO 123
Nott, Thomas 66

O'Connell, Alicia 143
Odda, Earl 1
Oddo 1
Ordinance of 1650 77
Oswald, Bishop of Worcester,
  Archbishop of York 2
Ouseley, Sir Frederick Gore, bt 104
Overbury, Thomas 119
Oxenton (Glos) 5, 65

Pagett, James 65
Painswick stone 11
Parker, Thomas, Lord Mansfield 84
Parliament, working with 78
Parrett, John 83
Parry, Thomas Gambier 104, 106, 124
Paulet, Richard 61
Payne, Thomas 54
Perry, David 129
Perry Lithgow Partnership,
  conservators 131
Pershore Abbey 1, 2
Peyton, John 84
Pert, Mr, burial of in Abbey 68, 70
plague(s) 1
Philip, HRH Prince, Duke of
  Edinburgh 123, 141
Plantagenet, George, Duke of
  Clarence 53
Plantagenet, Richard, Duke of
  Gloucester, later King Richard III 53
Pope(s) 36
  dues to 90
  Gregory X 41
  Innocent III 29
  John XXII 41
  'perceived papist practices' 81
  petition to 57
  'popery' 76
Powell, Professor Susan 143
Privy Council 72

Presbyterians
  Hill, William 81
  the nation's church? 74
  Toleration Act helps 83
  wary of Quakers 77
Protestant, Protestantism 74
  Abbey becomes 75
  ideas surface 57, 60
  protestation or covenant 74
  Toleration Act helps 83
  Tracy an exponent of 57–58
Pugin, Augustus 99, 105
Puritans, puritanism 74, 95
  Abbey becomes 75
  altar position 73
  box pews & galleries removed 106
  cleric 71, 72, 73
  cutting altar stone in two 85
  Geary suspended for 73
  loosening grip 80
  protest over alcohol 71
  pulpit later removed 106
  removal of Abbey font 77
  Thanksgiving Days 76
  Toleration Act helps 83
Pyrry, Alexander 63

Quakers (Society of Friends)
  Fox, George 76–77
Queens
  Adelaide (wife of William IV) 94
  Anne 84
  Anne Boleyn 58, 59
  Catherine of Aragon 57
  Charlotte (wife of George III) 35, 89
  Eleanor (wife of Henry III) 34
  Elizabeth I 63, 66, 68
  Elizabeth II 1, 35, 123, 124, 132, *142*, 143
  Elizabeth of York 62
  Isabella of Angoulême 31
  Jane Seymour 58
  Margaret of Anjou (wife of Henry VI)
    53–54
  Mary (r. with husband William III) 83
  Mary (Tudor) 35, 57, 66
  Maud (Matilda) 5
  Maud (Matilda), Empress 23
  Victoria 93, 95, 97, 108, 110
Queen Anne's Bounty 90
Queen Margaret's School 136, 138, 143
Queen Mary's Almsmen (*see Founder's
  Almsmen*)

Rawlins, Darsie 12, 122
Raywood, Joanne 141, 144
Reading Abbey 58
Rees-Mogg, Mrs 119
Reformation 57
Regularis Concordia 2
Restoration 77, 78
Ricketts, John 85
Ripple Parish Church stalls 101
Robert the Bruce 39–40
Robinson, Anthony 126
Roger, earl of Hereford 7
Romsey Abbey 12
Rouen, France 51
Rudhall of Gloucester 122
Ruffle, Wendy 136, 143
Runnymede 29

St Agnes 36
St Barbara 51
St Bartholomew's Day 79
St Basil 36
St Benedict, ikon of 129
St Catherine's Chapel 44
St Cornelius 36
St Dunstan, figure & chapel of *119*, 126
St Edmund, chapel of 44
St Elizabeth the Virgin 36
St Faith's Chapel 44
St George's Chapel, Windsor 123
St James, priory of, Bristol 15, 24–25
  Prior Robert 57
St Leonard 51
St Margaret of Scotland, chapel of 44,
  93, 113
St Mary (*see Blessed Virgin Mary*)
St Mary, Cardiff, Castle Chapel 27
St Mary Magdalene 51
St Mary's Lane, Tewkesbury 3
St Nicholas' Church,
  Stanford-on-Avon 87
St Paul's Cathedral, London 125, 141
St Peter's Abbey, Gloucester 2
  Abbot of 10, 17, 57
  east end of 44
  educating monks 57
  wealth of 59
St Thomas Becket, Archbishop of
  Canterbury 27
  relics of 34
St Wulfstan of Worcs, relics of 34
Salviatti, Guilio 110

INDEX 171

Samson, Bishop of Worcester 9, 16, 20
Samson Pontifical 16, 17, *18*, *19* 20
Schleswig-Holstein, Princess Victoria of 110
Scott, Sir George Gilbert 85, 100, 105
  examines Abbey 100
  reports to meeting 100
  Will, request in 105
Scott, George, Gilbert, (younger) 105
Scott, John Oldrid 105
Second Act of Supremacy 66
'secular' clergy 2
Severn, River 53
  fishery on 61
Seymour, Sir Thomas, Baron of Sudeley 66
Shuston church 51
Slapton, south Devon 46
Smith, Francis, Abbey surveyor 85
Smyth, (Smith) Thomas, Abbey churchwarden 77, 80
Society of Friends (*see* Quakers)
Somerset, duke of, Protector of the Realm 66
Stanway, manor of Tewkesbury Abbey 2
  Garter Banner of Gen. Lord Ismay 123
  manor at 58
  quarry at 11
  vicar of 91
Stoke Orchard 122
Stroud, Thomas 65
Stuntney, Cambridgeshire 125
Sudeley
  Barksdale, Clement 76
  Lord 99, 104
  Sudeley Castle 24, 58
Supplication for the Beggars 59
Suppression of Religious Houses Act 60
Swarbrick, Thomas, organ builder 87

Tait, Archibald Campbell, (A.C.) Archbishop of Canterbury 104
Tattersall, James 89
Taylorson, Mr 116
Taynton, Oxfordshire 62
Teck, duke & duchess of 110
Te Deum, singing of 20
Test and Corporation Act, Repeal of 95
Tewkesbury
  Almshouses, Sir Francis Russell 93, *94*
  attacked by earl Waleran 24
  bailiffs take over bell-tower 70

Barton Road 116
Battle of the Boyne aftermath 83
Battle of 53–56
  anniversary, 500th 123
  Requiems in perpetuity 62
becomes a 'free burgh' 26
bishop of, Snow, Martyn 132, 133
Bloody Meadow 53
bonfire night & fireworks, 2021 145
buildings in poor condition 56
'Celebrate', Fresh Expression of Church 136
cholera outbreak 94
Christian settlement at 1
Church Street 116
Churches Together in Tewkesbury (CTIT) 129
Collins, Thomas, builder 98, 101, 103
  commitment to Scott proposals 106
  memorial to & window *112*, 113
  moves monks' stalls back 101, *102*
  reconstructs cloister bay 109, *109*, 111–113
  removes galleries 102
  restores Abbey Gateway 98
Council, old borough
  bailiffs
    attend services 73
    claim to pay ministers 76
    part of Parish Assembly 73
    provide new pulpit 75
    see Abbey accounts 66
    relinquish authority to churchwardens 84
    Dobins, Mr Bailiff 84
    Hayward, Mr Bailiff 85
    Kemble, Mr Bailiff 85
  buys lordship of the manor 56, 75
  given a Charter 68
  licence for Abbey plays in jeopardy 71
  'nomination' of Abbey clergy 66
  no councillor prosecuted for Nonconformity 73
  Nonconformist inclination of 68, 75
  Roman Catholics barred from town offices 73
  Town Clerk
    Collett, Henry 83
    Hill, William 72
Convention, Priests' 120
Crown Steward of 58
Cull, James 98

Edgecombe, Edward 90, 99, 105
Festival 119
Flood, 2007 (*see* Great Flood)
Fox, George comes to 76–77
Free Grammar School, in Abbey 68
Gaston, The 53
Girls' High School, old buildings 123
granted a Charter, 1300 39
Great Flood, 2007 *135*, 135–136
Gupshill manor 53
High Street 116
Hitch, Dr, Mayor 101
Holy Trinity Church, Oldfield 97, 122
Indenture 62
Justices 73
Justices of the Peace 76
lords of the Manor of Tewkesbury
  Beauchamp, Henry 51
  Beotric (Brictric, Berthric, Brihric, Beorhtric) 4–5
  de Clare, Eleanor 41–45, *45*
  de Clare, Gilbert I 29–30, 31, 32, 36, 42
  de Clare, Gilbert II (Red Earl) 37
  de Clare, Gilbert III 37, 39–42
  de Clare, Richard I 29–30, 31
  de Clare, Richard II 34, 35, 37
  de Mandeville, Geoffrey 27, 29–30, 31
  Despenser, Hugh II 41–44
  Despenser, Hugh III 45–46
  Fitzhamon, Robert 5, *5* 6, 7, 9, 14, 37, 44
  Fitzroy, Robert 14, *14*, 15, 17, 23, 24–25
  Fitzroy (Fitzcount) William 14, 15, 23, 25–7
  John, Prince (given up when marriage annulled) 26–30
  manor reverts to Crown 66
  Neville, Isabelle 53
  Neville, Richard, sixth earl of Warwick 51, 53
  Plantagenet, Edward 56
  Plantagenet, George, duke of Clarence 53–56
  Queen Maud (Matilda) 5
  Seymour, Sir Thomas, Lord Sudeley 56
  Snow, Haylward (Aethelward Meow) 3
Lower Lode 53, 54
market cross 81
market place in 76
marriages secularized 76
Members of Parliament
  Dowdeswell, John E., MP 93–94
  Dowdeswell, William, MP 87

Gage, Lord, MP 87, *88*
Hicks-Beach, Sir Michael, 9th
    Baronet, MP 106
Lechmere, Sir Edmund, BT, MP 104
Martin, John, MP 93–94
Russell, Sir Francis, MP 93, *94*
Yorke, John, MP 104
Memorials, First World War 115–116
    Cartland Calvary 115, *115*
    Memorial altar 115, *115*
    Town centre Cross 116
Methodist minister 122
Minster 2–3, 9
Nonconformists 66, 94
organ committee 87
Pageant 119
Parish assembly 73
'parish church' 63
parish priest, funding for 63
Park 27, 53
Prince (later King) John visits 26
    develops deer park 27
Prior's Park 136
Queen Margaret's Camp 53
Queen Margaret's School 136
    'Celebrate' at 136
    pandemic at 143
religious attitudes post-Dissolution 70
Roses Theatre box office 145
Swan coaching Inn 85
town cemetery opened 101
Town Hall
    luncheon at 118
    meeting about Abbey renovation
        99–100
    procession from, to Abbey 122
White Hart Inn 85
Tewkesbury Abbey – General
affected by Coronavirus 138–143
Abbey as parish church 12
Abbey (Choir) School 123–125
    Amherst, Miles 123, 134
    Dean Close School saves choir 134
    Gardner, Neil, headmaster 134
    Nicholas, Benjamin, Director of
        Music 134
Abbey Foundation 147
Abbey Gatehouse/ Gateway 98, 107
    converted into holiday flat 125
    restored by Thomas Collins 98
    used for classes 98
Abbey House 51, 71

chapel in, used in pandemic 138
opened in flood emergency 136
returned for use by vicar 106–107
view of Oriel window 57
Abbey Lawn House 121
Abbey Lawn Trust 121
Abbey Lodge 90, 107
Abbey 900th Year Celebration Dinner
    in nave 143–144, *144*
Abbey ringers
    ring for Charles II 78, 79
    ring for Oak Apple Day 78
    ring for King William III 83
    ring for naval victory 83
Abbey Visitor Centre 122, 128
    flood emergency 136
    meeting rooms & offices 131
    Gough Room 122
    refectory, (later tea-room), opened 131
    'pop-up' shop 139, 142
    'Touching Souls' sculpture 131
Abbots (*see main index, Abbots of
    Tewkesbury Abbey*)
Abbots' manors 58
access for wheel-chair users 136
Act of Supremacy enforced 58
Alfred, monk in charge of Abbey
    building 10
Anniversaries of consecration 117–118, 123
appeal launched 128
Archaeological consultant 125
Archiepiscopal visitation 73
architectural styles, church 99
Augmentation, King's Court of 63
barn 107
BBC at Abbey
    Antiques Roadshow 136
    Choral Evensong(s) 136
    Christmas TV service 136
    local radio 136
    Songs of Praise 136
bells 37, 63, 72, 80
    become chimes for clock 122
    change-bell ringing 105
        competition begun 124
        Davies, C.D.P. 105, 118–119
        Grandsire Triples 105
        Glos & Bristol Association 118–119
    chapel dedicated to St Dunstan
        118–119, *119*
    'Flat 6' bell added ('Helen') 126
    quarter peal rung for festival 143

recast 122
rehanging all eight bells 98
restrictions on 71
ring in new millennium 132
    and New Year's day 132
ring of 12 bells 118
ring warning about climate 145
ringers represented on PCC 114
ringing chamber 98, *98*
    Cull, James 98
    old clock room used 98
rung at coronations 94, 97
rung after defeated rebellion 83
tenor bell cracks 75
tolling bell marking HRH Prince
    Philip's death 141
tonal qualities cause concern 122
trebles given 113–114, 118, 139, *139*
uses of bells 76
bell-tower (campanile) *69*
    in poor condition 56
    becomes town jail 68, 70
    sketched by J.M.W. Turner 90–91
Birdsall, Neil, Abbey architect &
    surveyor 124
    designs railings for Gage Gates 132
    first Quinquennial inspection 124
    holy water stoup 125
    high altar beam 129
    new seating, Lady Chapel 138
Blessed Virgin Mary with Child,
    altar stone dedicated to 72
    statue of 11, *12*
Blunt, J.H. 103
Boys' and Girls' Brigades 125, 145
Bruckner, Anton motet, '*Locus Iste*' 147
building changes
    chapel on north-east side of north
        transept 32
    double chapel on east side of north
        transept 32
    possible first Lady Chapel 32
    Early English style 32
    Decorated style 32
    St James' Chapel 32
    St Nicholas' Chapel 32
burials
    banned by Order in Council 101
    cause Abbey wall problems 101
    increased use in chancel & nave 85
    of duelling army officer 85
    of Mr Pert 68, 70

INDEX   173

Tewkesbury Abbey cont.
buttresses, including flying 85
  Camera Cantorum song school 124
  Caröe, W.D. 114, 115–116
  'Celebrate' 136–138, 143
    development of ministry 147
    effect of pandemic 143
    Pioneer Curate at 138
  central tower (exterior) 11 (13)
    building of second stage 14, 25
    rebuilding of battlements 71
  central tower (interior) 11
  chancel roof lowered 72
  chantry priests stipends suppressed 65
  chimes 'worn out' 87
  choral society/ choirs 97, 101, 114
    Abbey Choir 124
      Christmas TV broadcast 2010 136
      Christmas Eve service 2020 139
      Consecration Anniversary Sung
        Eucharist 145
      Etherington, Carleton, choir
        director 131, 138, 139, 141,
      help Abbey School Choir 124
      overcome pandemic problems,
        138–141, 142
      regulations concerning pandemic 142
      Sunday Choral Evensong resumes 143
      YouTube special carol service 139
    Abbey School Choir 124
      appears on TV in 1980 124
      Radio 3 choral evensong 125
      saved by Dean Close School 134–135
    Tewkesbury Abbey Schola Cantorum
      (TASC) 135
      Bell, Simon, choir director 139, 141
      first Choral Evensong 135
      girls as choristers 142, 143
      regulations concerning pandemic
        142, 143
      represent Great Britain 135
      sing Evensong at Lambeth Palace 144
      special Radio 3 Choral Evensong 135
      YouTube special carol service 139
  'church ales' 68
  Church Street shops 51
  churchwardens
    addition, 2019 138
    authority 84
    Brydes, Henry 94
    Cooke, Richard 77, 81
    expense of graves 70
    Hanford, Mr 99
    levy parish rates 70, 71, 73, 74, 75, 93, 99
      call for abolition 94
      resistence to paying 94
      soldiers hired to collect 75
    make beer available at plays 71
    Martin, Hugh 94
    Moore, Benjamin 99, 110–111
    Moore, Thomas 111
    'neglect' of displays 73
    Nonconformist elected 73
    obtain Faculty for an organ 87
    Peyton, John 84
    prosecute Nonconformists 73
    remove font 77
    rent out churchyard 73
    repairs to west window 77
    represented on PCC 114
    Smith (Smyth), Thomas 77, 80–81
  churchyard
    lowered in part 105
    manure from 73
    rented as pasture 73
  clergy at, from 1540–1662 70
  (see also *Ministers & Vicars, 1662–1845* 93)
  (see also *Vicars, 1845–present* 126)
    Audrey, John 70–71
    Banckes, 'Parson' 70
    Beard, Stephen 66, 70
    Blackwell, William 70
      Nonconformist 72
    Burroughs, Thomas 75
    Coxe, John 70
    Crondall, Nicholas 70
    Curtis, Richard 70–71
    Davis, John 65, 70
    Drake, Richard 66, 70
    Fox, Humphrey 70–71
      accused of Nonconformity 71
      suspended 72
    Franklyn, Thomas 70
    Geary (Geree), John 70
      author of book 76
      puritan in outlook 72
      suspended 73
    Greene, Robert 65, 70
    Grove, Charles 81
    Grove, Frances Emily 81
    Johnsons, William 70
    Lonsby (Losbie), Edward 70, 72
      has Abbey re-whitewashed 72
    Nott, Thomas 66, 70
    Pyers, John 70
    Sherewood (Sherwood), John 65, 70
    Wells, John 70, 80
      disputes with George Fox 77
      Independent views 75
      rejects 'Christmas' 76
    West, Samuel 70
    Whitehead, William 70
    Wight, Nathaniel 70
      prosecuted by own churchwardens 73
    Williams, John 70
  clergy marital situations 66
  clergy, retired 136, 138
  clergy 'secondaries' 68
  clock 87, *108*
    Jubilee Clock 87, 108
      face lowered 109
      face refurbished 132
      mechanism of *108*
    Moore, Samuel 87
    sexton to wind up 90
  cloister in poor condition 56
  Collins, Thomas 101, 103, 104
    commitment to Scott proposals 106
    memorial to and window *112*, 113
    moves monks' stalls back 101, *102*
    reconstructs cloister bay 109, *109*,
      111–113
    removes galleries 102
    restores and renovates Abbey
      Gateway 98
  Compotus Roll of Henry VIII
    presented to Abbey 118
  confirmation, large numbers for 94
  cottages 107
  closure of monastery 60, 63, 65
  consecration & dedication 16–22
    blessing of the pavement 20
    holy oil, use of 22
    holy water, use of 21
    laity involvement 20, 22
    lustration 21
    Mass of consecration 22
    relics, use of 21–22
  consecration cross at west end 12
  Court of Augmentation, King's 63
  Craik, Mrs, memorial 109, *109*
  curate(s) 115, 138
    Hamilton, Sebastian 142
    Hepworth, Robert 111
    Tattersall, James 89
  Davies, Harry, sub-sacristan 114–115

deathwatch beetle 119, 122
discovery of pre-Romanesque wall 3
Dissolution of 60–61
door, north, lobby to 114
Dowdeswell Gates 87
east end *42, 43, 64*
Edgecombe, Edward 91, 99, 105
Elizabeth 11
   distributes Royal Maundy 123
   possibly assists appeal 124
Elm trees damaged 105
excommunicated by bishop 32
fair at 72
Feast of the Holy Relics 34
festival
   850 years since Consecration 123
   Commemoration, 1881 106
   of music 97
   of thanksgiving for restoration 106
Festival of Lights 145, *146*
fires at 27
   bell-tower 39
   principal gate 34
   various buildings 37
flooding in Abbey 135–136
Fresh Expression of Church 136
Friends of Tewkesbury Abbey
   Fitzhamon Lecture 2021 141–142
   foundation and objects of 119
   Friends' Festival 143
   Founders' Book facsimile published 143
   Warwick Chantry restoration 119
Gage Gates
   conserved & restored 132
   evening prayer at 136
   Festival of Lights 145
   given by Lord Gage, MP 87
   Green Man on 50
Gambier Parry, Thomas 106, 124
General Synod 126
   ordination of women 126
   views at Abbey 126
Girls' Brigade company affiliated 125
Godfrey, Francis 113
Graebe, David 131
Green Men 50
guilds of 114
guide to Abbey, first 90
Harper, Professor John 141–142
Healing family 107
Henry VIII stays at 58
Honourable Company of Gloucestershire

Celebration Dinner in Abbey nave
   144, *144*
Indenture with Henry VII 62
killing of Lancastrians in 53
Lady Chapel (first) 32, 61, 62
Lady Chapel (second) 44, 45, 61, 62–63
land around Abbey sold 65
Landmark Trust 125
lay ministry developed 131, 136
   the future of 147
   Reader ministry 114, 131, 136
lay staff 132, 138
   reorganization of 139
lead, value of 63
library in 60
'liturgical resources' 68
Lord Chancellor role 66
Mass 23
medieval painting rediscovered 131
Memorials, First World War 115–116
   Cartland Calvary 115, *115*
   Memorial altar 115, *115*
method of building 10
ministers & vicars, 1662–1845 93
(*See also clergy in charge of the Abbey 1540–1662 70*)
(*See also vicars, 1845-present 126*)
   Eaton, Robert, 'the Elder' 80, 83
   Eaton, Robert, 'the Younger' 80
   Evanson, Edward 88
   Jenes, Penry 85, 95
   Jones, Henry, 'the Elder' 85
   Jones, Henry 'the Younger' 88–89, 95
   Knight, Robert 89
   Matthews, John 83–85
   Tattersall, James 89, 95
   White, Charles 89–91, 94, 95, 97
monastery, wealthiest 59
monastic buildings, area of *74*, 107
monks of the Abbey 46
   Bernard 29
   daily offices 23, 24
   dormitory roof collapses 31
   education of 57
   Gilbert 31
   'gluttony and drunkenness' 37
   Gunfrey, Prior 31
   Henry de Sipton, Prior 34, 36
   John Beeley, Prior 57
      pension 60
   John Wych (Wakeman), as Prior 57, 58
   monastic rule enforcement 58

'monk rector' for Tewkesbury 63
monks from Cranborne 9, 46
numbers of Abbey monks 56, 65
obedentiaries 23, 37
   almoner 23
   cellarer 23
   guest-master 23
   infirmarian 23
   novice-master 23
   precentor 23
   prior 23, 29
   sacrist 23, 29
   Peter of Worcester 29
   possible purchase by town 60
   Robert Cheltenham pension 60
   Robert Cisseter or Cirencester 57
   sign Act of Supremacy acceptance 58
   visitation 37, 39
monks, knitted 141
Morris, Dr Richard, archaeological
   consultant 125
Morris, William 105
Mother and Child, statue of 11, *12*, 122
music festival 90
national committee for restoration of
   Abbey 104
   London Committee established 106
   meets at Lambeth Palace 104, 106
nave
   bosses on vaulting 46
   clerestorey of 11
   dendrochronological dating of
      timbers 84
   re-roofed 57, 70
   'ruinous' condition of 41, 83, 84, 119
   triforium 11
   vaulting 11
north door
   Festival of Lights 145
   path to, paved 87
   possible changes to 145
north porch 11
   lights to Gage Gates 132
   paving around west end 132
   plaque concerning flooding 136
north transept (*see also transepts*)
   entrance to Camera Cantorum *33*
   re-roofed, 1521 57
ordination at 93
ordination of women, views on 126
Overbury, Thomas 119
   announces urgent work needed 119

Tewkesbury Abbey cont.
  investigates Lady Chapel site 119
  parish rates (*see churchwardens*)
  parishes presented to 27
  Parochial Church Council 74, 114
    women presidency 132–134
  patron saint of 4
  patronage
    by Beotric 5
    obligations involved 34
  patterns of Sunday worship 143, 145
  Peers, Sir Charles 119
  Peregrine Falcons 137, *137*
  pews
    re-pewing 90
    pew rents 68, 102
  pilgrims to 1
    problems, financial, concerning 34
  plan of, 1821 *xii*
  quire parapet, restoration of 119
  reconsecration 55
  re-founding 2
  renovation and reordering of Abbey,
    Victorian 99–101, 104
  renovation and repair, general,
    ambulatory, re-roofing 128
    Camera Cantorum roof 136
    chancel & transepts roofs repaired 124
    deathwatch beetle 119, 122
    eastern chapels' renovation 119
      re-roofing 128
    nave repairs 119
    quire parapets' renovation 119
    stonework and lead roofs, 1956 122
    tower repairs 119
      appeal for 124
      roof repaired 136
      tower pinnacle 124
      west face re-pointed 136
    wall, north aisle, collapse 71
      south aisle needs attention 71
    Warwick Chantry renovation 119
    west end turrets 136
    west end windows 136
  sacrilege in 53
  sub-sacristan (*see Davies, Harry*)
  screen *111*
  Scott, Sir George Gilbert 85, 100, 105
    examines Abbey 100
    his proposals adopted 103
    reports to meeting 100-101
    Will, requests 105

Scott, George Gilbert (younger) 105
Scott, John Oldrid 105
  designs doors 109, *109*
  designs nave pulpit 106
  moves wall, designs screen 110, *111*
servants of the Abbey at the
  Dissolution 60
services online 141, 145–147
sexton,
  dispute with verger and clerk 90
  winds up the clock 90
site of 3–4
spire/ steeple
  collapse of 68
  possible rebuild 99
steward of Abbey lands 57
stone used 11
structural problems 101
surveyors to the Abbey
  Birdsall, Neil 124, 125, 128, *128*
  Smith, Francis 85
  Taylor, Eric 126
  Taylor, Helen 126
time taken to build 12
tower, central
  first storey 11
  floodlit 125, *126*
  pinnacles of 93
  roof repaired 136
  second storey 14
  urgent work on 119
  west face re-pointed 136
transepts 11
  Romano-British stone used *11*
  roofs and walls repaired 93
  support to north 85
  support to south 85
verger, appointment of 90
  Bannister, W.G. 103, 105
  dispute with sexton and clerk 90
  head verger to Bristol Cathedral 110
  role during Coronavirus (Covid-19) 138
Vestry of 74, 87
  agree Scott's sons continue work 105
  compromise on pew allocation 102–103
  critical of musical standards 97
  prepares to be replaced 114
  reintroduction of sidesmen 103
  whole of Abbey interior 'be restored' 103
vicars of, 1846 to present 126
(*See also clergy in charge of the Abbey,*
  1541–1662 70)

(*See also Ministers & Vicars 1662–1845 93*)
  Davies, Charles Greenall 97, *100*, 126
    Abbey building requires much
      repair 98
    also priest-in-charge, Walton
      Cardiff 97
    rural dean of Winchcombe 97
    canon of Gloucester Cathedral 97
    prepared to face reordering
      problems 99
    sweeps away Puritan features 106
  Gough, Edward Pountney 118, *118*, 126
    appointed Hon Canon of
      Gloucester 121
    defers retirement 122
    founds Friends of Tewkesbury
      Abbey 119
    introduces incense 118
    memorial, high altar cross 122
    reservation of Sacrament
      introduced 118
  Moxon, Michael 125, 126
    appointed Queen's Honorary
      Chaplain 125
    Chaplain to the Queen at Windsor 125
    posts at St Paul's Cathedral,
      London 125
  Pouncey, Cosmo Gabriel Rivers 122,
    123, 126
    introduces Holy Week services 122
    Parish/Family Eucharists
      introduced 122
    Musica Deo Sacra week begins, 122–123
    rededicates Grove Organ 124
    supports idea of Choir School 123
  Purefoy, Brian 122, 126
    farming his first career 122
    given responsibility for Tredington
      & Stoke Orchard 122
    Grove organ rededicated in his
      memory 124
  Robeson, Hemming 104, 106, *110*, 126
    vice-chair, national committee 104
    becomes Archdeacon of Bristol 110
    benefactor, with sister 106
    biography 104–105
    cenotaph 11, 113
    corbel of, dedicated 114
    gives screen *111*
    founder, Tewkesbury High School 110
  Sheringham, Harry Alsager 110, 126
    also incumbent of Walton Cardiff 110

biography 110
corbel of, dedicated 114, *114*
exchanges livings 111
Priest in Ordinary, Queen Victoria 110
Smith, Ernest Frederick 114, 126
  appointed vicar of Yate 118
  brief biography 114, 118
  clergy colleague CF 115
  dedicates Town Memorial 116
  Easter Vestry Address, 1915 114
  files for bankruptcy 118
  introduces Choral Eucharist 114
  introduces full vestments & copes 118
  rural dean of Winchcombe 114
  Walton Cardiff additional
    responsibility 118
  was in American Episcopalian
    Church 114
Tavinor, Michael Edward 125, *126*, 126
  appointed Dean of Hereford 132
  brief biography 125
  develops lay ministry 131
  inducted as Vicar of Twyning 131
  introduces Common Worship 132
  views over ordination of women 126
  walks from Tewkesbury to
    Hereford 132
Wardell-Yerburgh, Oswald 111, *113*, 126
  biography 111
  canon of Gloucester 111
  dies unexpectedly 113
  gives treble bells to Abbey 113–114
  memorial to 114
  Reader ministry, support of 114
  rural dean of Winchcombe 111
Williams, Paul Rhys 126, 132
  Abbey School Choir saved 134
  Abbey School closes 135
  appointed deputy Lieutenant
    of Gloucestershire 143, *142*
  awarded Lambeth doctorate 143, 144
  canon of Rochester 132
  evolving broadcasting role 136
  Great Flood of 2007 *135*, 135–136
  outlines priorities at annual
    meetings 143
  reflections on future after 2021 145–147
  revising patterns of Sunday worship
    143, 145
  pandemic problems 138–142
  women presiding
    at the Eucharist 132–134

  worship styles of Abbey &
    'Celebrate' 136–138
visitation of clergy 97
visitors to 1
  arrive because of online services 147
  Burney, Fanny, (Madame d'Arblay) 89
  Close, Francis 97
  general numbers in 1904 113
  George III and Queen Charlotte 89
  lock-down, during 138
  Planta, Miss 89
  Schleswig-Holstein, Princess Victoria
    of 110
  Teck, duke & duchess of,
    with Princess Mary 110
  Turner, J.M.W. 90–91
  Witts, Francis E. 91
War, First World 114–117 (*see* Memorials)
  Roll of Honour 114
west end
  idea of two west towers 13
  seven arches 13
  turrets, pinnacles require attention 136
west front
  as it looks today *81*
  reconstruction in Norman times *80*
  turrets restored 93
  restoration, 1907 114
west wall 83
west window (*see Tewkesbury Abbey –
  internal*)
Williams, Catherine 136
Williams, Harrison 138
worship styles of Abbey 136–138
Tewkesbury Abbey – internal
  abbot monuments/ tombs
    Cheltenham, Richard, tomb of 56, 93
    Wakeman, John, cadaver of 93
  altar, high 36–37, *36*, 99
    cut in two 85, 106
    enhanced role of 105
    gate behind, marking Elizabeth II
      Golden anniversary of accession 132
    high beam and dossal curtain for 129
    made into seats 85, 106
    memorial to Canon Gough 122
    painting used as reredos 106
    position of 73
    rails around 73, 105
    returned to original role 106
    smaller altar 85, 106
    stone for, discovered 72, 106

    700 years marked 120
  altarpiece, Doric 85
    moved 99
    Pelican in her Piety moved 85, *85*
  ambulatory
    Brien (Bryan), Sir Guy de
      monument restored 126
    cadavar in 66, *67*
    conservation of 125
    Festival of Light 145
    green men in 50, *50*
    Henry III Despenser tomb restored 126
    'Our Lady Queen of Peace' statue 126
    Pharisee & publican picture 107, *108*
    tomb of Abbot Cheltenham 56, 93
    views looking north *61*
    views looking south *61*
  Baker, P. Bryant, RA 113
  bosses *17*, 32, 46, *47*, 54, *82*, 100, 103, 104
  Boulton, R.L. 113
  Bournemouth University 126
  Brien Monument (Bryan) 93
  burial of Mr Pert 68, 70
  Camera Cantorum 103, *104*
    floor tiles for 103
  central tower – interior 46, *47*
    possibly removing central vaulting
      99–100
  chancel, services held in 75
    problems over use for burials 84
    new pulpit in 76
    renovating the seven windows 118
  chantry chapels
    Beauchamp (Warwick) *49*, 51
    beheading/ defacing of figures 75, *75*
    stone altar dedicated 124
    Founders 46, *49*
      floor tiles of 103
      stone altar dedicated 124
      given gate 124
    Holy Trinity 46, 51, *49*
      'kneeling knight' 124
      restoration 124
      stone altar dedicated 124
  'chapel' above current Lady Chapel *10*, 11
  chapels 11, 32, 41
    Holy Cross Chapel 125
    St John the Baptist & St Catherine's
      Chapel *133*
    Green Men in 50
    holy oils aumbry added 126
    'I am that I am' altar 126, *133*

INDEX   177

Tewkesbury Abbey cont.
  tomb of Abbot Cheltenham 56, *93*
  1980, used as chapel 124
  windows marking monks
     coming to build Abbey 132, *133*
  St Catherine's Chapel 44, 125
  St Dunstan's Chapel 118, 119, *119*
    figure of *119*, 126
    frontal for 129
  St Edmund's Chapel 44
    stone altar installed 132
    triptych over the altar 132, *133*
  St Faith's Chapel 44
    Crucifix in (Peter Murphy) *128*
    Green Men in 50
    memorial tablet to Victoria
     Woodhull Martin 120–121, *121*
    Moore memorial window 111
    Moore memorial plaques 111
    Robeson cenotaph 113
    stone altar 119
    wooden reredos 119
  St James' Chapel
    becomes Abbey shop 125
    floor of 103
    Freemasons' pay for restoration 103
    grammar school in 68, 103
    painting/ reredos transferred to
     106, 124
  St Margaret's Chapel 44, 46, 99, *121*
    altar belonging to 106, 120
    Pelican in her Piety 85, *85*, 99, 129
    Reservation of the Blessed
     Sacrament 128
     sacrament house *121*
    window given to 113
  St Nicholas' Chapel
    floor of 103
    Freemasons pay for restoration 103
    grammar school in 68
    school moves 103
  Upper Room (formerly Sacrist's
    Room) 128–129, *128*, 131
choir stalls 45, 101, *102*
Clarence vault, possible flooding 136
clerestorey in nave 46
Comper, Sir Ninian, high altar cross 122
congregational seating 70
cope chest 120, 121, *121*
cope, Florentine, presented 119–120
Creed display 73, 85
Denny, Tom 132, *133*

Despenser Monument, restoration to 93
Dimitrova, Silvia 132, *133*
displays in, required by Archbishop Laud
  Creed 73
  Lord's Prayer 73
  Royal Arms 73
  Ten Commandments 73
distempering of 93
drama productions in 119
'dressing' the Abbey 80
east end, pews and balconies in 99
Feddon, Bryant 126, *133*
floor of Abbey relaid 106
floor tiles 46, 103
font 77, 95
  moved 83
  placed in present position 105
  removal of 77
  return of 80, 81
  font cover 83, 105
  Jeemes, John 83
Free Grammar School (St James'
  Chapel) 68
  gallery for pupils of 72
  moved elsewhere 103
galleries/ balconies 68, 72
  crowded 105
  removed 105
gallery, singing 97, 99
grave sites of Battle victims
  Audley, Sir Humphrey 55
  Baron, Master Henry 55
  Edmund, duke of Somerset 55
  Edward, Prince of Wales 54, 55
  George, duke of Clarence 56
  Hampden, Sir Edmund 55
  Isabelle, duchess of Clarence 56
  John, marquis of Somerset 55
  Lewknor, Sir John 55
  Newburgh, Sir William 55
  Thomas John, earl of Devon 55
  Tresham, Sir Thomas 55
  Vaux, Sir William 55
  Whittingham, Sir W. Robert 55
  Wrottesley, Master Henry 55
grave sites of others 85
Grove, Charles 81
  gives eastern ambulatory window
    107, *108*
  gives west window 96, *96*
  gives windows in north & south nave
    aisles 108

presents lectern 105
Gurney stoves 129
holy water stoup 125, *125*
Induni, Bruce 126
Ismay, General Lord Ismay, KG
  Garter Banner in Abbey 123
Jones, Kenneth and Associates, organ
  builders 129–131
'kneeling knight' (Lord Edward
  Despenser, KG) 45–46
Lady Chapel (first) (probable) 32, 61
  ceiling of Camera Cantorum *33*
Lady Chapel (second) 44, 45, 61, 62–3
  site of marked 119
Lady Chapel (third) 11, 23, 105, *120*
  altar cross & candlesticks 138
  altar for 106
    stone altar 120
  change of seating 138
  Craik (Mulock) memorial 109, *109*
  ikon, St Benedict, in recess 129, *129*
  medieval painting rediscovered 131
  statue, Blessed Virgin Mary &
    Child 120
  Venetian mosaic 110
lighting system 138
Lord's prayer display 73, 85
masons' marks 12
Miller, Alec 120
misericords 20, 45
monks' stalls moved 71
mosaic, Venetian 110
Murphy, Peter 128
  crucifix, St Faith's Chapel 128, *128*
  crucifix, Upper Room 128, *128*
  ikon of St Benedict 129, *129*
Musica Deo Sacra Week 122–123, 138
  Etherington, Carleton 138
  David Ireson 138
nave
  burials in 95 (see also in chancel)
  enhanced role of 105
  Festival of Lights 145
  festival of scriptural plays in 71
  floor uneven 98
  Gospel spots 132
  Parliamentary forces commandeer? 75
  paved 93
  vaulting in 11, 46, *82*
    above *82*
    cleaning of 129
  west end of south aisle returned 106

oculus 20
ordinations held in
   Diocese of Gloucester 120
   Methodist 129
organs 68
   Grove Organ *107*, 122, 124
      bought by Charles Grove 107
      exhibited in London & Liverpool 107
      originally water powered 107
      played by George Riseley, Bristol
         Cathedral 107
   Milton Organ 77, 87, 99, *130*
      built originally by Thomas Dallam 87
      enlargement, restoration, 1947 122
         celebratory recital 122
      from Oxford to Tewkesbury 87
      Jackson, Francis 122
      organ moves 100, 103, 107
      major rebuild, Kenneth Jones 128,
         129–131
         screen/ gallery, David Graebe 131
      Ouseley, Sir Frederick Gore,
         advises 104
      part goes elsewhere 87
      pedal organ added 91, 97
      played by S.S. Wesley 104
      renovation 138
      repairs to 97
      stops added 91
      swell organ added 91
organ gallery/ screen 87, 100, 104
organists/ directors of music
   Belcher, John 131
      founds Abbey Choir Assn 131
   Baker, Percy 115
   Cleavely, James 87
   Etherington, Carleton 131, 138, 139
      composes anthem for
         consecration anniversary 145
      Epiphany *YouTube* recital 141
   Peterson, Michael 123
   Stubington, Huskisson 122
pelican in her piety 85, *85* 99
pillars 12
Perry, David 129
Perry Lithgow partnership,
   conservators 131
pews, state of 105
   removed 105
pulpit 95, 99
   in quire *92*, 99
   new 75

pulpitum 20 *38–39*
quire 41
   access for wheelchairs 136
   box pews in 99
   ceiling colour-washed 93
   description of, by Witts 91, *92*
   floor examined 103
   gas gives way to electricity 114
   Henry, duke of Warwick, buried in 51
   Hodges, Thomas & clerestorey 93
   pulpit in *99*, 99
   services in 75
   'sun' bosses 54
   tiles in 103
   'Tudor Flowers' 103
   vaulting & windows 43
registers 113, 132
ringing chamber, new, created 98
Robinson, Anthony 126
Rood 12
round-headed lancet windows 20
Royal Arms in 72, 73, 78, *79*
Royal Maundy service 123
sacrist's room 44
sacristy 44
   door, security of 55, *56*
   'fragments window' in 44, *45*, 118
   Green Men in 50
sanctuary 41, *117*
   brasses noting tomb sites 103
   floor of 85, 103
   floor tiles 103
   reconstruction, twelfth century *116*
   renovating the seven windows 118
   vaulting & windows 43
sedilia 78
   nave sedilia 102
   sanctuary ones mutilated 85
shop (*see chapels, St James & St Nicholas*)
sound system 138
stained glass 5, *14*, *43*, 44, *45*, 96, 108,
   108, *133*
stone pulpitum or screen 12
stone surfaces lime washed 68, 72
Ten Commandments display 73, 85, 99
Thanksgiving Services
   for funds and urgent renovation 119
   VE Day, 1945 122
   RBL and USA flags received 122
   appeal completed (1997) 131
tomb of Abbot Richard Cheltenham 56

transepts
   allocation of seats in 102–103
   galleries in 72
   Green Men in 50
   organ on floor of north transept 104
   pews & balconies 99
   Upper Room 128
   vicar's stall 118
Wagner, (Anton) Anthony *119*, 126
Wakeman cadavar 66, *67*
   conservation of 125
west end
   drama productions in 119
   Garter Banner of Gen. Lord Ismay,
      KG 123, *123*
west end window 96, *96*
   Festival of Lights 145
   new window 83
   urgent repairs on 79
windows
   at east end *43*, 44
   central east end window 44
   eastern ambulatory window 107, *108*
   north & south nave aisles 108
   rose window 110
   triangular window 110
   worshippers in 1908 113
Thames, River 29
Theoc (Thecus, Theocus) 1
Theulf, Bishop of Worcester 16–22, 23, 117
Third Act of Uniformity 79
Thomas John, earl of Devonshire 55
Tintern, Abbot of 32
Toddington, Towers, William 76
Toleration Act 83
Tractarian movement, Anglo-Catholic 95
Tracy, Richard 58
Tracy, William 57
   Will of 58
Tredington 53
   Abbey 'secondaries' as chaplains 68
   parish & chapel/ church 65, 122
Tregonwell, John, commissioner 58
Trial of seven bishops 83
Tresham, Sir Thomas 55
Turner, Henry 70
Turner, J.M.W. 91
Twyning 3
   parish joins Abbey
      and Walton Cardiff 131
Tyndale, Edward 57, 65
Tyndale, William 57

Unitarians 83
  Williams, George 88
United Reformed Church
  Bach, John 81
  former congregationalists 77
  former Independents 74
  Wells, John 75
United States of America
  Forces flag received, Thanksgiving Service 122
  Martin, Victoria Woodhull 120, 121
Urban, Bishop of Llandaff 16

Vaus, Sir William 55
VE Day 1945 122
vicars of Tewkesbury Abbey
  (see *Tewkesbury Abbey – general*)
Vikings 2, 7
Visitations, Archideaconal 83
Visitor of the Black Monks 57

Wagner, Anton (Anthony) 119, *119*, 126
Wakeman, Bishop (see *Gloucester, bishops of*)
Waleran, earl of Worcester 24
Walton Cardiff parish & church/ chapel 65
  Gorle, James, becomes curate of 93
  Sheringham, Harry, incumbent of 110
Wareham 2
Warham, William, Archbishop of Canterbury 58
War, First World 114–117
War, Second World 121
Wars of the Roses 53–56
  Battle of Barnet 53
  Battle of Tewkesbury 53–56
Warwick earldom
  Beauchamp, Anne, eventually Dowager Countess of Warwick 56
  Beauchamp, Henry, duke of Warwick 51
  Beauchamp, Richard, fourth earl of Warwick 51
  Beauchamp, Richard, fifth earl of Warwick 51
  Neville, Richard, earl of 51, 53
Wessex, royal family of 5
Westminster Assembly established 74
Westminster, Bishop Thurlby of 65
Westminster Abbey
  coronation of Charles II 79
  Lady Chapel 32
  surveyor of 119
Whittingham, Sir W. Robert 55

Whittington, Mr 72
Whittington, Sir John 61
William, duke of Normandy 5, 6, 7
William of Malmesbury 10, 15, 21
Williams, Catherine 136, 147
Williams, Harrison 138, 141
Wilson, Alice *143*
Winchcombe Abbey (later parish church) 2
  Helme, Carnsew 76
  Henry VIII visits 58–59
  disputation in 76
Winchester 2 19
  Aethelwold, Bishop of 2
  Chapter Library makes presentation 118
  Council of 2
  monastery 10, 14
Winterbotham, Lindsey 93
Witts, Francis E. 91
Wolsey, Cardinal Thomas 57
Woodhull, Zula 121
Worcester Cathedral 2
  prior of 39
  wealth of 59
Worcester 19, 24
  Bishops of
    Cantilupe, Walter 36, 72
    Carpenter, John 51
    Gifford, Godfrey 37
    Latimer, Hugh 60
    Orleton 41
    Oswald 2
    Samson 9, 16, 20
    Theulf 16–22, 23
    William of Blois 32, 34, 36
    Wulfstan 10
Worcester College, Oxford University 57
Worcester, earls of 24
Worcestershire, estates in 5
Wrottesley, Master Henry 55
Wulfstan, bishop 10

York, Oswald, Archbishop of 2
York Minster
  Jackson, Francis, organist of 122
York, House of, rose of 51
  army of 53–55
    pursue Lancastrians into Abbey 53
Yorke, John MP 104
YouTube use of, 138, 139, 141, 147

A Said to have been the Chapter House.
B St Margaret's Chapel.
C St Edmond the Martyr's Chapel.
D St Faith's Chapel.
E Chapel, name unknown.
F The Vestry.
G Entrance from the Cloister.
H Effigy in Armour, unknown.
I Countess of Warwick's Chapel.

K Chapel of Robt Fitz Hamon, the second Founder.
L Monument of Lord & Lady De Spenser.
M Old Stalls.
N Tomb of Guy D'Obrien.
O Figure of an emaciated Monk.
P Chapel of the Holy Trinity.

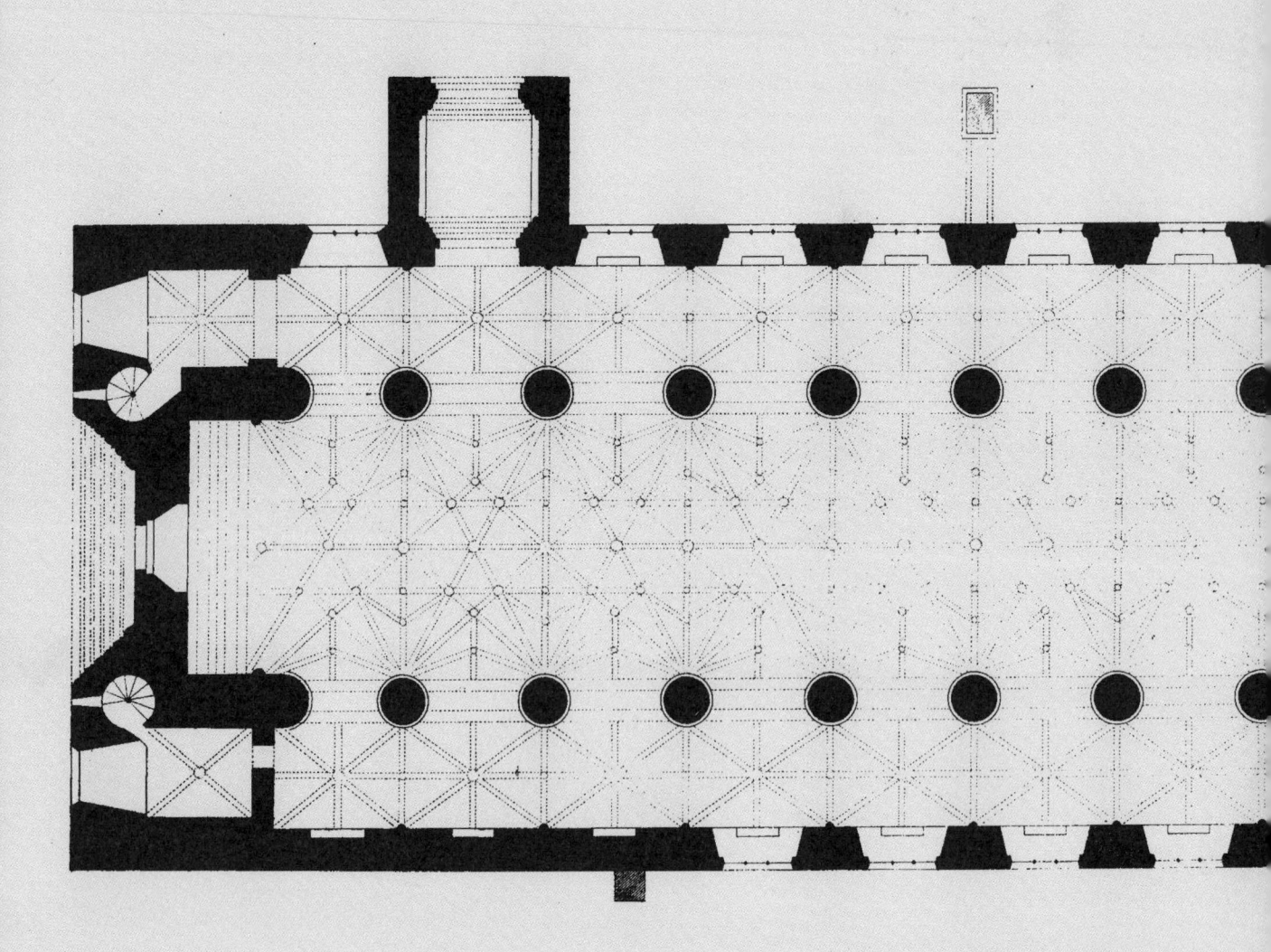